Totally Within

Thomas Strawser

Published by Spiritual Engineering Inc

https://spiritualengineering.us/

ISBN-13: **978-0-9755-6954-2**

Introduction

Do you feel like something is missing in your life? Well, the bad news is that you're probably correct; you've likely got a hole inside of you that nothing seems to fill. Money, power, fame, relationships, or church attendance may bring temporary relief but the emptiness returns. This is a spirit void, a God hole that can only be filled by a personal relationship with spirit. This emptiness, coupled with the fact that many are not attracted to organized religion, have left millions seeking a path for personal growth, a practical spiritual approach that actually produces results in the real world.

The good news is that you live at the greatest time in history of this planet to find the solution that actually works.

We stand at the beginning of an age heralding a revolutionary spiritual awakening. Many are discovering the powerful truth that every person has an unsuspected reservoir of inner spiritual energy, that can transform their life. This is the very power that can break the chains to addiction, transform self-centeredness, and melt all misery. But it is only a potential power, lying dormant and still, until *we make the choice and take the action* to unleash this awesome super energy and then keep the conduit open to allow it to flow every day.

This is our birthright as a child of the divine; this hidden inner life-force bestows a new freedom and power to control our mind, elevate our thoughts, feelings, and attitude and to live in the moment, in the NOW.

"Totally Within" daily affirmations, thoughts, meditations, and prayer help you connect *to your inner power*, keep the connection open, and experience personal growth. It offers: 1) A simple, easy-to-remember daily concept and 2) Practical exercises to increase awareness of the indwelling spirit and to allow this power to guide you to solutions and transform your life. For example:

There is no law that you must allow people to "push your buttons."
After all, they are YOUR buttons.

Do you give other people the power to make you angry? To make you feel guilty? To make you ashamed? Do you react to what others say, how they look at you, or what you think they think about you? Do you silently accept what "they" say you should do; how you should live your life; what your goals, dreams, and aspirations should be? And then withdraw to complain or inwardly simmer because of what "they" say, do, or think?

Every feeling, every beautiful or painful emotion you have *is inside of* you and no one else. No person has ever held your head and forced you to swallow a spoonful of anger or guilt or any misery.

They simply offer each of them. You are responsible to accept or reject the offering; you are responsible for all your feelings and reactions. You can allow anyone to "push your buttons" or you can accept the truth that *these are* your *buttons* and no law or ethical code requires that you allow other people to control them.

Each day also contains a short prayer and a suggestion that we pause for a few minutes and just breathe:

Daily Relaxation Breathing Technique:

Find a comfortable position, close your eyes and take a deep, deep breath; hold it for a few seconds while feeling all the tension in your body moving to the back of your neck and upper shoulders. Exhale very, very slowly while silently repeating "Peace....Harmony....Relax... Relax... Relax..." Visualize the tension leaving your body as the breath flows gently outward; actually feel your muscles relaxing, getting looser, going limp. Take another deep breath—hold it—and exhale very slowly while repeating "Peace.... Harmony.... Relax....Relax: Repeat three more times.

With this as with many things, results are based on action, not belief or agreement. Try it for thirty days and start your transformation.

Dedication

I dedicate this to all my spiritual helpers, especially my divine indwelling spark, my guardian angel, and the women who contributed to my spiritual growth. The spiritual giants emblazoned on the pages of history are often men but it is the women who are truly the spiritual torchbearers, quietly and inexorably lighting the path that guides humanity forward. Many such women have blessed my life. My mother Mary, a loving, wise, and gentle person, taught me values and principles, demonstrated the power resulting from an unassuming spiritual life, and encouraged an early freedom to explore for God; my wife Barbara stood beside me in my darkest times and faced an oncoming and certain death with poise, peace, and courage; and Berkeley Elliot, an outspoken and loving, spiritual mentor who expanded my concepts of God and life.

I make a special dedication for my wife Patricia, a true spiritual companion and partner. She is my cheerleader, advocate, loving critic, and *amore me de vita* who lit a fire of love within me the first hours of our meeting, a love that shall never extinguish or grow dim. Miss Patty demonstrates a profound and awesome ability to unify her life with these concepts and constantly challenges me to live these principles—to "walk the walk." Sharing our lives, supporting each other in our individual and partner growth, and helping other people experience the transforming embrace of a practical spirituality has blessed me with a life beyond my wildest dreams.

Acknowledgements

"Thank you" to Rebecca Hillan and Christine Colborne for devoting time and effort to reading, re-reading, and correcting my many errors.

Contact information:
tjstrawser@comcast.net

If you enjoy these daily thoughts/meditations, sign up for free "Daily thought" short version emailed directly to you. Just send an email to the above address.

January 1

People believe what I do more than what I say.

Actions, not words, produce results. Making promises, talking about values, and holding great intentions are as smoke in the wind—here for a very short time and then gone if our actions do not support them.

Honesty, loyalty, integrity, compassion, truthfulness, love, and forgiveness are great words but require consistent and repetitive action to become part of our character. If we desire to be the best version of ourselves, to progressively reflect our heritage as a child of God, our deeds must align with our language and intentions; each day we strive to identify where we fall short and then commit to improve. But this is a two-way street. We also need to give other peoples' past performance and current efforts—what they actually have done and are doing—much more credence than their words.

Disappointment, frustration, and misery often result from believing promises and rhetoric instead of demonstrated acts.

Prayer: My inner spirit, my God, my guardian angel, please help me this day. Help me to become aware of every word, every action, and my attitude. Guide my deeds that they may be loving, compassionate, kind, gentle, and fair; let each act align with your plans.

Take three relaxing breaths; ask your inner spirit to guide your meditation; pause for a few minutes in silence.

January 2

"The transient pleasures that come from the world bear sorrows to come; not in them do the wise find joy. "(The Bhagavad Gita 5 V 23)

What are the sources of happiness? Age-old wisdom suggested that we have four primary sources for happiness:

1. possessing—acquiring "things", relationships, power, or money;
2. winning—being recognized as a "winner", as being number one, as being important or better than others;
3. serving—doing good; serving or helping other people;
4. transcending—striving to be the best we can be; seeking a connection to something greater.

We can find some happiness at any of these levels. However, happiness experienced in the first two levels is gained from external sources. It is always temporary and is like satisfying an addiction. Maintaining this happiness always requires "MORE".

Happiness resulting from the third and fourth levels comes from within. Being dedicated to helping others gets us away from being the center of the universe, moves us from a selfish, self-centered lifestyle to an inclusive awareness of the needs and rights of all humanity.

The highest level of happiness results when we realize we have a transcendent value, that every righteous choices add to our personal mosaic. We face multiple choices each day; the world tires to convince us that "possessing" and "winning" are the greatest achievements in life. However, transcending helps us to discover the "Great Reality" deep within and strive for higher values—integrity, honor, compassion, forgiveness, and loyalty—rather than sacrifice principles for short term gratification.

Prayer: My wonderful source of inspiration, power, and peace, guide my thoughts, words, and actions this day; grant me peace and help me to be receptive to your leadings.

Take three relaxing breaths; ask your inner spirit to guide your meditation; pause for a few minutes in silence.

January 3

It is what it is!
Reality does not require our approval.

So simple it is almost an insult. However, we may know this but fail to apply it to our life; we focus on what we want, what we think *should* happen, what is fair, how other people should appreciate us and so on. We miss the simple truth that *reality is reality and does not depend on our wants, opinion, or approval.*

We can accept what we're facing exactly *as it is at this moment* or we can whine, gripe, complain, blame, or whatever. None of these affect the reality of the situation or advance a solution. Accepting does not mean agreement or approval, does not imply that the situation is "according to God's plan", or that it will stay this way forever. Acceptance does require that we recognize and accept the facts, the reality of what is in front of us. Problems are much easier to solve when dealing with reality instead of living in a land of fantasies or waiting for what should happen.

We might ask our self: Do I have contention in any area in my life? Have I fully accepted the reality of the situation?

Prayer: My heavenly parent and indwelling spirit, please help me accept the reality of my situation today. Help me to feel your love, mercy and peace. If my times are troublesome, let your strength and presence carry me over the rocks today; if times are good, help me to feel grateful but not take undue credit.

Take three relaxing breaths; ask your inner spirit to guide your meditation; pause for a few minutes in silence.

January 4

Life gives us pain but misery is optional—and self-inflicted.

Pain includes grief, sadness, and mourning; misery embraces fear, worry, anxiety, anger, resentment, remorse, envy, jealousy, self-pity, pride, and most guilt. Misery can start with untreated pain that has become infected or it can be initiated and propagated by selfishness, self-centeredness, or self-righteousness.

Life gives us pain. Loving other people makes us vulnerable to pain. We will lose people to death and separation; we will hurt, sometimes so much that it seems our heart and soul may break into shreds or never heal; however, we know that with time, the healing balm of God's love, and the love of family and friends, we can survive and flourish.

But misery is optional—and it's self-inflicted. Selfishness, self-centeredness, self-righteousness, self-pity and other forms of self-directed will are the primary causes of misery. This is one of the most life-changing truths we'll ever discover. We create many of our own problems and can minimize all those upsetting feelings by replacing our self-directed will with God's will. We sincerely ask for help and open our self to receive it; then our inner spirit, the "kingdom of heaven within," supplies the strength and guidance to release and avoid misery. We no longer have to volunteer for these harmful emotions.

Prayer: My magnificent spiritual parent, my marvelous source and destiny, I thank you for the spark of divinity that you gave me to guide and strengthen me. I feel your presence and know that you will grant me healing; please transform any selfish or self-centered thoughts to love, tolerance, and patience.

Take three relaxing breaths; ask your inner spirit to guide your meditation; pause for a few minutes in silence.

January 5

If what we're doing doesn't produce the results we want, we might consider changing.

Wisdom: *a reliable ability to decide with soundness, discernment, prudence, and intelligence; a sense tempered and refined by experience, training, and maturity.*

Wisdom requires learning from experience and not repeating mistakes.

Appearances indicate that the world is in chaos, that turmoil and misery prevail. In the United States, 48% first-time marriages, 67% second marriages and 73% third marriages fail; 40 million people suffer anxiety; over 43 million people abuse alcohol or prescription drugs; and loneliness has doubled in the last 20 years. Following what the world tells us to do yields chaos and turmoil; it simply does not work! The root cause for this misery—the first domino that starts the whole stack falling—is self-directed will. Unhappiness is inevitable when selfishness, self-centeredness, and self-righteousness dominate the individual and the culture.

There is a better alternative. Personal spirituality directed by the "kingdom of heaven" within—the divine spark within—the Buddha within—provides purpose, values, and practices that can uplift each of us. Our relationship with this inner divinity is a personal, intimate contact and can be practiced within an organized religion or exclusive of it. Our peace and joy in this moment, this day, and our entire life rest on this foundation.

Prayer: My loving and powerful inner spirit, make me aware of your presence this day. Let me pause and speak with you. Quiet my mind, sooth my emotions, and bring peace to my soul.

Take three relaxing breaths; ask your inner spirit to guide your meditation; pause for a few minutes in silence.

January 6

Live and let live.

Actually living is more than just existing—more than being a passenger along for the ride. Living is not blindly accepting what the world tells us is important but requires that we develop our personal values, goals, and priorities. It encompasses action, not procrastination; it demonstrates love and service, not indolence and inertia. Living means that we recognize and accept our own shortcomings and are willing to improve; we feel the joy and the pain of life but do not have to suffer misery; we share our life with others and actively participate in their lives.

"Let live" includes not getting too upset about what others do or say or fail to do or say; we avoid unreasonable expectations of other people, situations, or ourselves; we strive for patience, tolerance, humility, and caring actions. This does not mean that we are a doormat for other people; when necessary, we always stand for our values with quiet poise, integrity, and dignity.

Will I live this day or slide through it? Can I grant everyone else the freedom to live their day?

Prayer: My loving and merciful divine parent, please be patient with me. Help me to go forth this day with love, peace, and exuberance to enjoy a wonderful day; grant that I accept the frailties and humanity in myself and in all my spiritual family.

Take three relaxing breaths; ask your inner spirit to guide your meditation; pause for a few minutes in silence.

January 7

Imagined fears can ruin our day; the dreads of imagination are always worse than reality.

Few things that consume us with fear, anxiety, or worry ever happen the way we imagine. A single thought of what might happen enters our consciousness; our mind grasps that thought and nurtures it, spawning a family of fear-driven offspring. Morbid, fearful feelings follow the thought and start the downward spiral. It makes little difference whether the concern is real or imagined because everything appears real to a fear-driven mind.

We have a choice whether to release the thought or to continue to participate in the misery. Do we want inner peace or want to stay mired in emotional chaos?

If we truly want a better day, we'll take action: We pause, pray, and ask for help to guide our mind; we call a friend, read a book, listen to something uplifting and positive; we take a walk or volunteer in a soup kitchen; we use our physical, mental, and spiritual resources to change our emotions. Our decision-action sequence opens the door for our inner spiritual power to do its job; we give it the opportunity to expulse the fear and replace it with love, hope, compassion, forgiveness, and peace.

Prayer: Dear God, please remove this fearful thought; grant me peace; and illuminate my mind to see the truth about my challenge. If this is an imagined dread, erase it from my mind. If this is an immediate threat to my physical, mental, or spiritual well-being, reveal the solution that leads me to be the child you want me to be.

Take three relaxing breaths; ask your inner spirit to guide your meditation; pause for a few minutes in silence.

January 8

Un-returned love is not wasted but flows back to soften and purify the heart of the lover.

Love is an active and healthy concern for a person's well-being; a desire to do good for others. When we bestow love to someone, the acts and feeling of love flow *from us to them.* Nothing about the definition requires or even suggests that we may receive love as a reciprocal act. It's not about us. It's a bonus when we do receive love in return, either from the object of our love or someone else. The definition also offers some additional guidance. Our act of love should truly enhance a person's well-being, should contribute to his or her physical, mental, and spiritual growth; love should help but never enable.

Love is an eternal quality that flows from the divine source to us, through us, and to another person. We can become an open conduit for this divine value. As we bestow it with wisdom—with no need or expectations—we receive beautiful gifts. This divine quality nurtures and refreshes our very being as it flows through us, softening and purifying our heart and soul, helping us to become the best version of our self.

Prayer: I pray that I may open my mind, heart, and soul to receive the love so freely given from my spiritual source. Open my heart; let this beautiful quality flow outward from me to those in the most need of love. Help me bestow love with wisdom, expecting nothing in return.

Take three relaxing breaths; ask your inner spirit to guide your meditation; pause for a few minutes in silence.

January 9

Wherever you are, be there.

Life is always better if we can stay focused on THIS moment. We cannot change a thing we did five minutes ago; we cannot control any person or event in tomorrow. Our mind and actions in this precise moment are all that we can realistically hope to control. God lives in eternity but he responds to us in the moment of NOW.

Yesterday and everything about it is gone forever; tomorrow is but a possibility. This moment, the one we are living *right now* is truly all that we have. Our body always stays in the moment—it is always in the NOW. Our mind is the only part of us that time travels. It journeys into the past, re-lives events, and returns with guilt, resentment, and regret; or it journeys into the future and brings back anxiety, dread, and fear. Once our mind has developed this time-travelling habit, training it to stay home may be difficult. We access our inner spiritual power and ask for help; we strive for constant awareness and appreciation of every happening of every moment.

Living in the moment actually improves our abilities in the real world. We still make plans but don't waste energy worrying about things we cannot act on today; we appreciate what we have instead of floundering in turmoil of what might be; we face reality and find solutions for challenges instead of escaping in daydreams.

Prayer: Father, help me appreciate and love your world, others, and myself in each small moment as it passes; guide my thoughts; help me keep them in the NOW, in the very moment-by-moment experiences of this day.

Take three relaxing breaths; ask your inner spirit to guide your meditation; pause for a few minutes in silence.

January 10

Would you rather be happy or right?

Sometimes we may feel a need to prove our self "right," to win a disagreement to make the other person realize that we are knowledgeable or important. We may need to be right because we don't have enough self-worth to accept that we might be wrong; we may not understand that making mistakes does not diminish our value as a person or as a child of God.

When we feel good about our self, we are more patient, tolerant, and loving with others; when we don't have that inner void that yearns to be filled, we are more accepting, non-judgmental, and caring. This state of healthy self-love removes much of the need to be proven "right" that dominates the self-driven person. We can choose to be happy instead of worrying about who is "right."

Today, if you feel that urge to prove yourself "right," pause for a moment to see why it's so important and see if perhaps being happy might not be a better option.

Prayer: Dear God, I pray that you would help me be gentle with every person I meet today and myself. Help me not to believe that I have to be right, to prove something, to be better than another person. Guide my thoughts to love, tolerance, and patience and my actions to kindness.

Take three relaxing breaths; ask your inner spirit to guide your meditation; pause for a few minutes in silence.

January 11

Today is the first day of the rest of your life.

Did you make a mistake yesterday? Did you do something you really wish you hadn't done? No one on this planet can go back in time and change what has happened even five minutes ago. If necessary, we may have to apologize or make amends; then, we must completely release the error. This day—this moment—is our starting point. It is a new day that has never been used and we will never have another chance at this day for the rest of our life.

We pause, bring our mind into this moment, take three relaxation breaths and acknowledge five people or things for which we are grateful. We ask our inner spirit to help us keep our mind in this moment and to give us guidance and strength to be a better person; we must learn from yesterday but not dwell on the glory or mistakes of the past. We commit that we will not allow the past, another person, or any situation steal time from this day; we will not accept feelings of misery—anger, worry, guilt, fear, shame or other debilitating reactions. We can start this day in the morning, at noon, or anytime; it does not operate on a clock. It is *our* day to live.

Prayer: My divine source, help me to accept that making mistakes is part of being human; let your transforming power ease any contention about my past. Fill me with the hope that I can change, the desire to become the best I can be, the willingness to act, and the strength to overcome all barriers to my progress.

Take three relaxing breaths; ask your inner spirit to guide your meditation; pause for a few minutes in silence.

January 12

To thine own self be true.

This may be an old saying but is still essential to enjoying the best life possible. If we are not true to our values, we are a ship without a rudder, blown hither and yon by the winds of the world; if we are not true to our ideals, we have no anchor to hold us fast in times of uncertainty and turmoil. Then we compromise everything to achieve temporary goals; the opinions of others control our life.

We must know our self before we can be true to our self. We must honestly understand our values, purpose, ideals, assets, and liabilities; then, we must accept our self exactly as we are. Yes, we have made mistakes. We are not perfect but we are a child of God and trying our best; we accept the glory and blemishes of being us and nurture the desire and willingness to improve. We identify our core values and strive to demonstrate them in all parts of our life.

When necessary, in spite of fear and trepidation, in spite of being one against the many, we stand and speak for the principles that are important to us. As a child of the divine, we demonstrate humility, trustworthiness, honor, courage, integrity, truth, ethics, compassion, mercy, and honesty.

Prayer: My God, help me to honestly examine the qualities I hold dearest in life and elevate these to reflect the values you want me to embrace. Give me the courage and the strength to stand for these against all opposition, and the prudence to think, speak, and act according to your will.

Take three relaxing breaths; ask your inner spirit to guide your meditation; pause for a few minutes in silence.

January 13

**Prayer is a cornerstone of a spiritual life;
Experiencing a conscious contact with divinity elevates our humanity.**

Prayer is an essential part of changing our life. It accesses an additional reservoir of wisdom and power to soothe our emotions and to provide direction, courage, perseverance, strength, and hope.

Prayer is simply talking to God—a direct communication from the individual to the divine source, an opening of the human-to-divinity conduit. Billions of people in a multitude of religions have recognized the necessity and rewards of prayer for thousands of years. Consider the possibilities of prayer as cited by one source: Prayer can be

> *an expression of thanksgiving, an avoidance of emotional tension, a prevention of conflict, an exaltation of intellection, an ennoblement of desire, a vindication of moral decision, an enrichment of thought, an invigoration of higher inclinations, a consecration of impulse, a clarification of viewpoint, a declaration of faith, a transcendental surrender of will, a sublime assertion of confidence, a revelation of courage, the proclamation of discovery, a confession of supreme devotion, the validation of consecration, a technique for the adjustment of difficulties, and the mighty mobilization of the combined soul powers to withstand all human tendencies toward selfishness, evil, and sin.* (Urantia Book p 2088)

Prayer: Dear God, help me communicate with you more often. Help me lift my thoughts in prayer to seek strength, give thanks, ask for help or whenever I am moved to talk with you.

Take three relaxing breaths; ask your inner spirit to guide your meditation; pause for a few minutes in silence.

January 14

There are very few Big Deals.

Are you tense, anxious, worried, or stressed out? Does guilt, regret, or remorse consume you? Then you're making a big deal out of something. A "Big Deal" is a situation or event that appears to be life-altering but often is simply our over-reaction, something that we manufacture out of trifles often as a response to an unresolved misery (guilt, anger, fear, etc. trigger Big Deal reactions.) Life has very few Big Deals—death or serious illness of a loved one, addiction, divorce, bankruptcy, and so on—events that will negatively impact our lives for years into the future.

A quick check to put the current upset in perspective: We pause and ask our self: Will this problem impact my life a year from now? Will I even remember it (and what caused it) one year from today? If the answer's no, then it is not a Big Deal.

We pause a moment to see why we're reacting like this: Do we have any form of fear or other misery that we need to release? Are we allowing our mind to exaggerate small things, to create fear where none should be? Have we lost the connection to our spiritual power? Are we living in the moment?

Then, we seek the power and guidance of our inner spirit to release this and replace the anxiety with serenity. The number of "Big Deals" in a day is inversely proportional to our spiritual condition; we have more upsets if we are not in fit spiritual condition.

Prayer: Wonderful, beautiful, and all powerful God, please direct my thinking this day and help me not to react and make big deals out of small challenges. Help me remember that my inner life determines my peace of mind more than exterior events.

Take three relaxing breaths; ask your inner spirit to guide your meditation; pause for a few minutes in silence.

January 15

It's not any of my business what people think of me.

When another person judges or criticizes us, we should seek to understand their motives, values, and experience. We pay attention to those who love us, want the best for us, and share our goals and values. However, everyone is human. Their opinion reflects their life history, maturity, and how they feel about themselves in this moment; they act based on their own values, challenges, motives, and desires. We have no control over any of these. If someone calls us a lemon, that does not make us a lemon.

We can only try to control what we think, do, and say. We must manage our own behavior and attitude; we stay focused on our pursuit of spiritual and emotional maturity and do not give credence to the detractors. We will make mistakes and should not let these overburden us; we avoid self-righteousness—we listen to the criticism of those we respect and who are walking a path similar to ours but avoid being overly sensitive to the misguided disapproval of others.

Prayer: My loving inner spirit, help me spend this day with you—aware of your presence and feeling your love and acceptance of me. Guide my thoughts, words and actions that all may be worthy of your approval. If, in my humanness, my actions are less that your ideal, bathe me in your love and lead me to righteousness.

Take three relaxing breaths; ask your inner spirit to guide your meditation; pause for a few minutes in silence.

January 16

A glass full of vinegar can't hold honey.

We cannot be loving and angry at the same time; we cannot be full of gratitude and also have guilt, anxiety, fear, or resentments. When these miserable feelings start bothering us, we focus on the positive things in our life.

Write a gratitude list. This action changes our attitude quicker than a thousand thoughts. We feel the misery melt as we take pen in hand and start to write. We pause as we write the name of a person we love or someone who loves us and reflect on our appreciation for that person. We consider how walking, seeing, living, and breathing are blessings; we feel the love and security from knowing that we are children of a loving God.

Peace pervades our heart as we reflect on the truth that these are the really important things in our life. We enjoy an overwhelming gratitude as we trace the times that God's grace filled us with hope when hopeless; with direction, when wandering; with a word or act of kindness from someone when desperate; and with love when alone and feeling unlovable. Honey replaces the vinegar inside in our heart, mind, and soul.

Prayer: My divine parent, please wash the bitterness, envy, anger, guilt and all negative, hurtful feelings from my soul. Replace each with love and gratitude. Help me be aware of the seen and unseen blessings in my life. Thank you for loving and helping this child.

Take three relaxing breaths; ask your inner spirit to guide your meditation; pause for a few minutes in silence.

January 17

Stop worrying. Eliminate "If", "What if "and "If only" from your vocabulary.

Worrying contributes nothing to solving problems. In fact, it often prevents or interferes with finding real solutions. But worry becomes a habit, an automatic reaction when faced with things we can't control. It starts as a single thought but can quickly grow to dominate our mind and is much easier to control before it grows into a giant.

The words "If", "What if" and "If only" often precede worrisome thoughts. "If" she does this, it'll be a catastrophe. "What if" this happens? "If only" they would do this. It's hard to worry without using these words. Eliminate them from your vocabulary. Write them in large print and put them in conspicuous places—on a mirror, your dresser, the refrigerator, the dashboard of your car. Every time you notice them, reflect on the inner contention generally associated with these phrases; become aware of them as soon as they appear in your thoughts and immediately ask your inner spirit to remove them.

Prayer: Dear God, please help me to stop this worrying that upsets me and causes inner turmoil. Help me recognize when I start thinking about "if, what if, and if only" and to turn to you immediately for help. I know that you can stop this harmful journey into concern over things I cannot control.

Take three relaxing breaths; ask your inner spirit to guide your meditation; pause for a few minutes in silence.

January 18

God's love heals our emotional wounds.

God's love naturally flows to our individual need and supplies the exact agent required to heal our specific suffering. The healing may be a direct response or may emerge as an option to see, think, and feel differently that we must pursue to facilitate the healing. Our finite need can never diminish this infinite supply of curative power. Our God is an artist, a lover, and an engineer—infinitely efficient and only supplying what is needed.

- When we are weak, he gives us strength; when strong, he presents opportunities for compassion, tolerance, and patience.
- When overwhelmed, he offers the ability to breathe deeply and feel peace; when frustrated, a moment of clarity.
- When afraid, he imparts comfort and security; when confused, a direction; when lonely, a bathing of divine friendship; when angry, a thought to quiet the fury.
- When tempted, he grants an insight to truth, honesty, loyalty, integrity, honor, and ethics; when suffering self-righteousness, he presents opportunities to gain humility.
- When despondent with self-pity, he offers balance, a more realistic viewpoint that acknowledges our blessings.
- In grief, he offers the certitude of love; the knowledge that his love for us is always with us and we simply have to receive its warmth and power.

Prayer: My loving inner spark, let your healing love flow to my need this day. Help me to trust and accept your care; to open my heart, mind, and soul, to your transforming power. Thank you for your divine care.

Take three relaxing breaths; ask your inner spirit to guide your meditation; pause for a few minutes in silence.

January 19

Do you live in the "*Someday Isle*"?

The *Someday Isle* is a little like Never-Never Land. Of course, adults don't really believe in Peter Pan and Never-Never Land; however, many supposedly mature people spend a lot of time in *The Someday Isle* where they may join the chant that pervades the land. "Someday I'll ... Someday I'll... Someday I'll..."

- Someday I'll quit doing things that hurt people I love.
- Someday I'll spend more time with my children.
- Someday I'll tell the truth and not have to be afraid of being caught.
- Someday I'll quit telling or listening to gossip.
- Someday I'll quit worrying so much.
- Someday I'll not be so sensitive to what other people think or say.
- Someday I'll show all my family how much I love them.
- Someday I'll quit expecting my partner and others to read my mind.
- Someday I'll truly trust God with all my concerns and not give lip service to my faith.
- Someday I'll .....

Don't confuse this nefarious place with having dreams and goals. The *Someday Isle* attitude represents things that we could do today if we were willing to do them but stay shackled by indolence and complacency. Illusions create misery; dreams create hope.

Prayer: My God within, grant me the power and the initiative to act; ignite the burning flame within me; help me to make decisions and act with insight, clarity, poise and equanimity.

Take three relaxing breaths; ask your inner spirit to guide your meditation; pause for a few minutes in silence.

January 20

Blaming other people for the way we feel gives them control over our life.

Yes, other people can do things that offend or hurt us but it's our choice on how we react. If we get angry at someone and say—*or even think*— "Look at what he did! He made me angry, he hurt my feelings" we are acknowledging that he has the power to control the way we feel. This statement or thought makes the other person responsible for the problem, which automatically makes them responsible for the solution; then, we cannot feel better until they apologize or change.

When we allow someone to control our feelings—say make us angry—the feeling burning inside of us and the thoughts dominating our mind are our real problem. Changing our perspective can change the way we feel; modifying our thoughts and words start the healing process.

We acknowledge the turmoil and take ownership of the problem and the solution; we accept that "*I am angry* at what he did." This gives us the responsibility and the power to change no matter what the other person does. With this awareness, we then access our spirit of God within; we admit our turmoil and ask for help to elevate our thoughts, words, actions, and feelings.

Prayer: My divine inner source, guide my thoughts, feelings, and reactions. Help me understand that I do not need to allow any person or event to control my feelings; open my heart and mind to your calming presence; empower me to rise above my human reactions and find that peace that passes all understanding.

Take three relaxing breaths; ask your inner spirit to guide your meditation; pause for a few minutes in silence.

January 21

If nothing changes, NOTHING changes.

If we keep doing what we've been doing, we'll keep getting the same results (and keep feeling the way we're feeling.)

Burning our hand on a hot stove brings immediate changes so we don't do it again; however, we may suffer emotional pain but continue to volunteer for the very acts that cause our misery. We may

- allow someone to repeatedly hurt our feelings,
- extend trust to someone after they have proven untrustworthy,
- want to stop a harmful behavior but keep entering situations that trigger the same actions, or
- want better relationships but keep repeating patterns that lead to failure or mediocrity.

The only person we can change is our self and we'll suffer a life of continuing misery if our happiness requires another person to change.

Effective change requires that we:

1. Identify and accept the real problem.
2. Evaluate alternative solutions and pick the best one.
3. Take action to implement that solution.

Prayer: My divine parent, please reveal the best direction for change, instill within me the initiative to start this new path, and grant me the power to accomplish any task necessary to improve my life. Help me to be willing to change and be receptive to your guidance.

Take three relaxing breaths; ask your inner spirit to guide your meditation; pause for a few minutes in silence.

January 22

Illusions cause discontent.

Someone says or does something; suddenly a worrisome thought spawns in our mind. We unconsciously react, thus giving power to the false idea that this is a real problem. Thus starts the crescendo of emotions and thoughts about the false problem.

As we mature, we learn to pause and evaluate if we are facing a real threat or an illusion by asking four key questions:

1. Is it a real and immediate threat to my well-being?
2. Is it my responsibility to solve?
3. Can I do anything about it today?
4. Do I really need to solve this?

If none of these can be answered "yes," it is likely an illusion. Consider: If it does not pose an immediate threat to our physical, mental, or spiritual well-being, or if we're not responsible for it, or if we cannot do something *today,* or if it is just a minor concern, THEN IT IS NOT A REAL PROBLEM TODAY, so let it go.

If it qualifies as a problem at some future time, deal with it then. Don't waste time, energy, and resources dealing with non-problems. Release the illusion, face the day with equanimity and poise, free of all fear.

Prayer: Dear God, help me to pause and not react to everything that happens; give me the strength to resist participating in the turmoil created by my mind; replace all discontent with the awareness of your love and the assurance that we can face any hardship and overcome any obstacle.

Take three relaxing breaths; ask your inner spirit to guide your meditation; pause for a few minutes in silence.

January 23

Through "silent agreement" we can tell a lie, sever a loyalty, or see something honest or good be lessened without uttering a word.

Yes, silence may be golden, but failing to stand for our core values costs a heavy price. Make no mistake: *Silence is a tacit agreement with what has been said or done.*

Like so many things, the motive for silence is more important than the act itself. "Why" we fail to speak determines the ultimate effect on our character.

If the occurring words or deed reflect something that is not important, or we have no belief or knowledge about it, social grace may let us pass on stating our opinion. However, failing to address an action that conflicts with our life purpose, beliefs, or values because we fear other people's opinions, repercussions, or we simply want to "get along" causes three problems:

1. Our silent agreement adds weight, strength, and credibility to something that offends us or that we feel is in error.
2. Each such act takes a piece of our integrity, ethics, and courage.
3. Repeated failures build character patterns until we are conditioned not to speak out against anything.

Spiritual maturity and common sense guide us when to speak loving, tactful, courageous words.

Prayer: Dear God, guide my mind this day. Help me to always stand for what is important; guide me to speak and act with poise, loyalty, and conviction but not be overly involved with the trifles of life.

Take three relaxing breaths; ask your inner spirit to guide your meditation; pause for a few minutes in silence.

January 24

Guilt often comes from expectations.

Guilt: *a feeling of culpability, of being responsible or blameworthy for harm or error.*

Like fear, guilt can be healthy or unhealthy. We can be overly sensitive to other people's expectations and feel guilty when we disappoint them; we can set unreasonable expectations on our self and feel guilty when we fall short; we can have misconceptions about God and feel unwarranted guilt through our misunderstanding. Unhealthy guilt can cause deep agony; we can experience severe, soul-disturbing feelings and have done absolutely nothing wrong.

If we have actually done something wrong, even healthy guilt can inflict unnecessary harm. We cannot allow it to mire us in despair and self-loathing nor to extend beyond an appropriate time. We need to right the wrong, make restitution, apologize or whatever; then we let this experience mold us into a better person, a more loving child of God. Our mistakes can bring the pain that spurs us to grow; our errors may initiate better judgment, patience, and tolerance.

Prayer: My loving spiritual parent, I claim my birthright as your child. I come to you in this time of inner turmoil and ask that you direct my thoughts. If I have strayed from the path of your choosing, guide me in making right all things; grant me courage, wisdom, and sincerity as I proceed. If I am overly sensitive, replace my misguided reactions with true understanding; pervade my mind with your love and restore peace to my soul.

Take three relaxing breaths; ask your inner spirit to guide your meditation; pause for a few minutes in silence.

January 25

Love people; use things.
Don't use people and love things.

Our world focuses on "things." We are bombarded with the concept that our life gets better if we obtain this certain "thing"; we are told that we will experience love and exquisite bliss if we buy this certain object. And it's a lie. "Things" can make our life easier or more enjoyable; using them may add to our pleasure but they can never be the source of deep and lasting happiness.

Loving other people and being able to receive love are essential in fulfilling our human potential. Loving relationships are the heartbeat of our very existence, a vital need to every individual. Love flows from the eternal source but must move through us to others to become a part of our own experience. Love is "an active and healthy concern for a person's well-being" and not a desire for, or an affection of, a thing.

Prayer: Infinite source and my indwelling connection to God, help me open my heart, mind, and soul to become more aware of the divine flow of your love; grant me understanding, compassion, and tolerance to bestow this gift to all I meet this day—especially to any that may offend or hurt me. Let me appreciate the material blessings, the "things" of life, but not be overly concerned with any of them.

Take three relaxing breaths; ask your inner spirit to guide your meditation; pause for a few minutes in silence.

January 26

The value of a vessel is its emptiness.

"Clay is formed into a vessel; the emptiness bounded by the clay creates the usefulness of the vessel.
Walls, windows, and doors make boundaries of a room.
The value is its emptiness, not the boundaries."
(Verse 11, Tao Te Ching, Lao Tzu)

If I have a pitcher of dirty water and want to fill it with clean water, the vessel has to be emptied. The vessel cannot carry the desired contents as long as it is full of something else.

The walls of the pitcher define its shape. These physical boundaries are what we see and identify as "the pitcher." However, the attribute that makes this vessel worth having exists inside its walls. *Its value lies in the emptiness.* It must be empty before it can hold something more valuable. Likewise, we can never receive the new while we are full of the old. If I am full of ME, I have no room for others—including God.

- If I am full of knowing, I cannot learn.
- If I am full of physical desires, I cannot receive spiritual insight.
- If I am full of misery, I cannot accept happiness.
- I can be filled with knowledge but void of wisdom.
- I can be filled with facts but not know truth.
- I can be filled with action but empty of results.

Prayer: Please remove from me any thoughts, opinions, preconceptions, or understanding that stands in the way of my peace and happiness; empty me of anything that impedes my usefulness to you or my fellows. Fill me with wisdom, peace, and an active love for all I meet this day.

Take three relaxing breaths; ask your inner spirit to guide your meditation; pause for a few minutes in silence.

January 27

Anger is a physical and emotional manifestation of spiritual immaturity.

Everyone gets angry—right? It's "normal". Using this excuse to justify anger guarantees we'll keep getting angry; we'll believe it's just part of human nature and something we have to tolerate. A better view of anger helps us understand that it is a trait that causes us problems and one which we can eliminate or minimize.

We become aware of each episode of anger and accept it as a human feeling that we want to change. We pause, take three very deep breaths and exhale slowly. We immediately ask our inner guide to help us not react and lash out, to let us see the underlying reason for our reaction, and to replace the anger with peace and tolerance. Our emotional habits require time and consistent effort to change and our anger will not likely disappear at once; however, if we persistently follow this process, our growth is guaranteed and we're grateful for each inevitable improvement.

We are not doormats. We do not allow others to use us or abuse us; however, we must find the peace, poise, and understanding to handle situations in a way that nurtures our inner self and a demonstration of spiritual power to all people.

Prayer: Grant me peace at this moment. Let your love quiet my mind and emotions and save me from responding in anger. Help me see that this feeling is inside of me and part of me; give me perception to understand that real or imagined wrongs done by others cannot affect me when I feel your presence and your love.

Take three relaxing breaths; ask your inner spirit to guide your meditation; pause for a few minutes in silence.

January 28

Shed the darkness of religious lethargy and enjoy the amazing adventure of personally experiencing divine power.

Religion without a vibrant, personal spiritual connection to the divine source is like the reflection of a flame in a mirror; it reproduces the image but has no heat. Half-hearted spirituality produces few results in daily living.

The personal spiritual quest is not dull, boring, and glum; it's an exciting adventure of discovering an indwelling source of power and guidance and finding solutions that actually solve the problems of life. This journey unleashes the additional source of spiritual energy that offers the greatest transformations possible in this life: this power moves us from addiction to freedom; from fear, anxiety, and anger to courage, peace, love, and tolerance; from weak and undirected drifting—blown hither and yon by the winds of life—to strength of character, certainty of purpose, and unquestioned principles.

This quest finds and welcomes the shift in attitude that views adversities as challenges, triumphs over insurmountable difficulties, and is willing to reach out the hand of love and compassion to the less fortunate.

Prayer: Dear God, break my shackles of lethargy, apathy, and rebellion; grant me the willingness to explore and find all that I might be. Guide my efforts to feel and experience the inner spirit you so graciously gave me. Grant me the good judgment to allow this spirit to transform my life.

Take three relaxing breaths; ask your inner spirit to guide your meditation; pause for a few minutes in silence.

January 29

Rejecting a religious doctrine does not reject God.

Many have rejected God and religion; some refuse to believe anything that appears to disagree with science; still others have no need for anything that doesn't fit "modern" ideas or improve their materialistic life. Rejecting organized religion or disallowing doctrines that are intellectually invalid or morally repugnant is not rejecting God.

Some see God as the only uncaused cause; as the creator and upholder of the supernovas, stars, and planets; as the source of all power and energy. In addition to this grand physical domain, he is the very source of life and gives each unique human mortal the "kingdom of heaven within" which offers an inner reservoir of unsuspected spiritual power. He also gives us free will to choose whether we want to participate in the universe plan, claim our birthright, and activate this unique internal power to transform our life.

This life-empowering relationship can be discovered and enjoyed within the context of a religious group or alone. Accessing this "kingdom of heaven within" floods us with the peace that passes all human understanding, provides unflagging courage in adversity, and grants long-lasting patience, enduring tolerance, and fulfilling love. But it's always our choice. Close-minded pride can forever block entrance into this kingdom.

Prayer: I pray that the creator of all things, the origin and cause of the universes, the source of all power, and the giver of all life touches my mind, heart, and soul. Let me feel your presence; melt any barrier that blocks my full acceptance of your gifts; fill my being with love, peace and security.

Take three relaxing breaths; ask your inner spirit to guide your meditation; pause for a few minutes in silence.

January 30

Unconscious decisions cause much of our misery.

We seldom make a conscious choice to worry or get angry or engage in many other emotional upsets. An event happens; we automatically react; we experience thoughts, feelings, and possibly take action *without making a conscious decision*; then, our mind justifies and reinforces our response. Past reactions to similar situations have formed an emotional reflex action—we react without thought or consideration and create problems for our self.

If we want a great life, we must change our automatic unconscious choices into conscious decisions.

Each time we find our self starting to react, when we feel the rush of anger, worry, anxiety, or guilt and remorse, we pause, take three relaxation breaths and ask our inner spiritual force to

- remove this contentious feeling,
- alter our thoughts and let them reflect that we are a child of God,
- make us more aware of these automatic reactions that cause us turmoil,
- give us the strength to break these patterns and
- grant us the wisdom and maturity to make conscious choices that benefit our life.

Prayer: My inner bastion of power, help me not to participate in reactions that are not good for me; let me become more aware when I am reacting without thinking. Give me the power, strength, and resolve to make conscious choices that align with your desires for me.

Take three relaxing breaths; ask your inner spirit to guide your meditation; pause for a few minutes in silence.

January 31

The less love in any person's nature, the greater his or her need for love.
(and sometimes, the more unloving are their actions.)

We sometimes encounter people who hurt us, try to use us, or even abuse us. We have a choice in how we respond. Accepting the simple truth that "Those who feel loved, act lovingly" offers a perspective that might temper our response.

All true love comes from the divine source, flows to each person, through that individual and then outward to others. The flow from the source is constant and un-ending but self-righteousness, selfishness, self-centeredness, and fear can block our feeling the flow of love for a moment, a day, or a lifetime. These spiritual maladies render any person incapable of receiving love, experiencing love, or letting the love flow out to another human being. Those who are hurting do hurtful things.

Consider the lack of love—and the need for love—in the acts of this challenging, unloving person and offer a reply based on this knowledge without sacrificing dignity, poise, and self-respect.

Prayer: Dear God, let all my acts this day be acts of love and not depend on other people's acts toward me. If someone is unkind, belligerent, or hateful, guide me so that I may share the love I feel from you and from my family and friends.

Take three relaxing breaths; ask your inner spirit to guide your meditation; pause for a few minutes in silence.

February 1

Whenever I am upset, there is something wrong with ME.

We must be responsible for all our feelings or forever feel un-peaceful. Yes, bad things happen; people inflict real or imagined wrongs; life is hectic and we get frustrated when people or events do not meet our expectations. But we must remember: "*We cannot control other people but can choose how we react.*" We slow down, take three deep breaths, and ask our inner spirit to help us understand why we are reacting this way and to lead us to a better response. Then, we ask ourselves:

- Have I lost my connection to my spiritual source? Do I truly feel that spiritual presence?
- Am I making myself, something I want or expect, or someone else more important than my spiritual values?
- Is my mind spiritually directed or I am reacting on self-will?
- Am I allowing my perceptions, expectations, other people's opinions, or temporary events to erode my peace?
- How important is it really? Is it an immediate problem that threatens my well-being? Is it really any of my business?

Prayer: I am disturbed. I ask that you quiet my mind, heal my emotions, and spread your infinite love to my soul and every fiber of my being. Let me feel your presence. Guide my thoughts to reflect on the blessings in my life; help me to understand that disappointment, loss, rejection, and adversity are opportunities for growth.

Take three relaxing breaths; ask your inner spirit to guide your meditation; pause for a few minutes in silence.

February 2

Let us hear with our ears but listen with our heart.

Our relationships vary from casual contacts, friends, to very intimate and loving associations. For each of them, it is important that we actually listen in addition to hearing.

Listening with our heart includes active listening; we give the person our undivided attention to demonstrate the value we place on them and on their words and ideas; we actually participate using questions and comments to clarify our understanding. Listening with our heart implies that we try to recognize the importance of the conversation to the speaker—is it idle talk or something that reflects a value, a sincere concern, or fear?

Such loving actions also include empathetic listening—seeking to understand the point-of-view, motivation, and dreams underlying the spoken words; we try to recognize and acknowledge the feeling associated with what is being said. Listening with our heart takes more time, effort, and emotional investment than simply hearing with our ears. But it is a key to opening extraordinary relationships with everyone we meet.

Prayer: My divine father-mother, help me listen and actually hear with my heart and soul today. Help me be more sensitive to discern the message from the speaker's heart and not just the words from the lips; guide my response into loving, compassionate channels.

Take three relaxing breaths; ask your inner spirit to guide your meditation; pause for a few minutes in silence.

February 3

Tomorrow's dread is not real today.

Worry and anxiety about tomorrow can devastate today's serenity. We start focusing on the future, thinking something "might" happen and it will result in the worst possible outcome. Our fear-driven thoughts develop into an obsession that makes it impossible to feel peace in this moment. When this happens, we can stay unsettled or we can change.

We can choose to get out of the misery and ask for the "God within" to change our thinking and our attitude. We ask our self:

- Is this situation really my responsibility?
- Does it pose an immediate threat to my well-being?
- Am I allowing fear to distort my evaluation?
- Should I release and accept that I have no control over it?

Then, we make a gratitude list, read or listen to something uplifting, take a walk and actually notice something beautiful, and look for someone to be nice to—we open a door or carry a package for a stranger; we call a loved one and tell them how important they are in our life. Illusionary fears cannot stand against loving actions, positive attitudes, and our inner spiritual power.

Prayer: Dear Spirit, direct my mind, transform my thinking and attitude so that I can release all these self-imposed fears that are hurting me today. Help me understand what actions I can take to melt my anxiety and actually do what is in front of me to do.

Take three relaxing breaths; ask your inner spirit to guide your meditation; pause for a few minutes in silence.

February 4

A campfire is easier to extinguish than a blazing forest fire; Handling small problems prevents big ones.

Common sense dictates that extinguishing a small fire is much easier than trying to control a roaring inferno. The same logic applies to our problems and discontent. Yes, there are problems that come out of nowhere; we have no warning until faced with the raging blaze that demands immediate resolution. But more often, something happens that provokes discontent or anxiety; it's not that bad so we ignore it; however, it keeps returning and gains strength until it bursts into a must-be-solved problem. We can either handle small problems or allow them to grow into giants.

We do not immediately attack *every* minor annoyance in our life but we evaluate each situation to determine: 1) What are the possible consequences if left unattended? 2) Will it keep repeating and be a recurring drain on our well-being? 3) Is it easier to handle right now and put behind us? 4) How important is it really?

This conscious, systematic evaluation and subsequent action can prevent many internal forest fires.

Prayer: My always present divine spirit, I may face situations that challenge my peace today. Help me discern if this annoyance is best ignored or is something I must handle now to prevent future problems. Help me to be patient, tolerant, and loving in my response; guide me to pause and ask for strength and guidance.

Take three relaxing breaths; ask your inner spirit to guide your meditation; pause for a few minutes in silence.

February 5

Our forgiveness for our self is in direct proportion to the forgiveness that we have granted others.

If we are not enjoying happiness, peace, and serenity, consider the possibility that we may suffer from "un-forgiveness." Do we experience any internal conflict, guilt, remorse, or regurgitated anger when we remember a past situation? We may be aware of these remnants of the past; they may linger like a shadow below the surface, unconsciously blocking the healing warmth of the sunlight of the spirit.

The teaching that we ask God to "Forgive us our debts *as* we forgive our debtors" directly indicates the *fact* of the reciprocity of forgiveness—we must extend to others the very quality we wish to receive (we give it out; we get it back.) The *truth* of forgiveness is that if we have sincerely asked for forgiveness, it has been granted; we have been forgiven but can experience the feeling of being forgiven only in direct proportion to the degree we have forgiven other people.

Prayer: My indwelling spirit, help me to forgive everyone including myself. Help me to accept that we are all truly children, trying to live this life as best we can; we will make mistakes that hurt us and others. Impress upon my heart that this day marks a new beginning for the rest of my life; I do not have to carry the burdens of yesterday nor fears of tomorrow.

Take three relaxing breaths; ask your inner spirit to guide your meditation; pause for a few minutes in silence.

February 6

A loving God does not give us problems but offers solutions.

He/she God

- does not cause pain but alleviates our misery;
- does not make us wander in the wilderness of confusion but offers clear purpose and direction;
- does not willingly afflict us but soothes and strengthens us when we are afflicted; and
- does not take people but receives them.

Wrong perceptions and expectations about other people cause us problems but keeping such erroneous ideas about God can separate us from the vital source of power needed to enjoy the highest quality life.

Yes, bad things do happen; nature (disease, natural catastrophes) may afflict us; accidents may hurt us or those we love; war or terrible events may paint the darkest picture of the world but God does not do any of these things. Our loving spiritual parent does not afflict his children—but has given each of us an inner guidance to direct our path, a spiritual energy that is capable of dramatic and life-changing transformations, and a healing love to soothe the hurts inflicted on our journey.

Prayer: Dear God, please let me feel your presence. Grant me the serenity to accept the things I cannot change, the courage to change the things I can, and the wisdom to know the difference.

Take three relaxing breaths; ask your inner spirit to guide your meditation; pause for a few minutes in silence.

February 7

We should never take the people closest to us for granted

and fail to extend the respect, courtesy, and love we feel for them. We need to treat the people we love and value as well as we treat co-workers and friends.

Close relationships can suffer from familiarity—that attitude of quiet indifference—if we fail to give them attention. We expect people to know that they are important to us because we occasionally say a few loving words or because we did something in the past that should have proven it.

We must continually demonstrate the value we have for the people close to us. Love is not a passive, taken-for-granted, it's-all-about-me attitude. We remember and acknowledge the birthday, listen with our heart when they need to talk, and give those unexpected flowers, a card, or small gift. We can prepare a special meal (perhaps with an unexpected romantic setting); we communicate—actually tell them how much they add to our life and how grateful we are that they share our time, our hopes, and the adversities we face. We can give a quiet loving touch or a hug that shows we care.

Prayer: My powerful and intimate inner spirit, help me be aware of the value of those people closest to me; help me do those little acts of kindness and love that add a sparkle to their day, acts that demonstrate the love I feel and importance I place on each of them.

Take three relaxing breaths; ask your inner spirit to guide your meditation; pause for a few minutes in silence.

February 8

We are going to live every day until we die; do we settle for mediocrity or reach for happiness?

Of course, we're going to live every day until we die. But what about today, this little twenty-four-hour time period right now? Are we really going to live it or slide through it?

Today, we'll make a number of choices. The quality of this day and the long-term impact of these decisions often depend on whether these choices are guided by self-directed will or by our inner spirit.

Self-directed will: things *must* happen in our self-imposed time requirements; people *should* act according to our needs or desires; and everything *appears* important. The results are impatience, tension, anxiety, worry, and intolerance.

Living with a spirit-directed attitude shifts our priorities and actions. It's less important that we get our way, be the center of attention, control everything, or rush to accomplish unimportant tasks. We do what needs to be done and experience peace as we do it. We take time to take a deep breath, be kind to someone, share a smile, and actually feel grateful for the friends and family in our life. We are going to live every day until we die—but let us be aware and make the best choice on how we spend *this* day.

Prayer: My potent and loving inner spirit, guide my thoughts, actions, and emotions this day. Help me stay aware of your presence and power in my life; grant me the prudence to pause when agitated and the insight to see with loving understanding. Let this be a day of peace, learning, and hope.

Take three relaxing breaths; ask your inner spirit to guide your meditation; pause for a few minutes in silence.

February 9

We face two defining questions in life:
What is my purpose for living and how will I achieve it?

We are children of a divine parent/creator. This heritage automatically gives each of us a common purpose plus a plan on how to best achieve that purpose. We are told to "Love one another as I have loved you." Such parental love sets a higher goal than the brotherly love denoted by the golden rule of "Love your neighbor as yourself." The first denotes divine love; the second, human affection. Achievement of brotherly caring is a worthy accomplishment but the love a parent for a small child exceeds even this.

We must choose to follow this anointed path and then take action that moves us forward. We increasingly allow our indwelling spirit to guide our mind; this helps us respond with our divine nature instead of our ego nature. We pause to consider if our affections for our fellow travelers reflect how we think God cares for us; do we extend the deepest compassion, mercy, and love of which we are capable—or do we falter and find excuses?

We are not God, not divine in this life, but hopefully we are becoming aware of his attributes and striving to love others as he loves us. A spirit-directed mind opens the floodgates of spiritual power that bear witness that God will do for us what we cannot do for ourselves.

Prayer: My loving Creator/Parent and infinite source, I ask that today, please renew my mind by the transforming power of your indwelling spirit; let me see your purpose for my life and find gratitude for your gifts that make it possible for me to meet this and any challenge.

Take three relaxing breaths; ask your inner spirit to guide your meditation; pause for a few minutes in silence.

February 10

Happiness and peace are impossible without integrity.

Integrity (noun): *the quality or condition of being sound; of being unimpaired, undivided, complete, or whole.*

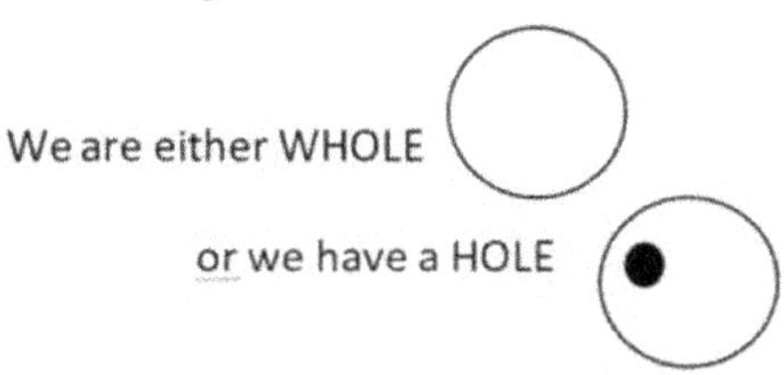

Many people feel this inner void; it's like something is missing. We try to fill it with answers taught us and sold to us by other less-than-whole people. We load the hole with power, money, toys, sex, fame, drugs, alcohol, harmful relationships, and myriad other phony fillers. Each time we get our current object of gratification, the void is filled for a short time; the inner tension and pressure abate but they always return because we have filled the void with temporary relief.

This is a spirit void and the only effective hole-filler is an active relationship with our divine inner spiritual spark. Substitute fillers always fail. The spirit guides us to a higher purpose, elevated values, and supreme practices; we enjoy goals, understandings, and meanings that bring us peace and security plus courage, strength, and energy to face and overcome misfortune This is the solid *something* we are missing, the spiritual substance that provides power and guidance, that yields the integrity we seek.

Prayer: My divine indwelling spark, help me feel your power in my life each moment of this day; fill the void inside of me with your presence. Open my heart, mind, and soul to accept the flow of love and peace from your source.

Take three relaxing breaths; ask your inner spirit to guide your meditation; pause for a few minutes in silence.

February 11

It's hard to balance on a two-legged stool.

You never see a two-legged stool. It takes three legs to provide stable and dependable support. Our life journey is similar. Using only the physical and mental aspects of our lives is like trying to sit on a two-legged stool—we achieve a short-term balance; then, the slightest disruption starts that uncertain wobbling once again.

Adding the third leg, the spiritual leg, provides stability, poise, and peace; we can sit and enjoy the moment without the scurrying to regain and keep our balance. An effective spiritual leg provides purpose, direction, and energy for life; it opens the conduit to access the 'kingdom of heaven within" and offers the "peace that passes all human understanding" in the face of inevitable adversity, tribulation, or success. Today, let's be grateful and stay aware of the stability added by our spiritual support.

Prayer: My spiritual source, I invite you to join me in my life this day. Let me be aware of you as I go through this day; let me pause, connect with you, and allow you to influence and direct my thoughts, my desires, and my actions.

Take three relaxing breaths; ask your inner spirit to guide your meditation; pause for a few minutes in silence.

February 12

The "outer life" may determine our worldly success but our "inner life" determines our happiness, peace-of-mind, and attitude.

The outer life is well known to each of us; it is the people, organizations, and things that touch all aspects of our life plus all the goals, values, and illusions we are told we "must" have. We also have an inner life—that internal part of us that contains our hopes, dreams, thoughts, emotions, and attitude.

Learning to really enjoy this thing we call life requires that we develop the skills to function effectively in both areas and harmonize the conflicting values and priorities. And that we do not have to allow the outside world to completely control and dominate how we feel inside.

We can join the fortunate few who have suffered adversity, disappointment, and hardship but have risen out of the ashes of pain to a new life. We pause and allow our inner spark to elevate our purpose, values, and practices from human to divine-seeking levels; we utilize the best of the worldly things while knowing that true peace comes from within. We let spiritual energy bring healing, strength, and recovery to the wounded soul; we let divine power replace fear with courage, desperation and despair with hope, and resentment and hatred with love, tolerance, and patience.

Prayer: My inner spirit please let my thoughts and actions demonstrate my commitment to my inner life. Help me to realize the transient nature of external events and not allow them to upset my peace nor erode my hope.

Take three relaxing breaths; ask your inner spirit to guide your meditation; pause for a few minutes in silence.

February 13

At any moment, life can throw a mud ball at me.

Life happens. We can be enjoying life or be barely getting by; then, something unexpected hits us. We get bad news; someone rejects us or something totally unfair or unreasonable happens. Do we give situations, events, or other people the power to determine the quality of our day? Of our week? Of our life?

If we trip and fall when hiking in the woods, do we pick our self up, nurse our wound a little, and travel on? Or do we stay there pounding the ground, cursing the limb that tripped us? Or do we go forward—and then return to that same spot to curse and stomp the limb, trying to understand how we could have let it happen, how that limb could do that to us?

We have a choice about how we act and react when something goes wrong; about how much we allow this situation to upset us. We can pause, relax, and ask our self "Did I have any part in this. Did I make a previous error that contributed to it? Am I being overly sensitive? How can I release this inner turmoil to minimize its effect on my day? How important is it really?" Honest answers reveal whether we face a real or imagined crisis. Either way, we then can go to our inner spirit reservoir for the guidance and strength to quiet our contention, make the best decisions, and move forward.

Prayer: I pray that I may accept the reality of this situation; let me see this with honest and long-distant vision; transform my thoughts to be loving, kind, gentle and peaceful. Grant me the power to move forward.

Take three relaxing breaths; ask your inner spirit to guide your meditation; pause for a few minutes in silence.

February 14

Do you view challenging people as villains or opportunities?

Experience teaches us that acquiring certain virtues can improve our life; we may develop a sincere desire to be more patient or tolerant. But often, learning patience requires experiencing situations that produce impatience and slowly learning to react differently; learning tolerance requires being around people that bother us and slowly learning to accept the person while being able to disagree with the action.

Patience is not a problem as long as we get what we want when we want it. Likewise, it's not hard to be tolerant as long as others are loving, agree with us, appreciate us, or don't try to force their ideas and values on us.

The challenges start when we find people that irritate us, make us fearful, or "push our buttons." These are our true teachers—they provide our opportunities to learn and practice patience and tolerance. God, or the universe, has an endless supply of these teachers and they will continue to appear until we learn the lesson. As soon as we allow another person to upset us, to cause us contention or irritation, we mentally repeat "Bless them, change me" and ask for help to see them as our teachers.

It's easier on us if we can learn with the first few instructors. We've made real progress when we view these people as teachers instead of a hindrance in that moment when we feel challenged.

Prayer: God, grant me the maturity to see a teacher in every person I encounter today; help me pause, be centered, and respond to any conflict with peace, poise, and love. Open my mind and heal my emotions so I take the positive lessons from all people.

Take three relaxing breaths; ask your inner spirit to guide your meditation; pause for a few minutes in silence.

February 15

Keeping rocks in your pocket adds weight to your journey.

It's just common sense: if we keep adding rocks in our pocket, the extra weight makes walking difficult and sooner or later, something has to give. We don't see adults with a pocket full of rocks; yet, quite a few carry the weight of resentments, guilt, remorse, or shame as a daily burden.

Everyone makes mistakes. We either 1) learn from these experiences and release the baggage or 2) carry the weight of past errors into every day of our lives. We may be conscious of this extra burden or it may be heaviness slightly below the surface of our consciousness that weighs us down.

If our best efforts have not broken the chains that keep us burdened by the past, perhaps only the mighty expulsive energy of a sincere spiritual affection can remove this burden. In the quiet, close your eyes; reflect on that weightless feeling of having all past errors removed; come to love and nurture the desire for that feeling of freedom; breathe in that cool, clean air of total release from the past; know in your deepest heart that this can be your life, that your inner spirit can dissolve these weights.

Prayer: My loving and wonderful inner spirit connection, I give you all my past—my errors and regrets, my memories of things I should have done differently, and words I wish I had said or had not said. Let your expulsive spiritual energy cleanse all feelings for these past regrets. I humbly ask you to remove anything that stands in the way of my soul progress. Take three relaxing breaths; ask your inner spirit to guide your meditation; pause for a few minutes in silence.

February 16

Actions—not intentions or promises—produce results.

Three frogs are sitting on a log and one decides to jump in the water. How many frogs are left on the log?

Of course, three frogs are still on the log. Making a decision to jump in the water is not the same as jumping in the water.

Action—the actual 'doing', the implementation of decisions, intentions, and promises—is the force that directly determines our quality of life.

First of all, we try to make the best choice. We gather information, use logical and sensible tools to evaluate the practical alternatives; then, we look at the motives and desires for making the choice: Do they originate from self-driven determination or do they align with our spiritual goals, values, and principles? Decisions based on fear, anger, or other emotional miseries often have harmful unintended consequences.

After that, we don't hesitate or procrastinate but take action. The doing—the implementation—is necessary to achieve any results. Action transforms decisions, intentions, and promises from ethereal, will-of-the-wisp clouds into solid existence.

Prayer: My spirit, my guide, help me use all resources to make choices that benefit my life and my soul; strengthen my desire and initiative to act; then, give me the power to move from the dead center of inaction, lethargy, and procrastination to accomplish my goals and purpose.

Take three relaxing breaths; ask your inner spirit to guide your meditation; pause for a few minutes in silence.

February 17

We do not have to accept a gift of stinky guilt or poisonous anger.

We'd have no trouble saying "NO!" if someone offered us a birthday gift of poisonous snakes but it's sometimes harder to decline gifts of feelings that other people try to give us.

We cannot begin to control other people but we can take care of our self. We actually do our spiritual maintenance in the morning and throughout the day instead of thinking about doing it. This helps us recognize a gift of misery and choose not to accept it.

For example, if someone tries to make us feel guilty, we pause, pray, and picture them handing us a gift-wrapped box full of stinky guilt; we politely decline to accept it and handle the situation with dignity, self-respect, and integrity.

We do likewise when someone tries to give us anger, remorse, or jealousy; we learn to accept only those gifts that contribute to our physical, mental, spiritual, or emotional well-being.

Prayer: Dear God, remind me not to accept gifts from other people that lessen my day. Help me have an instant awareness when I start to accept feelings that do not reflect my worth and stature as a child of the divine; grant me the peace and integrity to lovingly refuse un-beneficial gifts. It is my will that your will be done.

Take three relaxing breaths; ask your inner spirit to guide your meditation; pause for a few minutes in silence.

February 18

Life isn't always fair; so what do we do about it?
We can stall in self-pity and resentment or we can move forward.

Something happens and we immediately think of how unfair it is and say to our self "It's not fair! It's not right!" Here, we might pause and realize that the situation may truly be unfair or our sense of fairness may be distorted by 1) what we think 'should' happen, 2) what we believe is 'right,' or 3) how much we are participating in a current symptom of misery (anger, guilt, anxiety and so on). What is our best reaction when a real or perceived unfairness hits us?

Let us pause, evaluate our concept of fairness and try to honestly see if an impartial person might think this is unfair. If still disturbed, we discuss our reaction with someone we respect. If this act was obviously unfair, we may (or may not) try to correct the situation.

Then, no matter what the outcome, we have a choice: Do we whine about it, brood about it, and lose sleep over it or do we accept it, learn from it, and go on with living? Will we stay in the problem or move to the solution? Accepting what happened does not mean that we agree with it but that we recognize and accept the *fact* that this has occurred—denying the reality only keeps us in the problem. This may impact our life but we can strive to make the best of it.

Prayer: Dear God, if any situation appears unfair today, help me to pause and ask for your guidance to honestly assess my perceptions and preconceived ideas; let me understand that this may not be as important as I am making it.

Take three relaxing breaths; ask your inner spirit to guide your meditation; pause for a few minutes in silence.

February 19

Meditation grants us a moment to feel the spiritual embrace.

Meditation provides a unique opportunity to unify our physical, mental, and spiritual resources.

We sit quietly, take our relaxation breaths, and try to quiet our mind so we can feel the presence of our spirit; the mind may spew thought after thought but we tell it to be quiet, either with a sacred word, phrase, or personal method. This is the epitome of reaching for spiritual progress; we use our power of will to submit our mind to the directing influence of our indwelling spirit.

The intervals of quiet may seem small but success is realized through our persistent and consistent efforts. Wonderful things can be experienced in unbelievably small segments of time when we are seeking the spirit. We can feel brief intervals of quiet peace, a sublime and almost inexpressible sense of security and love; we may experience a spiritual embrace when something touches us, enveloping us in a cocoon of warmth and sweetness, giving us a 'knowing' that we have connected, that the essence of our soul is being held and embraced by divinity.

These seconds-long experiences may not happen every time we meditate but increasingly occur as we continue our practice. And this is all we're searching for—those intervals that validate our chosen path and give us the power to go on.

Prayer: My loving inner spirit, help me to be willing to meditate; give me the strength to keep trying and not give up so that I may get closer to you.

Take three relaxing breaths; ask your inner spirit to guide your meditation; pause for a few minutes in silence.

February 20

There is a difference between character building and character growth; one is doing it my way; the other follows the natural path.

Building indicates that we have the blueprint, that we are the planner and the "doer"; growth infers that we are willing to plant the seed, nurture and water it with the right thoughts and actions, and then let God and nature decide the direction and timing of the growth.

We've reached that point where we recognize certain actions, attitudes, and words that cause discontent or misery; we become willing to shed these traits and replace them with higher values and actions. Then, comes the hard part: we must release the control over how and when this growth occurs.

We ask our inner spirit for help, guidance, and strength to become the best version of our self; we acknowledge that this source of infinite power and love can do for us what we cannot do for our self; we know that this mighty expulsive energy can remove all obstacles to growth. We allow ourselves to develop according to the divine plan, the plan which opens the door to infinite possibilities instead of following our self-directed scheme.

The act is ours; the consequence, God's.

Prayer: My divine companion, remove from me any thought, word, or deed that impedes my serving you or helping another person; fill me with your divine intelligence and strength; let the water of your love refresh my soul and generate growth guided by you.

Take three relaxing breaths; ask your inner spirit to guide your meditation; pause for a few minutes in silence.

February 21

Pain may be a "touchstone of spiritual growth" but growth does not require pain.

Emotional or mental pain has one redeeming quality: it can move us to try something different, to grow and ease this terribly uncomfortable feeling. It may "push" us to change. However, experiencing the benefits that result from a spirit-directed life can also ignite a hunger that "pulls" us to understand and seek emotional and spiritual maturity.

As we experience the melting of resentments, we realize the terrible inner turmoil they caused and want to avoid them; when we see that an act of tolerance actually brings more peace than judging and condemning, we seek to become less critical; when we discover that helping a person brings us a feeling of warmth and gratitude, we seek more service; when we find that our spiritually mature prayers result in direct answers that benefit our life, we cherish the act of praying and would not cease for any reason; when we actually practice meditation instead of saying "Yes, I should do that" *and persist in spite of no apparent progress*—and then realize that our thoughts, words, and actions are improving, we commit to practicing and enhancing this awesome discovery.

However, if we "rest on our laurels," pain always returns; it's always there as an uncomfortable "push" in case we ignore the "pull" of the spirit.

Prayer: Dear God, help me not wait for pain to move me closer to you; let me embrace the wonder, beauty, and peace of sharing my life with you. Grant that I am conscious of your presence in every situation and relationship.

Take three relaxing breaths; ask your inner spirit to guide your meditation; pause for a few minutes in silence

February 22

Why—and how—do we react to people? Are we kind and loving, patient, and tolerant? Or something else?

If we get upset, is our reaction because someone attacked us physically or degraded one of our core values? Or is it because of pride or a need to be right? Do we respond with little thought, without being peacefully centered? People will do or say things that we see as hurtful or offensive; these can be real or imagined wrongs.

We should strive for emotional balance that helps us to

- suspend the instantaneous response that often is wrong;
- pause and find inner peace and guidance before we respond;
- take a moment to check if our emotional reaction is triggered by self-righteousness; and
- act with patience, tolerance, love, courage, and conviction.

We need not volunteer for abuse; we stand for our values but avoid being overly sensitive or reacting too quickly. We try to pause between the feeling and the response; then we act with courage, wisdom, and love instead of reacting.

Prayer: My loving spirit, help me accept my humanness; grant me guidance and power to grow more toward your ideal, to be what you would have me be, to love and exhibit your presence in all my responses to other people.

Take three relaxing breaths; ask your inner spirit to guide your meditation; pause for a few minutes in silence.

February 23

The answer to prayer is often just a change in our attitude.

Prayer is not meant to change the divine's attitude toward us but rather to change our attitude toward the divine, other people, and situations. We, not God, are the ones who need to release the shackles that hold us in bondage; we are the ones who need to develop our understanding, ennoble our purpose, elevate our intellect, and consecrate our will. Prayer opens communication with divinity and establishes the conduit to receive spiritual bequests. Sometimes our answers appear as:

A change in perception: If someone irritates us, prayer may not remove that person from our life but let us see a different view of things. We may read, hear, or feel something that lets us see the offending person's motives; this may temper our reaction or help us see how we are making a big deal out of a trifle. If a situation causes contention, prayer may not change the situation but grant us a new way of seeing the challenge; we may see an ultimate good or a benefit that we can glean from an unfavorable situation. Spiritual insight starts to replace human vision.

A new perception that shifts our understanding: We may suddenly see an answer that had eluded us; we somehow transcend our human understanding of the challenge and resolution; our attitude and outlook shift; prayer soothes our turmoil with a mental and emotional calmness that accesses increased levels of patience, tolerance, love, hope, and acceptance.

Prayer: My loving spiritual source, I pray that my mind opens and expands to understand the people and situations in my life as you would have me see them; soften my heart and judgment so that I reflect your infinite love; let the spirit of acceptance blossom in the deepest fibers of my being.

Take three relaxing breaths; ask your inner spirit to guide your meditation; pause for a few minutes in silence.

February 24

We participate in gossip by talking—or listening. Without the listener, gossip dies.

Do I have an inner void, a feeling of emptiness that makes me feel 'less than' other people? Is gossip one of my ways to compensate for this? Do I talk about other people? Do I share a confidence just to flout that I know something another person does not know? Must I try to harm another's image with my words or implications to make me feel better about myself?

Or have I matured enough to realize that the act of demeaning another person, breaking a confidence, or diminishing someone's value with my words reflect my own lack of integrity? Do I accept that many such acts are just efforts to build my value in my own eyes?

Finally, have I acknowledged the truth that *listening* to any such damaging talk indicates my immaturity? I only listen because either: 1) I agree with what is said, 2) I take vicarious pleasure in demeaning another person, 3) I need this unhealthy communication to fill my inner void to make me feel better; or 4) I am afraid to stand for my values that do not agree with such acts. Not a single one of these motives contribute to my growth. I must learn to walk away, to cease any participation in gossip.

Prayer: Dear God, my loving and powerful inner guide, deliver me from participation in any act which leads me to lessen the value of any other person or decreases my integrity. Make me immediately aware if I participate in any form of gossip; give me the strength and guidance to handle all such situations with the tact and truth that shields my soul from harm while presenting a growth opportunity for all participants.

Take three relaxing breaths; ask your inner spirit to guide your meditation; pause for a few minutes in silence.

February 25

The "Yeabuts" cause continuing misery—especially if they justify resentments, anger, or other symptoms of self-driven will.

"Yeabut—I have a right to be angry."
"Yeabut—you should see what she did."
"Yeabut—they aren't doing what they should do."
"Yeabut—it isn't right (or fair)."
"Yeabut—I need that."
"Yeabut—I don't have the time."

"Yeabuts" are masters of camouflage. They often hide selfish, self-centered, or self-righteous motives under a smokescreen of rationalization and justification or mask immaturity with seemingly acceptable excuses.

"Yeabuts" start with a tacit agreement. "Yes you're right...."; "Yes, I understand...."; "I was wrong...." Then, we sneak in the add-on, the "but" that validates, rationalizes, or excuses our action or lack of action. These sometimes obvious (but often subtle) offerings prevent an honest acceptance and evaluation of our mistakes and shortcomings. The "Yeabuts" are the crutch that supports the immature and weak; they stifle or outright prevent growth.

Prayer: My inner guide, please make me aware of "Yeabuts" today; help me to identify any words or thoughts that keep me from recognizing my self-driven attitudes. Grant me courage to fearlessly face my shortcomings and the strength to overcome any that block me from service to my fellows.

Take three relaxing breaths; ask your inner spirit to guide your meditation; pause for a few minutes in silence.

February 26

There is no law that you must allow people to "push your buttons."
After all, they are YOUR buttons.

Do you give other people the power to make you angry? To make you feel guilty? To make you ashamed? Do you react to what others say, how they look at you, or what you think they think about you? Do you silently accept what "they" say you should do; how you should live your life; what your goals, dreams, and aspirations should be? And then withdraw to complain or inwardly simmer because of what "they" say, do, or think?

Every feeling, every beautiful or painful emotion you have *is inside of* you and no one else. No person has ever held your head and forced you to swallow a spoonful of anger or guilt or any misery.

They simply offer each of them. You are responsible to accept or reject the offering; you are responsible for all your feelings and reactions. You can allow anyone to "push your buttons" or you can accept the truth that *these are* your *buttons* and no law or ethical code requires that you allow other people to control them.

Prayer: Dear God—the source of that infinite inner power that can transform my habits, patterns, actions, and thoughts—grant me control of my inner being; help me to not automatically accept the feelings offered to me by other people; guide me to be compassionate and loving but not allow anyone to dictate the way I feel or respond this day.

Take three relaxing breaths; ask your inner spirit to guide your meditation; pause for a few minutes in silence.

February 27

Make a "to be" list in addition to a "to do" list.

We get caught up in the rat race. We develop patterns that continually produce stress, anxiety, worry, and fear. We rush about, cramming as much activity as possible into each day; then, we crash, take a mood-altering chemical to help us relax or to sleep. Then repeat the same thing day after day. Yes, we must earn a living and take care of certain necessities but achieving the highest quality life is not simply filling the day with actions.

A "to be" list might help. Perhaps today, make a commitment to be more tolerant, compassionate, loving, patient, cheerful, kind or gentle; perhaps pick one or two values that are important to you. The "to be" list can also include specific actions that move us to fulfill the desired value. For example, if we want to be more loving, we commit to a definite act that will demonstrate love this day—we can show one person how much we value him or her, that we are grateful they share our life. We can extend an act of kindness without expecting anything in return; we can offer a hug, a massage, or prepare a special meal.

Prayer: My loving inner power, melt the hurry in my mind and soul this day. Help me be aware of values in addition to things; help me look for opportunities to practice the principles that are important to me; strengthen my resolve to take an action that reflects my true values.

Take three relaxing breaths; ask your inner spirit to guide your meditation; pause for a few minutes in silence.

February 28

**The good is often the enemy of the best;
we can settle for mediocrity or strive for excellence.**

"As a general rule, where circumstances do most for men, there man will do least for himself; and where man does least, he is least. His doing or not doing makes or unmakes him."—Fredrick Douglas

Settling for the good, or even the mediocre, has a definite ingrained appeal; indolence and procrastination are a part of the animalistic side of our human nature. Choosing to do as little as possible gives us an easier life but leaves us stuck in days of mediocrity and misery.

Choosing to excel gives us a chance to enjoy the best life on the planet but also introduces potential pitfalls. We must exert a continuous effort, but not become a slave to struggle; we strive for the best, but try not to waste effort solving unimportant problems; we have to act, but avoid becoming a control fanatic—trying to make things happen our way, in our time, and with the results we want. We accept inevitable mistakes, overcome hardship, and see disappointment as opportunity. We seek the best possible life and understand that this requires effort and discipline.

Prayer: My supreme creator, parent, and friend, guide me to realize that I only have this one life and have been given the power to choose how I spend each day. Help me accept strenuous effort, challenges, and even adversity as opportunities to become stronger.

Take three relaxing breaths; ask your inner spirit to guide your meditation; pause for a few minutes in silence.

February 29

It's hard to be spiritual when you've got diarrhea.

It doesn't sound erudite or wonderfully inspirational, but does reflect a practical truth. We may know or have heard of someone with a debilitating or fatal disease who is held as an icon of demonstrating profound faith. Facing long-term maladies may bring some of us to call on the reserves of faith and live with poise and grace; however, sometimes a temporary physical or emotional upset can divert us from our spiritual path and ruin our peace of mind.

We pause, and take a deep relaxation breath, hold it, exhale very slowly while saying "Peace, harmony, relax, relax..." and repeat this three times; we accept the short-term disturbance as being exactly that—a temporary manifestation—and acknowledge our certainty that our spiritual connection and peace will return. We take a physical act to help shift our thinking—we listen to` uplifting or inspirational music, force our self to write a gratitude list, or even divert our concentration with trivia (watching a comedy or interesting movie). We continuously repeat the short gratitude prayer of "Thank you, God, thank you, thank you."

Prayer: Dear God, help me feel your peace and presence when I suffer the fleeting disturbances that are inevitable in this life. Lead my mind to think of, and reflect on, the blessings in my life. Ease my conflict and pain and let me feel the calmness I seek.

Take three relaxing breaths; ask your inner spirit to guide your meditation; pause for a few minutes in silence.

March 1

Each of us has an indwelling divine presence that offers guidance, power, and security.

We have been told

- "Everyone has the Buddha within." (Awakening the Buddha Within, 1998, Das)
- "Nor will they say 'Look here or look there' for the kingdom of God is within you." (Luke 17:21 NKJV)
- "When a man sees that the God in himself is the same God in all that is, he is indeed on the highest path." (The XII, 27-28 The Upanishads)
- "We found the Great Reality deep down within. In the last analysis, it was only there that He may be found" and "...they have tapped an unsuspected inner resource which they presently identify with their own conception of a Power greater than themselves." (Alcoholics Anonymous pgs. 55 and 569 3rd Ed.)
- Every human being has a "fragment of God" within—and a birthright to claim this spiritual force. (Urantia Book)

We have a direct link to the creator of the universe; however, activating and using this connection depends on our individual choice and actions. We can ignore it, accept it as an idea that has some merit, or we may fully embrace this great reality. Our quality of life directly depends on this decision and the subsequent action.

Prayer: My loving and compassionate inner spirit, please help me be aware of your existence in my heart, mind, and soul this day; awaken me to the reality of your presence, power, and love. Help me to be a living testimony of the power and love of God abroad in this universe.

Take three relaxing breaths; ask your inner spirit to guide your meditation; pause for a few minutes in silence.

March 2

"Science without religion is lame, religion without science is blind."
–Albert Einstein

True science and spirituality need not be foes. Only mediocre scientists or fearful religionists deny or attack the other realm. Any scientific assessment is valid only for material things; it cannot measure anything that is not physical. For example, no scientific apparatus will ever accurately measure a mother's love for her child. Scientific instruments can measure heartbeat, respiration, and blood pressure; they can detect and quantify chemicals released when thinking about the object of love. These are all *physical* responses to love and not the underlying reality. Some quality of love exists beyond these components.

Likewise, science can measure some of the physical aspects of God but a spiritual quality exists outside this purely physical arena. Science will never prove or disprove the existence of such non-material reality.

Spiritual power is real but the only proof is personal experience; the validation lies in the transforming results experienced in an individual's life. Participation in this experience requires 1) open-mindedness and 2) access to a spiritual discovery process that delivers results and 3) implementing the process (actually doing the work). Have you experienced spiritual power?

Prayer: Dear God, open my mind, heart, and soul so that I may understand that the Infinite includes all things. Grant me the harmony to live in this material world as I discover the reality of spiritual power.

Take three relaxing breaths; ask your inner spirit to guide your meditation; pause for a few minutes in silence.

March 3

A thousand declarations of love mean less than one caring act.

- Do I speak of love but fail to demonstrate caring?
- Do I proclaim that everyone has a right to their belief and opinions but close my ears and mind to what they say—or even denigrate that which does not agree with my ideas?
- Do I say that I respect others but participate in gossip?
- Do I bemoan poverty but fail to act with charity?

Words and intentions accomplish nothing without action.

We may not be able to change the world but each of us has opportunities to contribute to others, to perhaps improve one small area of one person's life. We can give a "thank you" card for no reason, pause and listen with our heart when someone needs to share, or clean the toilet. We can serve a meal in a shelter, visit a lonely senior, give money or time to a worthy charity, or actually be patient and loving when we feel like rushing away or screaming. Our world overflows with words and intentions but has much fewer healthy, loving actions. A tender act benefits the recipient and the giver.

Prayer: My inner guide, help me to realize that without action, my desires and intentions are as smoke in the wind. Give me the "willingness to act"; strengthen me with your spirit and power to actually "do" in addition to loving and caring. It is my will that your will be done.

Take three relaxing breaths; ask your inner spirit to guide your meditation; pause for a few minutes in silence.

March 4

There is no companionship with the immature.

"If you find no one to support you on a spiritual path, walk alone. There is no companionship with the immature." (Buddha, the Dhammapada 5:61)

We may find times on this spiritual journey in which other people test our path. They may try to lessen or demean our value, ridicule our choices, tempt us to believe that the material life is all that matters, or offer conditional acceptance only if we align with their ideas, beliefs, or perceptions. We might feel the loneliness of standing for our beliefs, but we cannot allow the immature to distract us or shake our commitment. We need not participate in the immaturity.

We are never really alone. We are children of the Divine Source and share this journey with many of our brothers and sisters. We may need time and circumstances to find them. At these challenging times, we increase our quiet meditation, prayer, and reflection; we access our inner source of divine love, strength, and direction; we strive to live with love, understanding, and power as a living demonstration to the less fortunate.

Prayer: My inner source of strength, help me to feel your presence and stay aware of your love and compassion. Help me to see each person as a child of the divine and realize that as children, each of us may be immature at times.

Take three relaxing breaths; ask your inner spirit to guide your meditation; pause for a few minutes in silence.

March 5

You never see a U-Haul in a funeral procession.

We can't take anything with us. The house, the car, the toys, recognition, money, club memberships, and all the things we worked to acquire or achieve—none of it goes to the grave or beyond. So how important is it really? What do we barter to acquire these material possessions and self-gratifying objects? Are the days and nights of anxiety and tension, taking chemicals to sleep or relax, never taking time for family, for God, or for our self a good trade for these temporary, unimportant things?

We cannot change a single thing we did yesterday but we can change today. Let us pause, evaluate, and decide which actions help us fulfill the true purpose of our life. Are our daily values, goals, and practices selfish and self-driven? Or do we try to align with higher, divine attitudes? Will our actions today reflect more importance on things or on people? Will we focus on self-gratification or on loving service? If something stirs contention within us, let's ask our self: "How important is it really? Am I giving power to a temporary trifle?"

Living spiritually does not mean that we cannot enjoy the possessions and toys but that we recognize their appropriate priority.

Prayer: Dear God, open my path to that wonderful divine presence that dwells within me; let me feel the energy of love, the beauty of enlightenment, and the peace of assurance. Guide me to accept your love, embrace its sustaining nourishment, and use every opportunity to share it with the world.

Take three relaxing breaths; ask your inner spirit to guide your meditation; pause for a few minutes in silence.

March 6

"Lack of power, that was our dilemma."
(Alcoholics Anonymous 3rd edition, pg 45)

The alcoholic needs an additional source of power to stop drinking; the addict, to stop using; the self-focused person, to transform attitude, goals, and actions. Some of us may suffer with anxiety, anger, guilt, resentments, fears, or other emotional/mental turmoil that interfere with our life. We try to shed them but cannot; they keep returning. We need additional power.

Can you envision your life without these chains to misery? The good news is that we already possess all the power we need; it is sitting inside of us, ready to unleash a transforming energy that can strengthen and guide us. Prayer, meditation, and loving service open the connection to an infinite power source that provides a new energy that lets us access the best life possible. These same tools keep that spiritual conduit open to allow the continuous flow of energy so we can overcome each new challenge.

We must do our part to keep the connection strong and pathway clear—every day! We plug an electric light into the electrical power source and it changes from a light bulb into a light that illuminates the room; but it immediately goes dark when disconnected from the source of power.

Likewise, yesterday's prayer does not soothe today's challenges.

Prayer: I pray that I may stay aware and connected to the divine spark and power within me. Help me take the time, make the effort, and receive the blessings that are my birthright as a child of the divine.

Take three relaxing breaths; ask your inner spirit to guide your meditation; pause for a few minutes in silence.

March 7

Healthy love includes discernment, congruency, honesty, and enlightened forgiveness.

We learn to foster:

- *Discernment*: We learn to see the differences between mistakes and patterns. Everyone makes mistakes but can change and improve if they have the desire, a blueprint for change, and do the necessary work. Patterns are entrenched and more difficult to change.
- *Congruency:* We learn to help but not enable. If warranted, we lend a hand but do not interfere with another person's growth, freewill choice, or consequences of those choices.
- *Honesty:* We learn to distinguish truth from fact. Facts relate to the material world; truth is a spiritual reality. Facts can unnecessarily hurt someone; truth always frees and liberates. Telling correct facts requires that we ensure their validity and accuracy; imparting truth requires that our facts be correct plus we examine our motives for the communication and how it will be received by the recipients.
- *Enlightened forgiveness;* we learn to forgive and not to forget. We release all emotional attachment to the event but never forget the actual experience to avoid repeating the same mistake. Wisdom is born of experience. Fools repeat errors; the wise learn from mistakes.

Prayer: I pray that I may develop the attributes of healthy love; let me bestow compassion with wisdom.

Take three relaxing breaths; ask your inner spirit to guide your meditation; pause for a few minutes in silence.

March 8

In our darkest moments—when we would rather die than to struggle on, when we have no hope—relief is only a prayer away.

A person now convinced of the rewards of a spiritual life writes: *I lay in the darkness sobbing, my heart broken, wracked with anguish and pain; I had tried everything else and failed so I cried out to a God that I did not believe would help me to please help me. And nothing happened. I picked up the revolver, jammed it into my mouth and started pulling the trigger. A thought from nowhere flashed into my mind, burning through the alcohol haze and pain like a laser through smoke: "Wait, don't do this. You can find an answer." I did wait; over time and with effort, the answers came. And they were so much better than I thought possible.*

The prayer of desperation penetrates to the divine ear in spite of non-belief. The answers are not always what we want, expect, or think we need; they are rarely burning bushes or divine communications but are often simply opportunities to make some choices: Do I try something different or continue to follow my path of self-destruction and pain? Can I surrender my long-cherished 'right' to do things my way? Can I summon a drop of willingness and open-mindedness?

A simple prayer can unleash powerful spiritual assistance and provide the direction and strength to find solutions that work. Each of us is a child of the divine even if we do not feel that way in our dark times. Prayer works.

Prayer: My divine source, please help my un-belief. Relieve me of this oppressing bondage; grant me peace and guide me to a better life; let my heart, soul and mind find hope.

Take three relaxing breaths; ask your inner spirit to guide your meditation; pause for a few minutes in silence.

March 9

Nothing forces us to allow turmoil and despair to destroy our peace of mind; we have a choice.

Being human is not always easy. If fortunate, we have found a spiritual path that makes it less complicated but we still face challenges to our peace. We must deal with the world and its people; we will face turmoil, disappointment, grief, and the upsetting illusions made by our own mind.

Our body requires rest, food, and relaxation; it may seem that we don't have time for these but we invite misery if we get too tired, hectic, or hungry.

Spiritual exercise builds spiritual strength; taking the time for prayer, meditation, and serving others is a priority, not something that we do only when convenient. If we want to feel better, we pause and pray.

The world fills our mind with trash so we offset this with beneficial thoughts: Every morning and throughout the day, we acknowledge our gratitude for the blessings we have; we make a commitment to recognize selfish, self-centered, self-righteous thoughts and quickly move beyond them.

When our calm is broken, it's likely that our mind is a whirlwind; however, our inner spirit is a bastion of steadfast strength and can always supply the power and direction we need to change.

Prayer: Dear God, help me take care of myself and face whatever comes this day; grant me the certainty that you are the source of my true peace and strength and are always there for me.

Take three relaxing breaths; ask your inner spirit to guide your meditation; pause for a few minutes in silence.

March 10

"Must", "should", "need to", "ought to" and "have to" create stress and anxiety.

Our mental self-talk contributes to our emotional state. Thoughts of "must", "should", "need to", "ought to" and "have to" cause tension and stress. Often, we make self-imposed deadlines; then, we get stressed out when we cannot live up these expectations. Or we allow other people to make unrealistic and unnecessary deadlines or react when they try to force us to behave according to their rules. Yes, we may have things that must get done in a certain time but we need not blindly accept unimportant schedules or imposed value systems.

Today let us not allow trifles to overwhelm us. We look for the stress-triggering words of "must", "should", "need to", "ought to" and "have to" when we start to feel tense, irritable, or stressed. Are they truly appropriate in this situation? Will there be a catastrophe if we fail to meet the deadline or a disaster unfold if we miss accomplishing this task? Is someone trying to make us live according to their standards and values?

Then we can pause, take a few deep breaths, say a prayer, and allow our inner spiritual power to re-align our attitude, priorities, and thoughts. We never have a truly valid reason to let anxiety dominate our day.

Prayer: My loving inner spirit, help me to pause throughout this day and establish a peaceful connection with you. Help me resist the urge to hurry and to quietly and peacefully take one step at a time.

Take three relaxing breaths; ask your inner spirit to guide your meditation; pause for a few minutes in silence.

March 11

Irksome people or situations are opportunities for growth (and possible answers to prayer.)

Often, instead of granting us specifically what we asked for, prayer gives us a chance to achieve it. The spiritual domain provides the opportunity to learn—plus the strength to accomplish the objective and the inner reassurance that we can do it.

For example, asking for patience may not make us a shining example of patience overnight, but may provide multiple chances to practice and improve this attribute; asking for tolerance may find us in a flurry of situations that force us to choose whether to be tolerant or intolerant—to be loving, accepting, and forgiving or be judgmental, self-righteous, or bigoted. We may not actually encounter more opportunities for change but become more aware of the ones we do face. Our response is always our choice.

Prayer helps us accept our temporary short falls, guides our mind to a better perspective about the situation, elevates our attitude, and supplies strength to overcome the responses we wish to change.

Prayer: Help me see obstacles as opportunities, adversities as challenges to improve, and those causing me contention as my teachers. Grant me the insight to understand that all these can contribute to my progress.

Take three relaxing breaths; ask your inner spirit to guide your meditation; pause for a few minutes in silence.

March 12

An extraordinary relationship exhibits 1) shared core values, 2) the willingness to grow individually and together, and 3) personal freedom.

Shared core values are an important part of the best relationships. A mutual commitment to God, integrity, honesty, and truth coupled with loving, tolerant attitudes toward others offers a firm basis for building extraordinary relationships. A loving relationship is a living entity that either grows, stagnates, or dies. As such, it provides growth potential for each individual and for growth of the union, the partnership.

Each individual must nurture his or her own personal spiritual growth; this requires some quiet and alone time for investigation, meditation, reflection, and processing. The resulting security and peace provide additional tools to overcome the challenges inherent in combining two lives.

Then a unique and powerful bond forms when the individuals share their spiritual growth; a quiet time of reading devotionals, sharing meditation, and having spiritual discussions produces a depth of understanding and commitment that does not occur in secular partnerships.

Prayer: Dear God, help me realize the value of relationships; let your love open my heart and mind; guide me to live to my fullest potential; strengthen my commitment to learn and grow; expand this desire so that I may support those I love.

Take three relaxing breaths; ask your inner spirit to guide your meditation; pause for a few minutes in silence.

March 13

If our day is dark, we can curse the darkness or we can seek illumination. One focuses on the problem; the other, the solution.

Misfortune, grief, and challenges are part of life. They may range from a shadow to the obliteration of all light, the terrible dark night of the soul from which relief seems impossible. But we always have a choice—do we stay in the darkness or do we move toward the light? Do we stay mired in misery or do we access our inner spiritual power to transcend to the heights of human/divine potential?

Focusing on the problem—the darkness—keeps us in continuing misery. Our thoughts obsess on the immediate quandary and we are pulled deeper into the problem; we cannot see the solution because our attention is on the problem.

As children of a loving divine parent, we are gifted with an inner reservoir of spiritual energy that can quiet our mental upheaval. We pause, take a deep breath, exhale slowly, and claim our birthright. We acknowledge our challenges and our limitations; we ask our inner source for peace, guidance, and the strength to move into the light; we express thanks for the help and grace that we are confident to receive.

Prayer: My precious and loving inner spirit, please quiet my mind; bring peace to my emotions; help me to sit in stillness. Illuminate my choice with perception; give me strength to overcome these adversities and guide me to the best solution.

Take three relaxing breaths; ask your inner spirit to guide your meditation; pause for a few minutes in silence.

March 14

Even a great spiritual truth may not pierce the armor of self-righteousness.

Self-righteousness—discounting other people's opinions, ideas, and concepts without due consideration, believing that we know all the answers—condemns us to a limited life. The "Don't try to change my mind with facts, opinions, or your experience" attitude can be blatant or subtle; but the automatic rejection yields the same results. Personal growth requires hearing and trying things that challenge our preconceived ideas or long-cherished views.

Some may reject personal, practical spirituality due to a total rejection of religion; others may not believe in spiritual power or are committed to science and the material life; still others, independent and self-reliant to the core, may rebel at any belief in God.

Nevertheless, it is an undeniable fact that many have experienced a higher quality life as a direct result of spiritual practices. They have discovered an un-suspected inner reservoir of power, guidance, understanding, and purpose that transcends human resources. Open-mindedness—the willingness to try—is a key to opening the door to this new life; self-righteousness guarantees everlasting ignorance.

Prayer: Dear God or whatever is within me, remove any barrier of self-righteousness; make me receptive to anything that can improve my life; open my mind, heart, and soul and guide my thoughts this day.

Take three relaxing breaths; ask your inner spirit to guide your meditation; pause for a few minutes in silence.

March 15

"Life is relationships; the rest is just details." Gary Smalley

We can accept that most of our thoughts and feelings revolve around relationships if we understand the three types of relationships: We have a relationship with God, a relationship with our self, and relationships with other people. This last type includes any association we have with another person that initiates a physical, mental, or emotional response in us.

Our choices and priorities about relationships determine our quality of life. When we allow our spiritual relationship to guide us, we receive the acceptance, direction, and strength to conquer any challenge; we find peace, courage, and honesty to build a healthy relationship with our self. Then, when we get to know and accept our self exactly as we are, we start to love our self with healthy love.

This yields a wonderful freedom; it severs the power the world and its people have over us—we are truly free. We do not depend on other people or things for our happiness or well-being; we know that they can add depth and meaning to our happiness and peace but cannot create or control it.

Today let us remember this priority of relationships; let us establish our foundation with God, be honest and true to our self, and love others.

Prayer: My inner spirit, help me to stay conscious of your presence today; guide my thoughts, words, and actions to let me enhance my relationship with you, with myself, and with everyone I meet.

Take three relaxing breaths; ask your inner spirit to guide your meditation; pause for a few minutes in silence.

March 16

Our mind can be our best friend or our worst enemy.

The power and influence of our mind has long been recognized. Over 2500 years ago, Buddha noted: "Hard it is to train the mind which goes where it likes and does as it wants; but a trained mind brings health and happiness." (Buddha, The Dhammapada 3:35)

Every day we encounter situations that cause thoughts or feelings, often an immediate reaction to the event. This initial thought-feeling generates more thoughts that focus on the problem; the feelings gain strength and become entrenched. A self-directed mind cannot solve problems started and exacerbated by that very same mind.

Breaking this addictive mental cycle requires that we control our mind and we often cannot do this using just our own desire and force of will; we must have additional power. We pause, access our inner spiritual power and ask for help to direct our thinking; this starts training our mental machine. This new source of power breaks the shackles binding us to certain thoughts and automatic reactions and then re-directs and elevates our thinking. The spirit-directed mind sees a different view, a more balanced and truer perspective and becomes our best friend.

Prayer: My loving divine source and indwelling spirit, please quiet my mind and ease my emotions; elevate my thoughts to be conscious of your guidance; make me aware of my blessings and simple actions I may take to shift my thoughts.

Take three relaxing breaths; ask your inner spirit to guide your meditation; pause for a few minutes in silence.

March 17

The "Big I" causes much of our misery.

Infection from the "Big I" disease occurs when my thoughts, words, and actions focus on my desires and my needs. My only concern for other people is how they affect what I WANT. It's all about I, I, I, me, me, me. How well has it worked? Marriages are failing and families disintegrating; we turn to chemicals to feel good and still suffer extremely high rates of anxiety, stress, loneliness, and misery.

We cannot enjoy great relationships, happiness, and peace of mind when we're infected with the Big "I". We must move beyond this self-importance to something that actually works—an awareness of the importance of other people and of God.

When we feel tense, irritated, or angry, let us pause for a moment and see if this is related to the "Big I". We ask our self, "Are my thoughts focused on how something or someone affects my desires, needs, opinions, or ideas? Is it all about ME? Is this causing my discontent?" Upon retiring at night, we review our day for the frequency and impact of these self-directed words, thoughts, and actions; then, in prayer, we ask God to relieve us of the "Big I".

Prayer: My inner spirit guide. please make me aware when I succumb to selfishness, self-centeredness, and self-righteousness. Help me see the needs, desires, and lives of others. Grant me the divine wisdom to feel and be a part of this great family of humanity.

Take three relaxing breaths; ask your inner spirit to guide your meditation; pause for a few minutes in silence.

March 18

Progress measures how far we've come—not how far we've got to go. Temporary setbacks are stepping stones to improvement.

We are human; our daily performance sometimes falls short of our expectations. We may revert back to our old ways, making choices and taking actions based on self-driven will. When this occurs, we may compare our performance to where we believe we *should* be and become disappointed, thinking that we know better and should do better. Instead, let us measure progress by how far we've come from where we started and not how far we've got to go.

If we are growing, we'll find that consistently living up to our ideals is impossible. Striving to live a spiritual life inherently means that our ideals always advance faster than our performance. As we manage to improve in one area, we see a different perspective; our understanding expands; higher and more refined ideals appear. We are constantly pursing a moving target that stays ahead of us. This gap between ideals and performance is natural and absolutely essential; it provides the space required for growth. Getting closer to our higher standards always takes time, practice, and maintenance.

Prayer: My loving spirit, you have helped me come so far from my past. I sometimes fall short of the life I try to lead, but I know that your love, patience, and grace do not depend on my perfection. Ease my troubled mind and my soul; give me the power and guidance to move forward.

Take three relaxing breaths; ask your inner spirit to guide your meditation; pause for a few minutes in silence.

March 19

Do we pause to consider the importance of "things, meanings, and values" in our life?

Sometimes we become so involved with daily living that we seldom pause to consider important concepts that impact our quality of life such as things, meanings, and values.

How much importance do we truly give to "things"—the material part of life? Do we depend on them for satisfaction or happiness? Can we find peace and contentment without "things"? Is our sense of personal worth based on acquiring them? Are they more important than our relationships or our values?

What about "meaning"—the intellectual understanding of all components of our life? Do we respectfully listen to opposing points of view? Do we give more credence to what people say or what they do? Do we give serious thought to our goals, values, principles, and relationships or do we unconsciously accept what others tell us to think?

Are our values established by other people, by society, by the media, by self-driven opinions or do they reflect divine ideals—concepts that originate from a "higher than human" source? Do our actions demonstrate honor, ethics, integrity, love, tolerance, compassion, and loyalty or are these just words that apply to a by-gone time or to other people?

Prayer: Dear spirit that lives within me, empower me to be the very best version of myself, to experience an ever-increasing nearness to your perfection. Let your will, not mine be done.

Take three relaxing breaths; ask your inner spirit to guide your meditation; pause for a few minutes in silence.

March 20

God supports spiritual progress; he does not gratify ease-seeking egos.

Misunderstanding what God does and doesn't do and about what we are responsible to do leads to frustration and doubt about the value of the spiritual life. God participates in our spiritual growth and development but does not satisfy our immature material or emotional desires. If we're broke, God won't help us hit the lottery. Nor does he violate someone's power of free-will choice and make them love us, forgive us, or appreciate us.

The divine response is 100% consistent, reliable, and dependable when we align our desires and requests with God's will or universal law; it is not as responsive when we try to bend or change the divine to fit our immature wishes. When we sincerely ask for help to improve ourselves, we get results. We may see an immediate improvement or the results may take some time to unfold but growth always occurs if we persist.

Spiritual direction and spiritual power are always available to us; they are only a prayer away. Quiet prayer provides emotional peace, mental clarity, and guidance to make the best decision. Choosing the spiritual alternative opens that "unsuspected" inner reservoir of strength that helps us overcome almost insurmountable obstacles.

Prayer: Dear God, help me realize and accept what is your job in my life, what you do and don't do. Let me shed any false expectations about you. Elevate my priorities and thoughts so that I may enjoy that peace that passes all human understanding. I choose to let your will be done.

Take three relaxing breaths; ask your inner spirit to guide your meditation; pause for a few minutes in silence.

March 21

It matters not what name we give God.
He (She) is more concerned with our spiritual progress than our salutation.

Can limited, finite beings adequately name the infinite? THIS is the First Cause, the One before all things, who separated time from eternity, space from infinity to give home to the universes. He/She is the origin and upholder of the stars, planets, and all contained in the cosmos, the over-soul of creation, and the designer of evolution. This majestic, powerful, creator initiated all forms of life and then, with love, bestowed a fragment of his very divinity, the "kingdom of heaven within," to each of his children.

The name we speak pales in significance compared to how we respond to our creator and indwelling spirit, how we use our power of choice.

If we believe, do we seek guidance for every part of our life or do as little as possible? Do we acknowledge our gratitude and take time to open the communication pathway to receive direction and power every day? Do we try to maintain a conscious awareness of God as we trudge through the day? Do we allow other people and situations to determine our peace and happiness or do we truly depend on our spiritual source for these? Let us engage our inner spirit and find the peace and strength for this day.

Prayer: Dear _________, thank you for creating and loving me; thank you for the gift of the "kingdom within," for all your children; help me seek this inner reservoir to guide my thoughts, elevate my ideals, and improve my acts with transforming power.

Take three relaxing breaths; ask your inner spirit to guide your meditation; pause for a few minutes in silence.

March 22

**The mind is the gateway to the soul;
It can ignite spiritual growth or breed self-driven will that causes incessant misery.**

Do you ever consider the true power of your mind? This is where we make the choices that determine the quality of each moment and each day. These decisions influence our education, relationships, career, and future. Do we use this marvelous thinking machine to open the door that leads us to the excellent life or do we choose to let it propagate misery and discontent?

This day, train your mind to act for your best benefit. Upon awakening, nurture thoughts of gratitude before getting out of bed; ask your inner spirit to direct your thinking; then, read something uplifting and positive to start the day and reflect on that reading.

Become aware of your thoughts throughout the day. Try to remove yourself from being the center of all your thoughts; avoid constantly judging how things and people impact you. Seek to see with spiritual vision instead of the eyes of self-centeredness; act with love and compassion instead of reacting with anger, self-pity, or selfishness. Contribute to the peace of another person; search for that small act of kindness that may bring a smile. Allow the spirit to raise your thoughts to a higher level.

Prayer: My loving inner spirit, please guide my thoughts this day. Balance my judgment with compassion; replace anger with a desire for peace, loneliness with the ability for friendship, and sadness with the desire to help. Let me be a living demonstration of your love, grace, and wisdom.

Take three relaxing breaths; ask your inner spirit to guide your meditation; pause for a few minutes in silence.

March 23

The only fights we win are the ones we walk away from.

How important is it to prove we are right? We must learn not to react while controlled by anger, guilt, self-pity, fear, or other symptoms of misery. If we cannot respond with dignity, poise, and love, we must walk away.

This doesn't mean that we allow other people to trample our dignity or diminish our self-respect, but we must find an elevated response. We pause, take three relaxation breaths, and access our spiritual center. We ask this divine source and power to quiet our immediate emotional reaction, to remove any thought or feeling that prevents us from feeling peace and to help us see the situation with a spiritual insight.

Acting lovingly when someone is attacking us is a practical way of returning good for evil. It's hard to do but really works. We may not win the argument but we feel better (sometimes they are so surprised that the argument simply dies). Besides, we don't always benefit by winning; today's unimportant triumph may generate animosity that causes future problems. Spiritual growth is always more beneficial than winning trivial disagreements.

Prayer: Dear God, grant me the serenity to accept the things I cannot change, the courage to change the things I can and the wisdom to know the difference.

Take three relaxing breaths; ask your inner spirit to guide your meditation; pause for a few minutes in silence.

March 24

The virus of love is benign and infectious; maybe our small acts can start an epidemic.

Love may be a spiritual virus. If true, then when we get infected with love and overcome with the symptoms, our contagion can spread. Spreading love has an advantage over other viruses; the more we spread love, the greater the quality and quantity of our remaining love. The more we give away, the more we have. We cannot change the world but we can change our self and then help other people. That's it. No big headlines but small changes that may actually do some good.

Bestow small loving acts. Smile, be friendly; be patient and actually listen to the cashier at the checkout counter; open the door for someone; help a senior with their packages; make an unexpected call to parents or someone in your past; put a sticky note on the refrigerator for a loved one; actually demonstrate appreciation with loving and unexpected actions. An unexpected act of love has the power to shift our attitude and the attitude of the receiver; then, this enhanced outlook can affect every person we contact and spread outward.

It is our duty as a spiritual warrior/priest to initiate small acts of love that offer light and warmth to everyone we meet.

Prayer: Dear God, guide me to love. Grant me the insight to see the action that you would have me take; grace me with the courage to choose that action even if it opposes the way of the world or the way I would choose.

Take three relaxing breaths; ask your inner spirit to guide your meditation; pause for a few minutes in silence.

March 25

Seek the approval of angels rather than the applause of people.

From childhood we are brainwashed with the false power of self. The media, the pseudo educators, the "experts," the economic and political elite proclaim the rewards of a materially-oriented lifestyle; they constantly tell us to buy something or how to act so that we receive the approval of others—even though the others may also be disillusioned, drifting, and desperate. This glorification of self prevents inner peace and diminishes the hope of a better life.

Don't despair, there is an alternative, a way that yields an enhanced life. Seek the approval of angels.

We move to this higher level as we allow our inner spirit to guide us toward divine values, purpose, and practices instead of accepting those established by unhealthy and unhappy people; we let our inner light illuminate choices that contribute to the best possible life. We keep a constant check on our motives and expectations; we elevate our purpose as we strive to be the best we can be; we avoid settling for mediocrity but strive for inner excellence; we find the peace that passes all human understanding.

Prayer: My loving and perfect inner guide and source of power, grant me the wisdom and strength to live this day for your approval rather than for the applause of men. Help me to see from a spiritual viewpoint and align my choices with divine values, purpose and principles.

Take three relaxing breaths; ask your inner spirit to guide your meditation; pause for a few minutes in silence.

March 26

Control your mind; bring your thoughts to this moment. Think gratitude.

For much of our life, our mind has controlled us. We have allowed it to travel into the past and the future; to indulge in thoughts that generate discontent, anxiety, guilt, fear, and other miseries; to erode our peace during the day and steal our sleep at night.

Right here, right now, start to take control of your mind. Pause; take three relaxation breaths; focus on the peace of your indwelling spirit at the center of your being; spend a few moments in silence; then, think gratitude.

Consider your physical blessings: Do you have shelter, food, and the necessities of life? Do you have anything beyond these necessities that add to your comfort and enjoyment? Think of your relationships: Do you have any person that loves you? Do you have anyone to love? Think of your spiritual life: If you have nothing else, know that you have a spiritual parent who loves you, who bestowed a very fragment of himself to live within you that can comfort you, give you the power to change your life, and illuminate a path of hope.

Assert your control over this mental machine inside your head and take charge of your life.

Prayer: My loving source and inner guide give me the power to think gratitude whenever my thoughts stray to darkness or contention; bring into my awareness the many blessings in my life and give me peace.

Take three relaxing breaths; ask your inner spirit to guide your meditation; pause for a few minutes in silence.

March 27

Making plans outlines actions; having expectations anticipates results.

We're trying to live a better life; we hope to move beyond the inner strife and contention. To accomplish this, we seek to add the spiritual experience to the worldly experience. However, we know that we still live in a material world and must function efficiently here while we expand and elevate our spiritual life.

Living in the NOW or responding with spiritual attitude does not eliminate the simple necessity of making plans. We are not living in some spiritual la-la land. We have to call and make that dentist appointment, make vacation plans, evaluate our income and plan our expenses, and on and on. Such planning does not oppose the idea of living in the moment.

We take the action this moment that is required for a prudent, intelligent approach to life. We plan the timing and execution of actions but avoid having expectations—we accept that we cannot control the outcome. We can act wisely and with best intentions; however, the results, the outcome may be influenced by things out of our control—other people's choices, acts of nature, and even random accidents. We adjust and accept to these changes with inner peace.

Prayer: Dear God, help me to take a beneficial approach to life. Help me separate the important from the trifles, not get overwhelmed with unnecessary details, plan actions that align with your purpose and not have expectations about the outcome.

Take three relaxing breaths; ask your inner spirit to guide your meditation; pause for a few minutes in silence.

March 28

**We can only see what is in front of our eyes;
we cannot see the history.**

- We see anger but not the earlier years of abuse or fear.
- We see selfishness but not the previous poverty of love.
- We see self-centeredness and self-righteousness but not the low self-esteem or the despair of self-loathing.
- We see the inability to engage in healthy relationships but not the lack of a spiritual core causing unhealthy self-love.

Yes, each person is accountable for their current actions; each person is responsible to recognize their mistakes and shortcomings. However, the unfortunate may lack the necessary humility to admit their deficiencies, the desire or the courage to change, or not have a viable process for change; they may reject a spiritual solution for living problems; or they may merely be having a bad moment or terrible day.

Whenever we encounter such objectionable conduct, it is our choice how we allow it to affect us. Do we share the light to provide illumination or contribute to the darkness?

Let us show

- tolerance, not anger;
- patience, not a quick response;
- love of the hard-to-love, not retaliation;
- the willingness to walk away, not engage in pointless conflict.

If we are among the fortunate; we must be an expression of truth.

Prayer: I pray that I can be a light today. Let me share the wonderful love and peace that you have given me; let me act as beacon of warmth and caring for someone less fortunate than I.

Take three relaxing breaths; ask your inner spirit to guide your meditation; pause for a few minutes in silence.

March 29

The immature never say "I am wrong or I am sorry."

Everyone makes mistakes. Many react as if making an error is a reflection of their value; they believe that it is demeaning to say or do something wrong, that it makes them appear "less than" in the eyes of other people. Sure, we may encounter some emotionally immature people who build themselves up when they see others falter or make a mistake. But what value is the opinion of such unfortunates?

We are *children* of God and perfection won't happen in this life. The only way to avoid mistakes is to live in complete isolation and do nothing (and that very act would be a mistake in itself). Any action we take presents the potential for a blunder. That's life!

Hopefully, we do not repeat the same error and actually gain some knowledge from the experience. We learn the value of saying "I was wrong and I'm sorry" and making any amends necessary to correct the situation. Admitting fault may—or may not—heal the response of the injured party but definitely contributes to our own growth.

Prayer: My loving and merciful spiritual parent, shatter any barrier that prevents my growth; help me recognize and accept when I have acted in error. Grant me the wisdom to understand what you would have me do and give me the courage to act. I choose that your will be done in my life.

Take three relaxing breaths; ask your inner spirit to guide your meditation; pause for a few minutes in silence.

March 30

A practical spiritual life is an exciting adventure that yields happiness, security, hope, and peace; it is not dull and boring or a vale of tears.

A practical spiritual life is an individual's personal relationship with divinity and may exist within, or separate from, organized religion. Does it really work?

Well, millions of people in over 160 countries have recovered from a "seemingly hopeless state of mind and body" through the program of Alcoholics Anonymous that facilitates a "spiritual experience" to overcome chronic alcoholism; many other twelve-step programs based on the exact same process have led additional millions into recovery from other addictions; plus, millions of others have transformed their lives with personal spirituality.

Other common results include: a shift from anxiety, hopelessness, and misery to a sense of security and peace of mind; developing the ability to not allow other people or outside events to control one's feelings; finding a process to live in the moment—to release past mistakes and not be anxious of the future; being able to face adversity with courage and to see challenges as an opportunity for growth.

So the answer is a resounding "Yes!" A spiritual life does deliver results. What has it done for you?

Prayer: Dear God, I come before you with a hope that you might have an answer. Melt any prejudice that remains in me; let me feel your loving presence and experience the power of your transforming embrace; quiet my disturbed emotions and grant me peace.

Take three relaxing breaths; ask your inner spirit to guide your meditation; pause for a few minutes in silence.

March 31

Most stress is self-inflicted;
don't volunteer for misery.

Stress: *the perception that we do not have the resources to meet the impending challenges we face.*

Our perception—how we see events in this moment—influences our stress; changing our perception often alleviates the stress. We can pause and ask our self:

- Am I crowding too much activity into too little time? What *absolutely* must be done?
- How important is it really? Am I over-reacting?
- Is it really a problem or is it an illusion (an imaginary problem triggered by unsubstantiated fear, misplaced responsibility, or habitual over-reaction)?
- If this is a true problem, can I identify additional resources?
- What is the *real probability* that 1) it will happen and 2) it will result in the absolute worst consequences?
- Do I have a strong spiritual connection?

We often have fewer real problems and more resources than we think. Remember that we have a powerful reservoir of inner spiritual energy to help clarify our thoughts and smooth our emotions while finding a solution.

Prayer: Dear God, help me remember to pause. Give me the strength to pray; grant me the intelligence and power to eliminate illusions and find solutions for any real problems. Let my thoughts, words, and actions today demonstrate your divine love and power.

Take three relaxing breaths; ask your inner spirit to guide your meditation; pause for a few minutes in silence.

April 1

The self-righteous walk a lonely path.

Self-righteousness: *having a disregard for other people's opinions or ideas or a total confidence that we are always right.*

Self-righteousness prevents personal growth and results in a lonely life. It blinds us to the possibility that we might be wrong or that other solutions may be better than ours. The attitude that "I already know the answer so don't bother me with facts or opinions that do not agree with me" keeps us in everlasting ignorance.

This character trait thrives on denial and almost defies self-recognition; it avoids risking a crack in our armor that might reveal a less-than-perfect being. We rationalize, justify, and reject the possibility; we offer the "Yeabuts" to avoid the truth: "Yeabut, I am right; Yeabut, she shouldn't have said that...." Often we must pray for help to be honest and take a detailed, objective review of our attitude and behavior; we search painstakingly for the hidden symptoms. If possible, we ask a close trusted friend or advisor to help us identify the warning signs of self-righteousness.

Prayer: My inner bastion, my source of power and light, my perfect guide I ask that you help me be willing to examine my thoughts, words, and actions for self-righteousness. Remove any self-deceit; give me courage to see and accept all facets of my character; grant me the strength to shed all self-righteousness this day.

Take three relaxing breaths; ask your inner spirit to guide your meditation; pause for a few minutes in silence.

April 2

Small changes often shatter the illusion of control.

Imagine that you're slowly driving down a country road when the steering wheel comes off the steering column—it's loose and free in your hands. In that split second, your mind does not accept the truth and you still try to turn the steering wheel with absolutely no effect. You feel an immediate, absolute, electrifying panic at this total loss of control. Hopefully, you're able to stop the car with minor damage and no injury. (You may not know the simple fact that often, only a single nut holds this vital piece in place.)

We often live with an illusion of control; we try to make things happen the way we want; we are adamant about the direction, speed, and course of our life (and possibly of other people's lives also). But this illusion can shatter at any time (it probably also has only one nut holding it together.)

Life's better when we accept that our only control is to turn our will and life over to a Higher Power; we release the illusion of control and depend on God for direction and strength. If, during the day we take back this control, we immediately give it back to God and accept that we'll go along for the ride.

Prayer: My loving God, help me to be willing to align my thoughts, words, and actions with what you want me to do; let me not stray into the illusion that I can really control my life or know the best answers for anyone.

Take three relaxing breaths; ask your inner spirit to guide your meditation; pause for a few minutes in silence.

April 3

**A lamp must be connected to electricity if it is to illuminate;
We must access our inner spiritual power to live our brightest life.**

We don't need to be an electrical engineer to utilize the power of electricity. We don't need to understand how electricity is made, how it's transmitted from the generating station to our home; or how it flows as unseen power in the wiring behind that little outlet box on the wall. If we want light, we plug the lamp into the power source, turn it on, and behold, the light appears and stays bright as long as we keep the connection. *The results do not depend on our belief but upon the action we take.*

Our inner spiritual power works the same way. A reservoir of unseen spiritual power resides within each person but we must plug into this energy if we want our light to shine. The results depend on action, not belief or understanding.

We must make the connection and then keep the link open and strong. We take time to pray and meditate every morning; we pause throughout the day and spend a minute with our indwelling lover and source of power; we increase our conscious awareness of our divine source and values; then, as we retire at night, we review our day and spend a few minutes in thankful communication.

Like the lamp, we lose our illumination if our connection to the power source is interrupted.

Prayer: To my indwelling, unseen spiritual power, help me open the channels that allow your energy to flow; enlarge my receptivity to your transforming power and remove any obstacle that stands in the way of my usefulness to my fellow mortal.

Take three relaxing breaths; ask your inner spirit to guide your meditation; pause for a few minutes in silence.

April 4

If you're not in an ambulance, it's probably not a big deal.

If we've paid attention to life, we've likely realized that most of the things that caused us contention at any moment—that made us angry, resentful, guilty, or afraid—were not life-threatening issues. In hindsight, most of them were really trifles but we over-reacted and got upset; then, perhaps we said or did something that made things worse. Even on those rare occasions when we actually face a "big deal", we don't get the best results if our emotions overwhelm us.

Even as we try to grow in spiritual and emotional maturity, we'll find times that we revert to being selfish, self-centered, or self-righteous; we get overly sensitive; we allow other people to dictate our feelings; we don't seek our spiritual center. Most likely, we are not in an ambulance heading for the hospital; no one we love is in a life-threatening emergency; the challenges we face will likely not truly devastate our life. We are merely making a big deal out of a trifle.

Let us pause, take a deep breath and say a quick prayer; we give our inner guide the opportunity to influence us, to transform the way we see and interpret the situation, and guide the way we react.

Prayer: Dear God please help me slow down and not react this very moment; grant me the peace that changes my perceptions and outlook. Help me align my thoughts with your divine thoughts and act with love, tolerance, and patience instead of reacting.

Take three relaxing breaths; ask your inner spirit to guide your meditation; pause for a few minutes in silence.

April 5

God's word is quietly spoken in the secret places of our heart.

We often find peace and hope when we discover the awesome "kingdom of heaven within". Then, the world interferes and we run into the problem of trying to keep this wonderful feeling. We live in a hectic, fast-paced world that almost exclusively focuses on material possessions and gratifying an insatiable ego. Yes, we are responsible for our material well-being—we must work, pay bills, and survive. However, we must also nurture our inner life if we want to enjoy the journey and cease struggling.

Make time to be still; pause, breathe deeply, and reflect for a few minutes. Develop an ongoing *conscious awareness* of the Infinite in all things—let the awesome splendors of life open your heart, mind, and soul; become receptive. Actually see and appreciate the grandeur of the sun, the beauty of a flower, the flight of a butterfly; behold and bow before the wonder of a baby, the energy in children playing, the breath of life and the spark of divinity in every individual that crosses your path this day.

This practice takes only minutes and the rewards are so great that no one can afford *not* to do it. God's word is quietly spoken in the secret places of our heart.

Prayer: My indwelling spirit, lover of my soul, my guide through this maze of life, and my source of power, help me feel your presence deep within me today; help me be fully aware of the simple, divine wonders.

Take three relaxing breaths; ask your inner spirit to guide your meditation; pause for a few minutes in silence.

April 6

Why celebrate birthdays?
Our only contribution was to stay alive another year.

We didn't make a wise or courageous decision; we didn't really have a good option. Wouldn't it make more sense to celebrate genuine accomplishments?

Let's celebrate "growth days" instead of birthdays. We can have a "growth party" when we have grown in some area. Let's make merry when we have grown a little more patient, are not as upset by traffic, or not as judgmental as we used to be. Perhaps we are showing progress in devoting time for meditation or skipped an opportunity to worry; maybe we have learned to love someone that used to trouble us. We may have grown into less of a "people pleaser"— we have started saying "no" and standing by it; we may have reclaimed our power over our feelings by not allowing someone to "push our buttons" when we would have previously been in turmoil. Let's celebrate the fact that we have found effective solutions that help us overcome the inevitable difficulties of life.

All these and many more are cause for celebration. We could even throw our friends "surprise growth parties" when we see that they have accomplished something.

Prayer: Today let me celebrate that I have discovered your divine presence in my life that has opened a new world I never knew. Thank you for your strength, wisdom, power, presence and love.

Take three relaxing breaths; ask your inner spirit to guide your meditation; pause for a few minutes in silence.

April 7

This day could always be worse.

Someone fails to live up to our expectations or says (does) something that offends our overly-sensitive nature; we face an expense which we don't see how we can pay; we don't have enough time to do what we need to do; our mind gets on the hamster wheel of fear, anxiety, guilt, or other misery and won't quit. Hopefully, we've learned that this moment is never as bad as it appears and know that we must break this cycle if we're going to enjoy a good day.

We pause and reflect on a really bad day we've had in the past, when we were overwhelmed with sadness, grief, depression, or gut-wrenching fear. We may have experienced days so dark that we saw no point in living. Don't dwell on these times but remember them for a moment for comparison.

We've all experienced these dark times and today—right now—is not nearly as bad as these. So today could always be worse. Not only that, but it contains a lot of good things if we can change our perception. Very likely you can see, walk, and talk; you are loved; you can bestow love, compassion, and mercy—free and wondrous gifts; you have hope—with your abilities, resources, effort, and your inner divine power, things can always improve. You're alive and you can change and with this change, you can experience a new and different life.

Prayer: My spirit Essence please melt my anxiety and regrets and fill me with your care and compassion; dissolve my difficulties so I may better do your will and become a benefit to you and others; help me see the abundant blessings in my life.

Take three relaxing breaths; ask your inner spirit to guide your meditation; pause for a few minutes in silence.

April 8

Today, say something true and beautiful to someone you love—and then to a stranger.
The ripple effect of a single act can touch hundreds.

It's human nature to love and need to be loved. Encountering tragedy or self-driven people may make receiving or bestowing love difficult; our own selfishness, self-centeredness, and self-righteousness may erect barriers to healthy love. But love is as essential to our development as air is to breathing. Today, let us be the spearhead of love.

Let's spread simple acts of kindness, respect, caring, and thoughtfulness that convey the value we have for that other person. Let us speak our appreciation for a personality trait—perhaps they are kind, optimistic, wise, or patient; we can acknowledge a physical attribute—a lovely smile, an appealing dress or haircut; we can recognize the effort they exert to sustain our family or keep our home; we can express appreciation for their support—perhaps they helped us in our job, in making a decision, or guided us to see a spiritual truth that expanded our life.

For strangers we can smile, open the door, carry a package, ask if we can help them, and look at them with serenity while sending beams of happiness, love, peace, and beauty to them. We can't change the world but today, we can change our self. We can show love.

Prayer: Help me to pour love to all people this day; open my heart so that I convey the value, respect and appreciation I have for each person. Make me aware that the stranger I meet this day is your child and let me greet them as I would greet you.

Take three relaxing breaths; ask your inner spirit to guide your meditation; pause for a few minutes in silence.

April 9

Belief is intellectually accepting an idea;
Faith is changing the way we live because of that belief.
Faith is action.

Belief precedes faith. It is the intellectual acceptance of ideas and ideals that establishes the framework for the purpose, values, and principles on which faith is built. What we believe directly influences our thoughts, words, and actions in all areas of our life. Beliefs can be rooted in truth or error; they can move the individual, groups, or civilization forward or they can yield misery and destruction. So how do we find a belief based on truth?

We can believe in spiritual awareness, not theology; in love, not apathy or hate; in values, not doctrine; in the guidance of our inner spirit, not the way of the world. We can use a simple yardstick to evaluate our belief: does it contribute to freedom, peace, and love for myself and for others?

Consider: Having the fundamental belief that "God *does* exist and is the loving spiritual parent of every person," sets the foundation and framework for a faith to live as if all humanity is one family, that *every* person is our brother and sister. God desires good things for all and each person has the freedom to choose his or her path to experience this divinity.

Prayer: My beacon of light, help my belief to be based on truth; guide me to hold sacred the life of all people, to recognize each individual as a child of divinity and encourage me to show love to every person. It is my will that your will be done in my life this day.

Take three relaxing breaths; ask your inner spirit to guide your meditation; pause for a few minutes in silence.

April 10

Actions, not words, reveal true values and priorities.

We all have those times when our actions fall short of our ideals. That's part of the spiritual/emotional growth process. But some of these may indicate an area ripe for personal improvement. We might consider:

- Am I late for appointments? Is my time more important than the other person's time? Do I do this to show how important I am?
- Do I keep commitments or find excuses as to why I do not?
- Do I do my fair share of the work or exert the least effort that simply gets me by?
- When I do something for someone do I expect nothing in return or do I make certain that others know of my action?
- Do I allow a person to quit speaking before I talk or do I interrupt?
- Do I actually give people my attention or do I divide my interest with gazing about, reading something, or texting?

Some small actions may reflect an attitude that harbors selfish, self-centered, or self-righteous motives. Any of us may slip and do some of these at times; however, let's examine these occurrences to see if they are exceptions or patterns of behavior that need our attention.

Prayer: I ask to be made aware of my small failings, that I see when I drift from my path of being loving, kind, considerate, respectful, tolerant, and patient.

Take three relaxing breaths; ask your inner spirit to guide your meditation; pause for a few minutes in silence.

April 11

We must share love; we cannot experience it in isolation.

Isolation is an emotional state, not a physical one.

Relationships are the most rewarding and the most frustrating of human endeavors. Loving other people makes us vulnerable to emotional pain. The ones we love are human—they die, betray us, break our trust, take us for granted, or choose a different path. It may seem easier to withdraw and not form close emotional ties. Then, we can claim the values of tolerance, patience, honesty, and empathy with little risk.

However, we can never enjoy the great rewards of receiving love without the investment of giving love. Love flows freely from the divine to our heart; but it can only be experienced as it flows *through* us to others. Love is always outgoing in all its satisfaction seeking. Contentment comes from *doing* something that benefits another person; we delight in the bonus from being loved. Feeling total, all-encompassing, unconditional love is one of the greatest rewards of human existence and more valuable than wealth, possessions, or power. Today, let us share our love.

Prayer: I pray that I can surrender my un-healthy ideas and expectations about love. Help me receive the divine love, let it flow through the very fiber of my being and then outward to those around me. Guide me to bestow love rather than seek love.

Take three relaxing breaths; ask your inner spirit to guide your meditation; pause for a few minutes in silence.

April 12

Never make a long-term decision while in short-term misery.

Most of us will face hurtful, disappointing, and frustrating times in our lives; hardship may overwhelm us; people may betray us. The actions of others or our own choices may bring despair and hopelessness; accidents of time and misfortunes of nature may bring anguish so deep that we cannot see hope for relief.

Experience teaches that great moments—and these sad times—are temporary, that the dark night of the soul will dissipate. These are times we must simply survive; we learn not to make long-term decisions that can negatively impact our life or the lives of loved ones while suffering short-term misery; we do not make decisions during such times that limit our future options. Choices dominated by darkness seldom prove beneficial.

We remember that we are truly a child of God. Our loving divine parent always loves us and wants the best for us. Uncontrollable events and our mental/emotional attitude can make us suffer but our inner spirit can spark a revival of hope and direction. This wonderful power can reveal the beacon of truth that we are loved and have a direct connection to an infinite and divine source. Let us delay any serious decisions until we overcome our current difficulties and can act with reason untainted by emotional misery.

Prayer: My divine creator, grant me the wisdom to not make important decisions while I am disturbed. Soothe my inner turmoil; let peace flow into my heart, mind, and soul; let the light of hope dispel the darkness and let me feel the warmth of your love radiate over me.

Take three relaxing breaths; ask your inner spirit to guide your meditation; pause for a few minutes in silence.

April 13

Knowing God does not require chemical shortcuts.

Each of us is blessed with an indwelling spark of divinity, a fragment of the very God we seek. This "Buddha within", this "kingdom of heaven within," the Great Reality deep down within" waits patiently until we search for the divine. Our path may be clarified by those who traveled before us. Reading about spiritual truths, prayer, meditation, and communing with other seekers can act as guiding lights; however, believing that any chemical may help find enlightenment is a false detour. We cannot circumvent the natural path. There are no shortcuts to God.

We live in a hectic, materialistic world; we may desire a spiritual life or just want inner peace but find it difficult to take the time that prayer, meditation, and service require. Discovering and living in a manner that transforms our life is a huge challenge; shifting from a materially-based life to a spiritual life takes effort, direction, and discipline. The animalistic side of our nature always seeks the easier, softer way and may find a mood-altering chemical attractive.

These may present a temporary break from reality but offer no concrete answers for solving the living problems we face. In fact they often prevent finding real solutions or actually create additional problems; they offer escape but retard growth.

Today, let us enhance our relationship with our inner spirit, the real power that can transform our life.

Prayer: Divine spirit, please help me to see what I must do; give me strength to persevere despite doubts and weariness; let me listen for my "still, small voice within".

Take three relaxing breaths; ask your inner spirit to guide your meditation; pause for a few minutes in silence.

April 14

**A self-directed mind discovers facts;
A God-conscious mind discerns truth;
A mature mind integrates both.**

Don't be distracted or confused when the secular world shouts "God is dead, only scientific facts are relevant" and the religionist answers "Only God is truth, don't bother me with science." These outlooks confuse facts and truth. Facts deal with physical certainty; truth, with spiritual reality. Facts are concrete and measurable; truth is neither since it originates from inner personal experience with divinity. Both are important and necessary to enjoying the fullest life possible.

We work, live, and function in a material reality—the outer world. We must adapt to the laws and guidelines of this if we want worldly success. Even if we achieve this "success," we may still find that something is missing; we still have a void inside us.

Then, we must seek the truth—the understanding, values, and practices that fill our inner void and yield the best possible life. We actively engage in our spirit quest; we read or listen to spiritual truth, spend more time in prayer, reflection, and meditation; we develop and nurture relationships with other truth seekers. As more is revealed, tolerance, patience and wisdom guide us to harmonize the material and spiritual viewpoints.

Prayer: I pray that I can synchronize the outer world with the spiritual inner world; help me recognize and utilize both truth and fact. Help me live wisely in the world but not let it control my feelings, dreams, and purpose. Direct my mind to the inner bastion of spiritual strength to find peace.

Take three relaxing breaths; ask your inner spirit to guide your meditation; pause for a few minutes in silence.

April 15

**Many problems are illusions;
they disappear when exposed to critical thinking.**

Let us consider a real problem as a real, direct, and imminent threat to our physical, mental, or spiritual well-being; illusions are false problems generated from fear, misunderstanding, or habits of reaction. Differentiation helps us distinguish between problems and illusions.

Personal Differentiation Process

- Is it really a problem? Is it a real and imminent threat?
- Is it my responsibility? Whose decisions and actions caused this? Am I protecting someone else from the consequences of his or her choices or actions? If I take no action, will the outcome cause direct harm? Is this really any of my business?
- Can I do anything about it today that will prevent or alter the situation? If I cannot take an action today, it's not yet a problem.
- Do I really need to solve it? We don't always have to find an immediate solution for nuisances or irritations.
- How big is it really? Am I blowing this out of proportion and over-reacting?

Prayer: Dear God, I know that you are always with me when I encounter tribulation and adversity. Fear, anxiety, guilt, remorse and other forms of misery lead me to see problems that may be illusions. Help me to quietly and peacefully release these phantoms.

Take three relaxing breaths; ask your inner spirit to guide your meditation; pause for a few minutes in silence.

April 16

Believing in "The Positive Power of Worry" is a fool's conviction.

"The Positive Power of Worry" or PPW theory represents the belief that spending mental and emotional energy focusing on what *might* happen emanates a force that goes out into the cosmos and actually stops the undesirable event from happening. This sounds ridiculous but people still spend a lot of time and energy worrying. The mind of someone deep in worry *does not* emanate an external energy that could affect anything but there are negative effects on the worrier.

Worry keeps our minds in turmoil with internal conflict, stress, and anxiety; it prevents sleep and rest; it leads to making mistakes in the moment because our mind is in the fearful future.

Breaking the chains of worry requires that 1) we accept the futility of worrying and 2) we re-train our minds. A physical action can shift our mental gears: We actually write a gratitude list and deeply consider each item we write. We take a walk and reflect on the beauty and wonder we see. We clean the house while focusing intently on the details of the task. We listen to or read something spiritual and uplifting and think about the peace and understanding in the words. If all else fails, we look for someone to help; serving others takes us off being the center of the universe.

Anytime the worry thought intrudes, we pause and ask our inner spirit to replace it with a thought that benefits us and to grant us peace; we claim our birthright as a divine child to live peacefully in the moment.

Prayer: My loving inner spirit, I pray that I recognize the futility of worry; remove my fear of the future and replace it with the peaceful, secure knowledge that today, all is well.

Take three relaxing breaths; ask your inner spirit to guide your meditation; pause for a few minutes in silence.

April 17

There is a vast difference between our needs and our wants. Our "wants" often upset us if we make them too important.

Our *needs* include basic levels of food, shelter, and clothing to sustain life; our *wants* can start with desiring a few more of these necessities and expand to anything imaginable. This power of "want" can be a positive force moving us to act, to achieve, to persevere, to overcome many obstacles; or, it can become distorted and push us to trade our integrity, honesty, truthfulness, and other values to get our way.

When we have current *wants* that cause us contention, we might ask:

- Why do I want ___?" Is my motive healthy and loving or selfish and self-centered?
- How important is it really? Is my want so strong that I'll trade my values for it? Will it contribute to my growth, the well-being of a loved one or me, or is it an added extra? (There's nothing wrong with wanting the extras as long as we realize their relative priority.)
- How do I handle the success or failure of getting what I want? Will I allow either to unduly affect my attitude, thoughts, or emotions?

Prayer: Dear God, I thank you for your grace and ask that you help me realize the blessings I have, that my true needs are taken care of. Let me not allow my wants and desires to interfere with my peace.

Take three relaxing breaths; ask your inner spirit to guide your meditation; pause for a few minutes in silence.

April 18

Extraordinary relationships must be built; they don't just happen.

Almost everyone wants great relationships. Failed and mediocre relationships result in misery—rampant anger, blame, resentments, grief, jealousy, envy, worry, and hopelessness. Extraordinary relationships must be built, they don't appear. Successfully building anything requires two things: 1) a plan or blueprint and 2) doing the necessary work.

Building any relationship is like building a house: first, we must build a solid foundation; second, we erect sturdy walls and last, we add the roof.

Everything rests on the foundation. In a relationship, this foundation is each individual's relationship with God—the universal force. Herein, we discover our personal concepts of divine values, purpose, and practices that establish the bedrock of our character; we receive additional (spiritual) power and direction.

The walls—the structure that supports all other relationships—is our relationship with our self. The importance of this self-relationship has been heralded for centuries with "Know thyself and to thine own self be true"; it was emphasized by the admonition to "Love your neighbor *as* yourself" implying that we are only capable of giving or receiving love *exactly as we love our self.*

Then we emplace the roof, our relationships with other people.

Prayer: Help me to be willing; help me exert the effort to discover and build my relationship with the divine spirit; give me the guidance, courage and power to truly know and accept everything about me; let me extend and accept love wherever I go.

Take three relaxing breaths; ask your inner spirit to guide your meditation; pause for a few minutes in silence.

April 19

Love is not ownership; it does not attempt to control.

Love is an active and healthy concern for a person's well-being and leads us to desire the best possible life for other people. It can be bestowed upon our family and intimates, shared with friends and relatives, and extended to acquaintances and strangers. But love never contains the tentacles of control, is not conditional based on the receiver following the wishes of the giver, nor does it exist for any selfish purpose.

Desiring the very best for those we love means that we encourage their personal growth and enhancement of life. Hallmarks of mature love include devotion, loyalty, fairness, honesty, trust, service, forgiveness, open-mindedness, selflessness, and demonstrated caring that supports personal freedom and selected privacy.

If the desire to manage another person's feelings, actions, or attitude invades our mind, let us pause and consider how God's love for us includes the wonderful freedom to walk the path of our choosing. Commit to the practice of love. Demonstrate this quality to at least one more person this day or this week—whatever is your capacity for extending love. Small, loving acts benefit the giver and receiver.

Prayer: Dear God, help me to love today; help me realize that this wonderful value never suggests ownership or even the slightest control of another person. Open my eyes that I may see the opportunities to show love; grant that I act upon these.

Take three relaxing breaths; ask your inner spirit to guide your meditation; pause for a few minutes in silence.

April 20

Today, let us consider what we have, not what we may be missing; to see blessings instead of disappointment.

Do you want to enjoy a great day, slide through a mediocre day, or suffer a day of misery? Given the chance, most people choose to have a good or possibly great day. One secret of having great days is to keep our mind focused on positive rather than negative facts; to think about what we *do have* instead of what we *do not have*; to count blessings instead of listing our failures and disappointments.

We start this practice right now! We acknowledge a number of specific people and blessings that improve our life or we get into the habit of repeating "Thank you God, thank you God..." for a few minutes. This starts us with an attitude of gratitude that can expand and permeate our day.

When thoughts start to drag us down, we force our mind to grasp a positive thought. We consider what physical ability we would miss the most if it was suddenly removed—our eyesight, the ability to walk, speak, or hear? And we are grateful for what we have. What close, loving relationship would we miss? Be grateful. What possessions would make living much more difficult if they disappeared? Be grateful.

Prayer: I pray that I focus on what I have instead of what I'm missing. Help me recognize and appreciate the special people in my life, the abilities I have been given, and the material blessings I enjoy. Thank you for your presence that brings peace to my life.

Take three relaxing breaths; ask your inner spirit to guide your meditation; pause for a few minutes in silence.

April 21

Hindsight is not 20/20.
We can only see what is; "what might have been" is fantasy.

We may have regrets and be absolutely positive that our life would be so much better if we had gone down that different path: "If I had taken that other job five years ago, I'd be so much better off than I am now." We may be correct; our circumstances may have turned out better if we had made that different choice. Or it may *not* have.

Choosing the alternative path would have started a completely different series of life events. It's possible, but unlikely, that everything could have gone as great as we fantasize. It's also possible that disappointment or tragedy could have appeared in that alternative outcome and we'd be worse off than we are right now. Perhaps a loved one could have been injured in an accident during the move; maybe the job was terminated shortly after we accepted it and led to a worse financial situation than we have now. Many other things may have happened that could have negatively impacted our life. We plainly do not know.

Human nature tends to romanticize and idealize the choices we *didn't* make. "What might have been" is fantasy. The only certain outcome is the one we are living today; don't dwell on what might have been.

Prayer: I pray that I can accept that I am human and will make mistakes. Help me to learn from these and not dwell on what might have been; guide me to make the right choice for the right reason at the right time this day.

Take three relaxing breaths; ask your inner spirit to guide your meditation; pause for a few minutes in silence.

April 22

Seek integration, not balance, of personality.

Each of us live and function in physical, mental, and spiritual life arenas; each of these contain a unique energy, open specific resources, and have a definite function in our life. For our best life, we learn to integrate these life forces which implies that we recognize the specific function of each arena and allow each to do what it is intended to do:

- The physical part of our life is meant to be *subordinate*. The physical things we want or think we need are not meant to be the ultimate driving force in our life.
- Our mind is designed to be *coordinate*. It co-ordinates between the material world and the world of the spirit, between the outer world and the inner world. It is here that we exercise our most powerful right, the right of free choice.
- Our indwelling spirit should be *super-ordinate* or directive; it provides the best direction for our choices.

Chaos and turmoil result when we follow the way of the world and allow our physical desires or our mental ideas to direct our decisions. As a spiritual seeker, we try to increasingly subject our mind and physical desires to spiritual guidance.

Prayer: My loving spirit, help me to use each gift, each area of my life, the way it was meant to be used; help me become the best version of myself.

Take three relaxing breaths; ask your inner spirit to guide your meditation; pause for a few minutes in silence.

April 23

I must accept myself exactly as I am but realize that I can improve.

We've all made some bad mistakes in our life and may have deep regrets, guilt, or shame about the past; we may also have shortcomings that still hurt us or those around us. If we have a desire to grow and be a better person, we must realize that any journey starts where we stand right now. We must know and accept our character assets and liabilities.

Revealing and accepting the truth about our self is not easy. It often helps to remember that each of us will remain a *child* of God throughout our entire lifetime. *We are children* learning to live a life that draws us closer to the Infinite. This happens through experience which inevitably includes making mistakes.

These errors don't reflect our value but may highlight specific traits which delay our development. If we tell lies, we must accept this flaw and the damage it causes; then knowing the problem, we can find a solution. Denying the problem will make us liars forever. Accepting the truth about our self, without guilt or self-recrimination, is essential for personal growth and also makes us more tolerant, loving, and patient with others.

Prayer: I pray that I honestly review my thoughts, words, and actions to see the traits that cause me problems; help me accept these and realize that I do not have to stay this way.

Take three relaxing breaths; ask your inner spirit to guide your meditation; pause for a few minutes in silence.

April 24

Another person should never be the primary source of our happiness—or our misery.
Others can add to our happiness but not create it.

The old saying that "Happiness is an inside job" holds inescapable truth. Any time we say or even think that "I'd be happy if she (he) loved me or if I had that *thing*", we guarantee un-happiness. If we need anyone or anything to make us happy, that same person or thing can make us unhappy.

Happiness depends on having a healthy self-love that rests on a strong and vibrant relationship with the "kingdom of heaven within," our inner source of guidance, strength, security, and love. This firm foundation enables us to develop wise and loving self-acceptance. Then this humble sense of self-value becomes the gateway to a great life.

Acts of other people and the disappointments of the world affect us much less when we experience the love of our spiritual source and love our self; we accept goodness but allow the negative and hurtful things to slide over us, without any attachment or reaction. People and things can add to the enjoyment of life but cannot create happiness.

Prayer: My inner spirit, let me feel your presence and guidance this day; help me accept myself as I am and love myself as a child of the Divine. Open my eyes that I may see all opportunities of happiness and joy.

Take three relaxing breaths; ask your inner spirit to guide your meditation; pause for a few minutes in silence.

April 25

Are you having fun yet?

What if—when we die and wake up someplace, the question posed to us is: "Did you have fun down there?" Will your answer be: "I didn't have time to have fun? I was too busy worrying and trying to control everything." We cannot expect a life of continuous laughter and joy; tribulation and challenges are part of life but many of us spend significant energy and emotion on trifles and on problems of our own creation.

We can develop skills that help us live with peace-of-mind throughout most days and then take delight and revel in the bursts of laughter, light-heartedness, and joy. We can

- start the day right by thinking of people, events, or things that bless our life—start with an attitude of gratitude;
- learn to lighten up. Taking our self too seriously or having too many "big deals" breeds discontent;
- quit waiting for fortune to smile on us, it's already beaming. Throughout the day, we accept joy from the taken-for-granted blessings—the people around us, the beauty of nature, the scent of a baby, the laughter of children; and
- open our heart, mind, and soul to our indwelling spirit.

Enchantment and delight await the loving and open mind.

Prayer: I pray that I may spend this day in peace; guide me to be kind, gentle, loving, and tolerant; help me not overreact to any person or event; make me aware of moments that offer an opportunity for gratitude, open my heart to delight in the smallest truth I hear, any beauty I see, and every goodness I witness.

Take three relaxing breaths; ask your inner spirit to guide your meditation; pause for a few minutes in silence.

April 26

Silence is the same in all languages.
"Be still and listen" offers God the chance to communicate in this universal dialect.

We live a hectic pace; we are overwhelmed with noise and bombarded with visual images; our mind generates a continuous stream of mental self-talk. The secular, materialistic world programs us to avoid natural silence and has done this so effectively that many people are uncomfortable in stillness.

The spirit speaks in the silence and the world prevents us from hearing. The most powerful force in the universe, the true source of inner peace, works in the still, quiet space of our mind. We must make the conscious choice to seek the stillness and then find anything that helps us accomplish this. We can take calming walks; sit in a beautiful, tranquil place in nature; relax in a dark room, breathing deeply and reflecting on the value of stillness; find and practice meditation techniques that calm us; search for, find, and use any tools that aid us in achieving inner silence.

We learn that inner silence leads to inner peace.

Prayer: I pray that I may learn to sit in silence; that I may practice this art until I experience the benefits it offers. My loving inner spirit, please help me quiet my mind, to cease that endless cycle of thoughts. Let me enjoy the stillness.

Take three relaxing breaths; ask your inner spirit to guide your meditation; pause for a few minutes in silence.

April 27

It's our choice whether to have a bad five minutes or a bad day.

Bad things happen to all of us; people disappoint us, hurt us, or break a trust; we encounter situations that offer fear, anger, worry, or other miseries. A few may be real problems but many are a flash-in-the-moment that triggers an immediate overreaction on our part. We have a very important choice to make when these hit us: Do I have a bad five minutes, a bad day, or a bad week?

When turmoil penetrates our peace, we find a quiet few minutes to pause, practice relaxation breathing, try to objectively look at the situation, and pray. We might say to our self: "Yes, this upsets me, but will I allow it to disturb my whole day, to put a contentious weight on my mind and heart, a burden that may lead to additional bad choices that hurt me or those I love? Or will I assert my freedom as a liberated child of divinity?

I proclaim: I choose not to let other people or situations have power over me; I choose to handle any problem that I can at this moment, to release the burden, and not have any additional emotional attachment to this." I claim my freedom and my peace.

Prayer: My inner spirit, grant me peace at this moment; help me to see this situation with a long-distant and spiritual outlook; guide me to understand that these disruptions are temporary upheavals and do not have the power to determine my life.

Take three relaxing breaths; ask your inner spirit to guide your meditation; pause for a few minutes in silence.

April 28

We enjoy better relationships if we recognize God as the managing partner.

Most of us want great relationships, especially those intimate loving associations we have or hope to form with that special person. The extraordinary relationship of our dreams is not a fantasy; it is achievable if we share similar core values and build on a spiritual foundation. Our spiritual parent is not a passive observer but becomes an important and active third partner. Actions, not intentions accomplish this.

If possible, share morning prayers and meditations. Acknowledge all accomplishments, spiritual, and emotional growth in the other person; share insights, longings, fears, and dreams; become a living demonstration of loyalty, love, compassion, integrity, and tolerance.

Invite God into all disagreements, contention, and major decisions. Perhaps reserve a chair at your table for God; make a sign for this chair that is a physical reminder of his place in your home. When faced with a major decision or disagreement, sit down with you partner, acknowledge God in his chair, say a prayer of gratitude and ask him to quiet any disturbance, help each person exhibit peace, patience, and love in the discussion, and grant guidance to make loving choices. The awareness that this brings, the truth that God is actually present, often eliminates rancorous words; it always elevates the process and the outcome.

Prayer: Let me gratefully accept the challenge of building a special relationship; help me show the appreciation, love, and joy that my partner adds to my life; guide us to always open ourselves to your presence, love, power, and knowledge.

Take three relaxing breaths; ask your inner spirit to guide your meditation; pause for a few minutes in silence.

April 29

The Infinite includes all things.

In contentions between spirituality and science or between different views of God, remember the story of the blind men and the elephant. Ramakrishna Paramahamsa describes one Hindu version of this story,

> *A number of blind men came to an elephant and asked, 'What is the elephant like?' and they began to touch its body. The man who touched its leg said: 'It is like a pillar.' Another who felt the ears said, 'The elephant is like a husking basket.' Similarly, he who touched its trunk or its belly talked of it differently. In the same way, he who has seen the Lord in a particular way limits the Lord to that alone and thinks that He is nothing else.*

People seeing different views or having different beliefs does not necessarily mean that one is right and the other wrong, but only that each may be seeing one part of the total reality. They never need to be foes; if they continue progressing, each may see the entire elephant. The Infinite includes all things.

Prayer: Dear loving Creative Source, help me accept that my way is not the only way; open my mind and beliefs to ideas and concepts that may enlarge my understanding of you and of all people.

Take three relaxing breaths; ask your inner spirit to guide your meditation; pause for a few minutes in silence.

April 30

Blaming others and making excuses prevents growth; being responsible and accountable advances it.

Responsible: *exhibiting the duty to take care of something; having good judgment and the ability to make decisions on your own.*
Accountable: *obligation to account for and justify actions or decisions*

"I didn't mean it"; "If he (she) hadn't done what they did, then I wouldn't have made the mistake"; "They talked me into it or I wouldn't have done it"; "The devil made me do it" and other excuses block all growth. Our manner and degree of evasion matters not; we are responsible and accountable for our decisions, actions, thoughts, and feelings!

Being responsible and accountable is not always easy; few of us want to take an honest and objective look at our mistakes. We start by praying for the honesty, strength, and courage to examine our acts. We look at our motive for each act: what was the underlying reason for our action or reaction?

Even if someone else played a part in the error, we focus only on the part we played; we accept responsibility for our part and make any appropriate apology or restitution; then we commit to change and improve.

We stay aware of our human tendency to offer excuses and blame, watch for the slightest indications, and take immediate corrective action when we see these.

Prayer: Dear God, grant me the strength, courage, and willingness to examine my tendencies to offer excuses and blame for my shortcomings; help me to release any traits that stifle my growth.

Take three relaxing breaths; ask your inner spirit to guide your meditation; pause for a few minutes in silence.

May 1

Stay aware of the value of values—and of people you love.

A long association can erode the worth we feel for a person or for a value; we simply start taking them for granted. We expect people to know that they are important to us because we utter a few endearing words. "They" should obviously know we love them no matter what our actions demonstrate.

Likewise, we may believe truth, loyalty, and integrity are important but what do our actions show? Do we listen to gossip? Do we speak out when our core values are abused or do we stay quiet in fear that someone may not like us? How about freedom—do we stand when liberty is diminished, when someone else's rights are threatened? Whether relationships, values, or freedom, we often do not appreciate their worth until we lose them.

A campfire quickly smolders and dies without additional firewood; anything vital to us must be stoked with the fuels of commitment, dedication, action, and appreciation if it is to endure. Today, let's not allow erosion of our values but pause and speak with wisdom, courage, and tact; let's not depend on yesterday's prayer to feed today's spiritual hunger; let's accompany our words of love with demonstrated deeds. Let our actions reflect the importance of our relationships and values.

Prayer: Dear God, help me reflect on why each of my family and friends are truly important; help me take action that demonstrates the value I place on them and all things that are important to me.

Take three relaxing breaths; ask your inner spirit to guide your meditation; pause for a few minutes in silence.

May 2

Integrity is essential to great relationships.

Integrity: *The quality or condition of being sound; of being unimpaired, undivided, whole, or complete.*

Integrity influences all our relationships. We are either whole or we have an inner void that we strive to fill. We try money, power, things, and people to fill that empty space but find only temporary relief; we develop an unhealthy dependence on them or need "more."

Developing integrity means that we do not depend on things or other people to fill our inner void. We fill this emptiness with a spiritual essence; it is what has been missing all along and is the only thing that can truly return us to wholeness. This allows us to feel good about our self; we find dignity, self-respect, and value; we experience a healthy self-love which gives us the ability to bestow and receive love. Peace of mind, security, and happiness become an integral part of our being; nothing or no one can greatly disturb us.

Having returned to wholeness, we then form relationships to share and augment this experience; other people and 'things' enhance our enjoyment of life but never create it.

Do you still depend on people or things to fill your inner void?

Prayer: My loving spiritual parent and indwelling guide, help me find and build that wonderful connection with you that fills the voids within my heart, mind, and soul; let me recognize and seek you as the solution to all challenges and as the source of all that is good.

Take three relaxing breaths; ask your inner spirit to guide your meditation; pause for a few minutes in silence.

May 3

Trading values for short-term gratification is always a losing trade.

Many of our day-to-day decisions are primarily concerned with our "wants." Do I have pizza or steak for dinner? Do I mow the lawn or watch the ball game? Most such choices have little long-term effect but some may influence other areas of our life. Deciding that "I don't want to go to work today; I think I'll call in sick even though I'm okay; everyone else does it" may give us some free time but also comes with a price.

Choices that erode our principles or reflect self-directed behavior can start establishing harmful patterns. We need to make it second nature to check our potential choice for motives and values:

- Is my motive selfish, self-righteous, self-centered, or fearful; or is it based on love, compassion, and service?
- Does this choice advance or retard my spiritual growth?
- Does it align with my core values?
- Does it harm anyone? If harm is unavoidable, will this choice lead to the least harm?
- Is it right or is it wrong?
- Would I feel good if I had the opportunity to explain the choice to God?

Compromising our values always has a price.

Prayer: My inner beacon of truth and power, guide me in evaluating this choice; help me see the material and spiritual implications of these alternatives; help me avoid wrong motives and be honest in my judgments.

Take three relaxing breaths; ask your inner spirit to guide your meditation; pause for a few minutes in silence.

May 4

Our mind shapes our life; we become what we think.

"Suffering follows an evil thought as the cart follows the oxen. " (Buddha, Opening of the Dhammapada)

Something happens and we react; we feel angry, guilty, jealous, hurt, anxious or afraid; our mind immediately conjures more thoughts justifying the feeling; and we are caught in the cycle. When we realize that our feelings follow our thoughts, we avoid those that interfere with our serenity.

For example, something happens and we get angry. We accept that we're upset and that continuing this disturbing emotion will result in an unhappy day.

So we take action to improve our thoughts: We pause, take three deep breaths, and ask our inner spirit to let us see, hear, or remember something that helps us. We force our mind to remember an act of love, to review something for which we are grateful, or to see a different perspective, a sympathetic view that discerns the underlying motive of the other person. We examine why we react this way: "Was I carrying an emotional weight before this happened? Am I being overly-sensitive? Does my reaction express a need to be "right"? How important is it really?" We might read, or listen to, some inspirational thoughts. We provide opportunities for our mind to shift to a higher level, to thoughts that are beneficial instead of harmful.

Prayer: I pray that thoughts of kindness, gratitude, beauty, and peace dominate my day; help me remember that I have the power to pause and change my thoughts and adopt a positive, loving attitude at any time.

Take three relaxing breaths; ask your inner spirit to guide your meditation; pause for a few minutes in silence.

May 5

A broken trust is more difficult to mend than a broken arm. Both are better avoided than repaired.

Reconstruction of a broken arm is straightforward: a physician sets the arm, puts it in a cast, and after some rehabilitation time, the break mends. A broken trust is harder to repair. Someone lies to us, fails to fulfill a promise, or betrays us. Disappointment and hurt follow; we ask "Is it possible to trust again?" We might consider:

- Was this act a pattern of behavior or a mistake? In-grained patterns are harder to modify than a single mistake.
- Did I have any part in this? Did I extend trust unwisely? Did I ignore previous indications of untrustworthiness? Did I have unhealthy expectations—did I believe someone would change just because I wanted them to change? Was I clear with my expectations or did I assume they understood?
- How important is it? Will it leave a lasting imprint on my life? Can it help me avoid larger disappointments?
- Are there positive signs of change? Has the mistake been acknowledged? What actions will help avoid a re-occurrence? Do I see progress on those actions?

Prayer: My indwelling spirit, soothe my troubled mind; relieve my disappointment and hurt; help me to see your love in all people. Guide me to extend trust wisely, to not have undue expectations and to be a demonstration of honesty, acceptance, forbearance, truthfulness, and love.

Take three relaxing breaths; ask your inner spirit to guide your meditation; pause for a few minutes in silence.

May 6

If we're coasting, we're probably headed downhill.
Whether riding a bicycle or living life, progress requires effort.

We may think that life would be easier if we could drift along, doing as little as possible, and sometimes do exactly that. We ease into complacency; we're comfortable and have no initiative to change. Some coasting can be beneficial but too much can establish habits that become difficult to change and we settle for a second-rate life.

Watch for some of the warning signs of extended coasting: a total loss of initiative—having no desire to improve or change anything; failing to act when action is needed; making excuses for procrastination and indolence; blaming others for our shortcomings and failures; allowing laziness, fear, or lack of direction to force us into unhealthy acceptance.

If we are suffering from this and want a better life, we commit to change and take action. We don't blindly act for the sake of action but direct our effort to achieve the desired results. We acknowledge that our inner spirit, the "kingdom of heaven within" can guide us to the highest goals, let us see the most beneficial opportunities, and provide the power to accomplish the change.

Prayer: Dear God, please help me find balance in my life, to rest when needed but not stay at ease too long. Grant me the initiative to arise and move forward, the strength to overcome lethargy and complacency, and the courage to conquer obstacles that block my forward motion.

Take three relaxing breaths; ask your inner spirit to guide your meditation; pause for a few minutes in silence.

May 7

Some say that success is just getting up one more time than we've been knocked down; But wisdom may sometimes dictate finding a different path.

We've all heard the platitude that we should keep trying and trying and never give up. This may be true—to a point. Perseverance is valuable; gaining a worthy goal is often achieved only after repeated disappointments but this does not mean that we *never* quit, that we *never* surrender.

We might consider: Is my goal righteous? Will it be a significant benefit if achieved? Why is it important? Does my perseverance come from self-directed will—do I fear that failure would diminish my value in my own eyes or my appearance to others? Do I resist giving up because it injures my pride? Am I too self-sufficient to ask for help? Does surrender automatically mean failure or can it offer opportunities that lead to ultimate success?

If the goal is worthy and we have exerted an honest effort, perhaps surrender (or weariness) can bring us to that place where we are open to ask for help from other-than-me sources. We might seek guidance and strength from our inner spirit; we might seek the counsel of wise friends, advice from experts, or assistance from spiritual advocates.

Prayer: I pray for peace in this effort and for the wisdom to know when to keep trying and when to give up. Soothe my disappointment and hurt; grant me the strength to persevere, the willingness to try again, and the humility to seek and recognize wise counsel.

Take three relaxing breaths; ask your inner spirit to guide your meditation; pause for a few minutes in silence.

May 8

A rude awakening often precedes a spiritual awakening.

A rude awakening often occurs in that moment when we come face-to-face with the consequences of self-driven will. Currently or sometime in the past, we made a decision and took an action that is bringing us misery today. Thoughts and actions based on self-driven choices inevitably bring anger, guilt, fear, shame, resentment, or other misery. These can deepen and let us to see the un-seeable: We are at fault; either we change or stay in misery.

Perhaps for the first time, we cannot deny the true source of our contention; we cease blaming other people or events and accept responsibility for our actions and feelings. Self-driven determination, reinforced by denial and justification, is not easily recognized or changed, but *must* be altered if we want a better life.

In this moment of clarity, we pause, ask for help from our inner spirit, and petition for guidance and power; we talk to a trusted friend or advisor to help assess our situation; then, we resolutely march forward, confident that we now have all the resources we need for our personal awakening and transformation.

Prayer: My loving inner spirit, grant that I accept my responsibility in this current turmoil; help me clearly see the changes necessary to relieve this contention and avoid a recurrence. By your grace, bestow patience, humility, guidance, and strength to help vanquish anything that stands as a barrier to my growth as a child of divinity. Let your will be done in my life.

Take three relaxing breaths; ask your inner spirit to guide your meditation; pause for a few minutes in silence.

May 9

What will you do today for spiritual growth?
Strive for more patience, tolerance, and loving actions.
Action—not intention—produces change.

Our world offers a lot of distractions. Living the best life requires that we function *in* this world but are not dominated *by* this world. Our spiritual attitude is the basic ingredient to achieve a happy and peaceful life. Herein we establish our purpose, values, and principles that determine how we act and react to all life situations; plus we receive the liberating energy to break the shackles of this material existence and rise above the turmoil.

We must sustain our spiritual core if we want peace. We start the day with prayer and meditation asking for peace, guidance, and strength. As we venture into the world, we take advantage of all the opportunities for growth. When facing anger, we respond with love, tact, and tolerance; when hurried and hectic, we strive for patience; when disappointed, we examine our expectations and acts; when attacked by fear, we pause and respond with courage and grace; when bombarded by distractions, we stay focused on the truth—much of the calamity and drama of the world are passing trifles. We are a child of divinity with a life purpose of learning to love.

Prayer: My inner spirit, help demonstrate divine qualities as I face this day. Let me be invigorated by tribulation, see challenges as opportunities, and respond to disappointments with love. Guide my thoughts with wisdom and my words and acts with tact, patience, love, and tolerance.

Take three relaxing breaths; ask your inner spirit to guide your meditation; pause for a few minutes in silence.

May 10

Bondage to yesterday's misery limits our freedom today.

Bondage: *slavery or involuntary servitude; the state of being bound by or subjected to some power or control.*

At some past time, we made a mistake, suffered a disappointment or hurt, or encountered a person or event that caused fear, anger, anxiety, guilt, or envy. We struggle for a time but finally breathe a sigh of relief and "let it go" But now, something triggers a memory, a thought takes hold; the old emotions flow and disturb our peace in the current moment.

Sometimes our 'letting go' is similar to flying a kite: we release the kite to the wind—but still hold the string, holding on to that little bit of control. We need to feel like we exert some degree of influence on the outcome; we do not fully release and 'let go'.

If we still have this tenuous connection and start to feel the misery returning, we can stop the progression before it consumes us. We ask God at once to remove this feeling and our contentious thoughts, talk them over with a trusted friend, and extend love and kindness to someone else.

Prayer: I pray to truly release all emotional and mental ties to past mistakes, disappointments, and contention. Grant me the courage to recognize any bondage that holds me to past misery and the willingness to completely release anything that impedes my growth today.

Take three relaxing breaths; ask your inner spirit to guide your meditation; pause for a few minutes in silence.

May 11

Do not focus on the darkness but bring light to someone's life.

Why wait for someone to die before we send flowers? Wouldn't it be better if they could enjoy them? We know we're not responsible for other people's feelings but at the same time, it is our responsibility to spread love, to bring a little illumination to dispel the darkness. We may not be able to change the world but we can take actions that may uplift someone today.

Sometimes a loving card can bring a light into the darkness; a sticky note on the refrigerator or dresser saying "I love you—thanks for being you" can gladden a heart; a simple note expressing appreciation may produce a smile and a tender memory. We call our parents for no reason other than we want them to know we love them; we invite a co-worker for coffee, ask about their life and actually listen to the response; we play with our children, do the dishes for our wife, or surprise our husband with a romantic meal. We express the value of relationships while we have them.

Then, we carry this light to strangers with small acts of kindness.

Prayer: I pray that I am aware of how much each person truly adds to the meaning and quality of my life. Guide me to reflect on the value of these relationships, the love I have for these people, and help me find small ways to show them this love today.

Take three relaxing breaths; ask your inner spirit to guide your meditation; pause for a few minutes in silence.

May 12

Thoughts held in mind produce others of like kind.
Think love, not anger; faith, not fear; peace, not contention.

Our mind is a rich breeding ground. Once a thought takes root, it multiplies faster than weeds in a garden. We have a momentary flash of anger; then, a single thought about the anger triggers more thoughts that justify and reinforce what we're thinking. Or we're a little discontent for no apparent reason; then, we notice something—perhaps a perceived slight or unrealized expectation; we think about it; thoughts of self-pity, unfairness, anger, or guilt plow open the ground and plant the seeds of similar thoughts.

Cows produce calves; horses have colts; like begets like. Beneficial thoughts produce beneficial thoughts; harmful thoughts produce more harmful thoughts.

Start the day with 'good' thoughts. Upon awakening, before our feet hit the floor, say a prayer of gratitude. Lie there and slowly review things and people that bless your life; then, make contact with your inner spirit and ask that it guide your thoughts today and they be divorced from selfish and self-centered motives.

Throughout the day, make a conscious effort to control your mind: Watch for the smallest disturbance in your peace and review the thoughts and the associated motives that are causing it; request power and guidance to make your thinking more tolerant and loving.

At night, give thanks for all the help and ask that your spirit to minister while you rest.

Prayer: Please bless this day with beneficial thoughts. Fill my mind with thoughts of truth, beauty, and goodness.

Take three relaxing breaths; ask your inner spirit to guide your meditation; pause for a few minutes in silence.

May 13

A vibrant spiritual relationship helps us avoid mediocrity.

We can live without any spiritual awareness or participation in a spiritual life; millions do exactly that. Others give lip service to the idea of living spiritually; some occasionally attend religious service but don't let this interfere with their secular life. A fortunate few practice spiritual exercises that actually transform their lives. Each day we must choose "How will I spend this day? Will I get by as easily as I can or try to live the best life?"

Living in awareness of the fatherhood of God and the brotherhood of all humanity elevates our attitude to the highest possible level; it results in the highest ethics, the ultimate integrity, and supreme loving. Today we can declare "I will treat myself and every other person as a child of divinity." With this foundation, we can acquire material possessions that aid our comfort and enjoyment but are not critical for our peace and happiness; we can forge relationships that add depth, meaning, and pleasure to our existence but are not the basic source for our peace and joy; we balance our dignity and self-respect with tolerance and patience.

Prayer: I pray I may hunger for righteousness. Make me aware of the fragment of God in each person I meet. Fill my heart, mind, and soul with compassion, love, and mercy balanced with prudence and spiritual insight. Today, guide me to act as a loving child of the divine.

Take three relaxing breaths; ask your inner spirit to guide your meditation; pause for a few minutes in silence.

May 14

We do not have to accept unacceptable behavior. Living spiritually does not require being a doormat.

Some may believe that acceptance is the answer to all of life's upsets but this wonderful trait must also be balanced with wisdom. Yes, acceptance is essential to a peaceful life but some things are simply unacceptable. Blindly and passively accepting continuous abuse, degradation, or outright harm for our self or other innocents is not virtuous and may actually contribute to the problem.

In all cases, we have to accept the *fact* of the situation—that it really is what it is; denying reality never solves any problem nor does such denial ever lead to long-term comfort. However, we do not have to accept that it is God's will or "it is as it should be" or refuse to take action that may change the circumstances. A child of God does not have to be a doormat for anyone but has the guidance to see the correct action and the strength to stay peaceful and loving while taking that action. The oft quoted Serenity Prayer offers some of the best guidance to face the turmoil in daily living.

Prayer: God grant me the serenity to accept the things I cannot change, the courage to change the things I can, and the wisdom to know the difference.

Take three relaxing breaths; ask your inner spirit to guide your meditation; pause for a few minutes in silence.

May 15

Faith and prayer will not eliminate the consequences of our actions but can yield serenity as we face those challenges.

We will make mistakes. Other people make mistakes. We can make a decision with best intentions and things can still turn out wrong. The choices and actions of other individuals, random acts of nature, and even accidents can determine the outcome of many situations. How do we utilize our spiritual beliefs to overcome the turmoil?

When disappointed or discontent, we honestly try to determine who is responsible. Have our own decisions/actions wreaked havoc in our life or spawned unnecessary problems and contention? Did we check our true motives prior to acting? Can we recognize and accept the responsibility for the error? If another person was truly at fault, can we see any part that we played—did we extend trust where we shouldn't have; did we make an erroneous assumption; did we in any way set our self up for this?

Mistakes are part of life and wisdom can always be gained from such errors. We pause and acknowledge our inner spirit as the source of peace and power; we ask for help to not overreact or be overly sensitive; we seek to learn from this situation and not repeat it.

Prayer: My loving and friendly higher power, help me accept that I am human and will make mistakes; open my heart and mind so that I can honestly evaluate and accept errors I make; grant me the wisdom to discover the best solutions and the strength to overcome any obstacle to my progress.

Take three relaxing breaths; ask your inner spirit to guide your meditation; pause for a few minutes in silence.

May 16

Let me strive for the best I can be; help me to:
ennoble my thoughts,
sanctify my purpose,
consecrate my will, and
purify my motive.

- *Our thoughts*—the silent self-talk that produces ideas, comparisons, dreams, and imaginary reality— are either guided by self-directed will or by divine will; they are selfish, self-centered, and self-righteous or loving and altruistic.
- *Our purpose*—the reason we have for living this life—must recognize the material life but also incorporate the necessity of spiritual growth. Does our purpose include increasing our capacity for love, spiritual awareness, and serving our fellows?
- *Our will*—the ability to make decisions and then initiate and consummate action—either functions as self-directed will (ego) or spirit-directed will. Experiencing the best life requires consecrating this wonderful gift: We choose to align our will with God's will.
- *Our motive*—the reason or cause for our current thoughts, words and actions, the "why" for everything we do—greatly determines the right or wrong and the possible outcome of every action. We must search for our true motives and seek pure, divinely aligned reasons for acting.

Prayer: Dear God, grant me the insight to understand my reason and purpose for this life, the willingness to open my heart, mind, and soul and be guided to the divine path.

Take three relaxing breaths; ask your inner spirit to guide your meditation; pause for a few minutes in silence.

May 17

A loving relationship is no place for taking or being a hostage. Participation in such bondage damages both parties.

Love—the active and healthy concern for a person's well-being, the desire to do good for a person—stands as the opposite of taking hostages or prisoners. We may intend to bestow love, but living on self-focused will can lead us into taking or being an unsuspecting prisoner. The situation may be obvious or it may be camouflaged and require a conscious evaluation. If so, we strive to be sincerely honest and objective without being overly sensitive.

Do we expect others to please us or make our life easier but make little effort for them? Do we expect acquiescence and accolades from people in our relationships? Do we, *in any way*, demand to know and control their time, friends, dreams, needs, and hopes? Do we allow others to do these things to us? Do we compromise our core values to keep the peace? Do we allow the pirating of our time, permitting others to repeatedly infringe on our personal time and space? Do we take and give selected privacy, the freedom to develop and grow as a child of God?

Prayer: I pray that I support the growth and development of every individual I meet and know. Open my eyes that I may see the chains I attach to the thoughts, words, actions, and emotions of my loved ones; sever any bond by which I bind another.

Take three relaxing breaths; ask your inner spirit to guide your meditation; pause for a few minutes in silence.

May 18

We cannot understand God
but can develop an understanding <u>of</u> God.

We use words of eternity—infinity—omnipotent—omniscient to discuss God. We say that he created everything and knows everything; that he's really the parent of our inner spiritual nature (Our Father); that he bestows to each of us the "kingdom of heaven within," a direct link to his majesty and power. We look with awe at the star-filled sky on a dark night; we stand with over-brimming love at our new-born's birth or fall to our knees in gratitude that his power broke the shackles of our addiction.

Each of us responds in our unique way as we relate to this being we call God. Our limited finite eyes only see a small portion of the infinite, but even that holds us in wonder, praise, love, and thankfulness. We may respond to the energy that creates and sustains the universe, the same power that can erase our fears, reinforce our resolve, and strengthen us through adversities. We may recognize the infinite cosmic mind and strive to elevate our mortal thinking to higher levels. We may acknowledge that he (she) is our spiritual parent and see all the beautiful implications of this parent/child relationship.

Or we may integrate all these outlooks plus others to develop our personal understanding while knowing that even our most enhanced comprehension is but a small glimpse of the wonderful infinite.

Prayer: Infinite source awaken in me the hunger for more understanding of you. Open my eyes that I may see more of the magnitude of your creation; embrace my heart so that I can feel your love and power; nurture my soul with your life-giving power.

Take three relaxing breaths; ask your inner spirit to guide your meditation; pause for a few minutes in silence.

May 19

An "I" counter would record how many times we say or think "I" or "me" during the day. The daily total might indicate our spiritual state.

How often do we say or think "I, I, I" and "me, me, me" during the day? Some focus on our self is healthy and part of our human nature. However, excess may indicate a harmful infection of the "Big I" disease, an illness of the ego. Selfishness, self-centeredness, and self-righteousness cause most of our misery and the degree of our "I" talk indicates the level of our self-absorption. We have no "I" counter but must make an effort to unveil this monstrous "Big I."

We can ask in morning prayer to become aware of thoughts or words that indicate too much consideration of our self. At night, we mentally review our frequency of using "I, I, I" and "me, me, me."

Throughout the day, did we exhibit peace, tolerance, and patience or were we focused on what we might gain or about what someone else should do for us? How often did we interrupt someone? What were we thinking about while driving or just relaxing? We strive for progress each day.

Prayer: I pray that I am aware of selfish, self-centered, and self-righteous thoughts; help me immediately recognize when I overindulge in the 'I' and 'Me' talk in my mind or in conversations. With this awareness, I ask that you purify my thoughts, adjust my attitude, and guide my actions so that I might demonstrate my love for other people.

Take three relaxing breaths; ask your inner spirit to guide your meditation; pause for a few minutes in silence.

May 20

Ignoring maintenance erodes our happiness and peace.

We have suffered hurt and disillusionment, perhaps been so far down that we thought we might never find our self-respect and dignity. Then, the miracle happened: We found a relationship with God; the past yesterday lost its hold on us, our fear of the future melted and we began to actually live in the present moment. Our relationships improved; we experienced a taste of that "peace that passes all human understanding"; we found tolerance, patience, and love replacing our old traits. We happily drift along and are surprised when we notice that we've allowed someone to irritate us, reacted inappropriately with a loved one, or are lying awake at night worrying.

Losing our serenity, feeling less and less of our vibrant, joyful, hopeful outlook often doesn't result from one cataclysmic event but frequently erodes a small piece at a time. It's easy to slip into complacency and assume that everything is alright. However, our wonderful spiritual life is not magic; without daily maintenance the world, its people, and our ego pulls us back into the darkness.

It's really very simple: Will we take time today to invest in the way of life that brings us the most rewards and greatest blessings, that keeps us from returning to our life of pain, mediocrity, and misery? Or will we choose to take this enlightened life for granted and let a little more slip away? Spend time with God today.

Prayer: My loving spiritual source, please let me take action to maintain our vibrant, loving relationship. Help me stay aware of your constant presence; let my words and action reflect your righteousness and love.

Take three relaxing breaths; ask your inner spirit to guide your meditation; pause for a few minutes in silence.

May 21

Use T H I N K as a guideline to evaluate thoughts and actions.

Ask yourself: Is it:

T	**True**	Does it align with higher, altruistic, even divine, values or does it reflect a self-important attitude?
H	**Honest**	Does it reflect an objective evaluation without rationalizing and justifying our motive or is it selfish and self-centered?
I	**Intelligent**	Is it an accurate appraisal of the reality as is exists or is it clouded by fear, fantasy, or self-driven views?
N	**Necessary**	Is thinking about this subject truly essential? Does it accomplish something positive and healthy? Does it contribute to truth, beauty, and goodness?
K	**Kind**	Is it considerate, benevolent, helpful, or loving? Or can it do unnecessary harm?

Prayer: My inner spirit, I pray that my thoughts reflect the values I am trying to achieve and move me ever closer to the life you envision for me. I choose that your will and plan be done in my life today.

Take three relaxing breaths; ask your inner spirit to guide your meditation; pause for a few minutes in silence.

May 22

Grace: *an unearned or unmerited gift.*

God, our spiritual parent, has an infinite supply of spiritual gifts available for his children. Appropriating some of these may be done through spiritual practices—we achieve peace and serenity by practicing prayer and meditation; then, we may tend to see these wonderful rewards as "earned" to some degree.

But sometimes life-transforming gifts inexplicably appear in our life. The alcoholic or addict initiates a small desire for recovery—and people, events, or situations appear and the door opens for a miracle; the parties in a strained relationship share a thought, a memory, or experience and suddenly the healing process starts. We may be sincerely trying to understand and do God's will but have hit a roadblock—and then a thought, a word spoken by someone, or something we read offers an insight that carries us forward.

Surrendering or developing a strong desire that aligns with the divine way may sometimes precede grace; other times it just appears.

We can also act as the divine; we can demonstrate unconditional love and bestow grace to others.

Prayer: My loving spiritual center, open my heart to the obvious; help me see the many acts of grace that bless my life and be grateful for them. Guide me to see opportunities where I may bestow grace this day.

Take three relaxing breaths; ask your inner spirit to guide your meditation; pause for a few minutes in silence.

May 23

The warmth of our inner divine spark can melt our fears and anxiety as wax before a flame.

God has gifted each of us a divine spark—the kingdom of heaven within. This wonderful resource is always subservient to our will; we must choose to access this inner reservoir of augmented guidance, hope, strength, peace, and power. A moment of deep need, recognition of our limitations, a surrender of our self-driven motives, or a sincere yearning to find true answers may open the door to this wonderful gift but commitment, time, and effort are necessary to enjoy the full potential.

Following the spiritual path is a continuing process of exchanging the way of the world for the way of the spirit. We trade selfishness for love, self-centeredness for concern of others, and self-righteousness for humility—we become teachable. As we make these exchanges, a quiet peace replaces turmoil and chaos; an inner healing melts our misery; a new courage vanquishes fear; a new strength supplants our human weakness.

We trade the worldly acquisition of "things", money, power, and recognition for a new purpose in life, an enhanced level of living. We enjoy a shift in perception—we see the material world as additions that can improve our comfort instead of as necessities for happiness, as a reality in which we must live but not as a force that controls our current peace and future destiny. We exchange doubt, confusion, and anxiety for certainty, clarity, and hope.

Prayer: My indwelling spirit, I pray that I may be conscious of your presence in my life today. Help me to pause five times this day and communicate with you; let me turn to you before I am troubled.

Take three relaxing breaths; ask your inner spirit to guide your meditation; pause for a few minutes in silence.

May 24

Compassion should always be guided by wisdom.

We see something; we feel for that person; we act to relieve the person's suffering. Wanting to help someone who is deeply hurting is a hallmark of an enlightened life but even a great trait can be detrimental if used inappropriately or activated by unhealthy motives. We might ask our self:

- What is my true motive?
    - Am I doing this out of love, a sincere desire to help?
    - Am I willing to do this anonymously?
    - Do I expect gratitude or accolades?
- Will my action help or will it enable?
    - Is the person I want to help responsible for this situation or a victim of circumstances?
    - If they are responsible, do they accept the responsibility or do they blame other people? (Blaming leads to repeating same actions with same results.)
- Can my acts serve a dual purpose—relieve the suffering and also demonstrate higher values and principles?

Prayer: I pray that I may be tenderhearted toward all of Gods children; that I may exercise the acts of compassion with wisdom and love.

Take three relaxing breaths; ask your inner spirit to guide your meditation; pause for a few minutes in silence.

May 25

A single deed can produce haunting thoughts for decades. Release all attached emotion but retain the experience.

We make a mistake that truly hurts our life or the life of people we love; we apologize, make restitution, and try to move forward. Or another person does us harm; we accept it, try to forgive, and go about our life. Sometime later a word, an event, or a person brings the memory rushing back. The old thoughts and feelings invade our mind.

Complete forgiveness for others and our self is essential if we are to release the past. We must achieve that state of detachment wherein we remember the event (to avoid repeating the mistake) but have no associated feeling about it. We pray to be honest, thorough, and willing; then

1. We write specifically about the event including:
    a. the thoughts, words, feelings, and actions associated with it;
    b. all perceptions, expectations, and motives that played a role in our action.
2. We review this with a trusted advisor or friend.
3. We make any warranted restitution.
4. We release the past: We acknowledge the error in prayer, asking our inner spirit to remove any emotional attachment to this event; we repeat this whenever the memory of the event disturbs us.

Prayer: Dear God, grant that I truly forgive so that I may completely live in this moment. Let your mighty expulsive power flow through me to break all shackles to my past.

Take three relaxing breaths; ask your inner spirit to guide your meditation; pause for a few minutes in silence.

May 26

A pint cannot hold a quart.
Every drop of anger, guilt, worry or any misery we hold decreases our capacity for happiness.

On a physical level, no one would believe a pint jar can hold a quart of water. But we sometimes fail to apply the same logic to our thoughts and feelings. We harbor resentments, guilt, fear, shame, jealousy and a myriad of misery and then wonder why we cannot fill our day with laughter, happiness, and joy. We fill our mind and emotion-stream with clutter without realizing that every smidgen of past misery, current chaos, and future fears eliminates the space for that exact amount of peace and happiness.

Enjoying the best day possible requires that we live in the moment; we must keep our mind focused on the exact instant we are experiencing *right now*; we spend no energy or emotion on past errors or future worries.

This isn't always easy and may not happen simply because we *want* it to happen. We must access our inner spiritual power and seek the mighty expulsive energy that can purge all these feelings of past misery and future concerns. As this force empties our mind and cleanses our emotions, we have room to receive happiness and joy; we experience the peace that passes all human understanding and become open to hope and wonder of life.

Prayer: My refuge and my source of life-transforming power, please remove the smallest traces of fear, anger, or any hurtful feeling linked to my past or my future; keep my mind in each moment as I go through this day.

Take three relaxing breaths; ask your inner spirit to guide your meditation; pause for a few minutes in silence.

May 27

Worry and anxiety take root in self-directed mind;
Peace and hope spring from a spirit-led mind.

Our will—our ability to engage in intelligent reflection, make decisions, and initiate action—is the foundation for our quality of life. This awesome power allows us to choose a life based on self-directed will or choose to follow the divine plan for our life—God's will. In choosing the elevated response, we do not relinquish our will; we consecrate and align our will with something that produces better results. Consequences follow every decision/action we make; poor choices lead to mediocrity and misery and good choices to peace, love, and joy.

Choosing the self-directed life moves us to be selfish, self-centered, self-righteous, and afraid; happiness, satisfaction, and peace are elusive and temporary. Using our power of free-will choice to ask for spirit guidance elevates our decisions/actions to higher values and divine purpose; the use of our mind shifts to a more meaningful level; we begin to experience our true potential. The change is progressive as we find peace in the midst of turmoil, courage that melts fear, strength to overcome seemingly insurmountable obstacles, joy in the experience of living, and knowledge to see answers.

Prayer: My divine source and all powerful friend, I know that you want the best for me. Help me to be increasingly willing to follow your way. Divorce me from any tendency to be selfish, self-centered, or self-righteous; help me be loving, tolerant, kind, compassionate, and patient today.

Take three relaxing breaths; ask your inner spirit to guide your meditation; pause for a few minutes in silence.

May 28

When praying is hard, try the five word petition that says so much: "Thank you, please help me."

We are human; at times, the world may overwhelm us before we can summon our spiritual strength. We may get so deeply discouraged, inundated with fear, or so lonely that we do not feel like praying. Or our minds may be filled with confusion; we know we should pause and pray; we should ask for strength and guidance, but have no words to utter; our minds cannot even construct peaceful thoughts. Five words can open the channel and release the relief we desperately seek; "Thank you, please help me."

This simple prayer says so much. "Thank you" expresses our gratitude and silently establishes our position—we are children of the divine; we acknowledge the blessings we have received by that birthright; we know that his grace and love brought comfort to many previous episodes of chaos and turmoil. "Please help me" is the cry of the hurting child that opens the channel to unlimited and unconditional relief. We do not have to give details of our problem or offer a litany of our pain; he already knows everything; we humbly, trustingly, and with confidence leave the time, degree, and manner of answer solely to the wisdom and care of our God who wants the best for us and knows the appropriate solution.

The sincerity of any petition guarantees access to the divine ear; the spiritual maturity determines the answer.

Prayer: My loving, compassionate, and wonderful God, "Thank you, please help me."

Take three relaxing breaths; ask your inner spirit to guide your meditation; pause for a few minutes in silence.

May 29

We cannot always "think" our way out of emotional upsets. Our mind cannot always ease upsets started and exacerbated by that same mind.

We think of something; we know that if it happened, we would suffer contention or distress. Then, we start to worry; the anxiety and fear fester and grow. Our rational mind acknowledges that this worry is futile, that it cannot actually change anything. We tell our self to stop it, but it keeps going. The very mind that started the problem now keeps feeding the concern; it does not have the power to release the obsession. So we call on our other resources to help shift our thinking.

Changing our physical actions can help change our thinking. A few things might include: taking a walk and actually slowing down to enjoy it; observing something beautiful and good or merely appreciating nature; writing a gratitude list of ten blessings that affect our life; reading or listening to something uplifting; or exercising.

While changing our action, we pause, take three relaxation breaths, and access our inner reservoir of spiritual energy. We know that this transformative power can alter our thinking; that this inner energy has the power to make our mind release the contentious thoughts to bring us peace.

This two-step process—combining physical action with spiritual energy—can ignite, cleanse, and guide a transformation in our mind.

Prayer: My loving and powerful inner spirit, I ask for help in controlling my mind. Relieve me of all motives that cause my contention; melt my fears and anxiety; remove those thoughts that do not benefit my growth today and guide my mind to align with my divine purpose.

Take three relaxing breaths; ask your inner spirit to guide your meditation; pause for a few minutes in silence.

May 30

Are we willing to improve our life?
Willingness must precede change.
Willingness opens the door; action produces results.

We may have an area in our life that causes some discomfort or outright pain; we really want to change but nothing happens. We can *want to* do something—have a desire to make a change—and stay unchanged indefinitely. We must acquire willingness; this means that we get to that place where we are *prepared and ready to take action* to achieve the change, not only desire it.

When we are ready to actually make a change in our life, we can sit down and write a list of all the reasons we *should* make the change (the gains) and also list the consequences of staying as we are; we burn into our consciousness the actual life benefits that can result from doing this.

Then we turn to our inner reservoir of strength, guidance, and power; we pray for the willingness to make this change in our life, that our inner motives and desires are transformed into a vibrant and ready state of true willingness to start and complete this beneficial act. If willingness is still elusive, we ask for the willingness to be willing. This never fails.

Prayer: Dear God, I ask for your help. Grant me clarity of vision that I may see the consequences of staying as I am; help me understand how my lack of willingness is hurting my life. Transform my weak desire into a committed willingness and guide me to the actions that can improve my life.

Take three relaxing breaths; ask your inner spirit to guide your meditation; pause for a few minutes in silence.

May 31

How will we live this day?

We may live 100, 1000, or 10,000 days or more from this moment. How can we experience each of these and know that it was time well spent? What determines the quality of our day? Is it the amount of money we made, the number of arguments we win, or the times we were proven right? Is it getting the promotion, acquiring the new car, or capturing that dreamed-of relationship? Or is it deeply realizing the love we feel for another person, of demonstrating his or her value in our life? Is it actually doing something for someone else instead of being totally immersed with our self?

I had the great blessing of almost dying in a remote mountain region, lying there for hours thinking that I would not likely live through the night. Not once did I think of the money I had made, the possessions I'd miss or about any of life's trivia. I thought of the wonderful relationships I had known and the blessing of experiencing God working in my life.

This incident illuminated the shift in priorities, understanding, and actions that had transformed my life: devoting time every morning to make that initial spiritual contact; pausing to maintain awareness of God throughout the day; making an effort to let loved ones know their value; accepting that I am not the center of the universe.

Today, let us focus on relationships and on things that have genuine value; let love ones know of our love and not get upset with trifles.

Prayer: My wonderful inner divine spark, guide my mind to choose wisely this day; help me realize that every choice I make either augments or lessens my character; grant that I make those decisions that align with your purpose for my life. Help me not to take myself too seriously.

Take three relaxing breaths; ask your inner spirit to guide your meditation; pause for a few minutes in silence.

June 1

Self-respect is not self-admiration; self-preservation is not selfishness.

We must hold sacred our value as a child of God, a descendent of the divine; we should maintain respect for our worth to God, to other people, and to our self. Nothing about self-respect is flavored with self-admiration—being prideful, believing and acting as if we are better than other people.

Recognizing our divine inheritance and the value of our life requires us to care for our well-being; self-preservation makes us responsible to avoid actions that could cause us undue or disproportionate harm. This reflects in caring for, and nurturing the physical, mental, and spiritual aspects of our life; we must take care of ourselves. We strive to live with humility, dignity, and love. This is quite different than selfishness which implies a lack of consideration for others; that we are concerned chiefly with our own profit or pleasure.

Prayer: My divine source, grant me the ability to walk this day with self-respect that is not tainted by pride; to have the maturity to take care of myself in all ways compatible with your will and shun all invasions of selfishness.

Take three relaxing breaths; ask your inner spirit to guide your meditation; pause for a few minutes in silence.

June 2

God speaks in whispers and leads with gossamer threads.

We might think that the God who creates the super novas, stars, and planets, the being who emanates the power that controls the path of universes could at least speak authoritatively and clearly when communicating with us. But it doesn't seem to work that way for most of us. We seldom have a message delivered by a burning bush that leaves no doubt about its origin and power. Our Father does speak to his children but we are often too busy or distracted to hear or not sensitive to the voice of the spirit.

We are created in the image of our spiritual parent; although we exist in a physical body guided by a mind and free will, we are also an embryo of spirit potential. We are spiritual babies who must grow in spiritual receptivity, comprehension, and practice and it is to this spirit essence that our spiritual parent speaks. We must often quiet the mental noise and physical distraction of our senses to hear the words of wisdom and feel the threads of power.

This divine communication may appear as a whispered thought that clarifies a decision or offers insight; it may be a gentle feeling, an urge, or a sense of 'knowing' the best path or the right answer; it may appear as words or deeds from another person that resonate within us to provide direction or answers. We must be open and receptive.

Prayer: I pray that I may be willing to be slow down and be still; that my inner spirit quiets my mind and my actions; that I find peace in the stillness. Let me be receptive; help me feel the gentle communication that fosters the growth of my soul and leads me to a better life.

Take three relaxing breaths; ask your inner spirit to guide your meditation; pause for a few minutes in silence.

June 3

**Irritations and discomforts will occur;
however, we can continue as we are <u>or</u> we can change.**

How much of our day do we feel happy and at peace? How often do we get upset over trifles or start the day a little uneasy for no apparent reason? This is not about serious challenges but refers to those times we simply feel off-center; perhaps we find ourselves over-reacting or being overly sensitive. Face it; we're human beings, not angels. It's our choice how deeply we allow our self to sink and how long we choose to stay there.

Three important factors affect this self-inflicted distress:

1. Awareness: We cannot solve any problem until we realize there is problem. We will not stay happy and joyous all the time so we try to become more sensitive to the least of a disturbance to our peace.
2. Decision: After awareness, we must decide if we want to stay where we are or do we want to change?
3. Action: We start with the fundamental source—we pause and pray; we ask that we see specifically what is shredding our peace, what physical actions we need to do, and for the guidance and power to improve our mental attitude and outlook. Then we do something positive for ourselves.

Prayer: Dear God, every moment of this day, help me be aware anytime I allow the slightest intrusion into my place of peace and to take action with you so that I may regain my serenity.

Take three relaxing breaths; ask your inner spirit to guide your meditation; pause for a few minutes in silence.

June 4

Spirituality is not a spectator sport; Watching a football game is vastly different than playing on the field.

Some view spirituality and religion similar to their involvement with a football game. Many are completely oblivious that the game is even being played—it's not important to them and they totally ignore it; some watch it on television with varying degrees of passion and interest; still others go to the stadium and share in the enthusiasm with a group of fellow supporters; a very few actually play in the game.

How do our actions demonstrate our personal connection with God? Has our secular culture so biased our mind that we ignore this awesome power and love? If we don't ignore it, are we an observer or a participant? Do we play in the game—actually expend the effort, demonstrate commitment, and stay willing to put forth that final effort to snatch victory from defeat? Do we demonstrate a passing interest, participate only under extreme personal stress, or are we actively engaged? Do we expect the rewards of a participant although our actions show us to be only an observer?

This day, this moment, let us take the time and effort to participate in the most important and rewarding activity in our life.

Prayer: Help me honestly assess my commitment to the spiritual life. Enhance my desire for the best life; let my heart and mind open to your guidance and fill me with passion to follow your divine will. Grant me strength to move forward when I feel overwhelmed, tired, and defeated.

Take three relaxing breaths; ask your inner spirit to guide your meditation; pause for a few minutes in silence.

June 5

We need never hurry to achieve spiritual growth or emotional maturity.

Do we enjoy peace most days or do we yield to the pressures of the world and join the parade to insanity? Stress, worry, and anxiety dominate the society but we have a choice in whether we participate in this unhappiness. Do we choose the way of the world or the way of the spirit?

Jesus never hurried; Buddha was never frantic; no true spiritual devotee rushes to accomplish unimportant tasks. Slowing down in this hectic world takes practice, strength, and commitment. When we find our self scurrying to meet real or imagined deadlines or feel the pressure on our body or emotions, let us pause and reflect on what is truly important. Is our real purpose in life to attain more things, satisfy a relatively unimportant deadline, or enjoy the day? Which action *in this moment* will contribute to our best life?

Rushing seldom contributes to our inner peace; pausing always does. Pausing for a moment to breathe, to inhale the peace of divinity, unleashes the power of the spirit to ease our emotions and re-direct our mind.

Prayer: Dear God, help me to slow down this day; open my eyes that I may see with spiritual, loving vision and not be blinded by the short-sightedness of the material world. Grant that I can disregard the trifles and accomplish all that must be done.

Take three relaxing breaths; ask your inner spirit to guide your meditation; pause for a few minutes in silence.

June 6

God is not Santa Claus.

- He doesn't keep a list of who's naughty or nice.
- He doesn't keep score and then visit once a year.
- He doesn't bring gift-wrapped presents from a wish list of toys and material desires.
- He doesn't put lumps of coal or other negative gifts in our stocking because we've made a few mistakes.

BUT

- His wonderful love has already forgiven his children so he doesn't need a naughty or nice list; we experience the feeling of that wonderful divine love and forgiveness as we develop healthy self-love and forgive other people.
- He is with us every second of every minute of every day; we simply have to learn to be conscious of his presence, power, guidance and love in our life.
- He continuously offers peace, courage, tolerance, patience, compassion, hope, and wisdom to each of his children.
- He gives us solutions, not problems; hope, not despair; peace, not turmoil, and love, not pain.

Let us pause and say "Hello" and "Thank you" to our indwelling spirit.

Prayer: Dear God, enlighten my understanding of your role in my life. Help this child to see you as the divine source and spiritual power that can gift me the strength to conquer all challenges, the love to heal all wounds, and the direction that leads to my best life.

Take three relaxing breaths; ask your inner spirit to guide your meditation; pause for a few minutes in silence.

June 7

We must sometimes surrender to win.

Paradox: *a statement that appears to contradict itself but may nevertheless be true.*

Stubbornness or the urge to overcome any challenge, to preserve against all odds may dictate that we never admit defeat. This can be a great quality in many cases but there are times that wisdom dictates surrender is a better option. Individual battles may be lost and sacrifices required in order to gain ultimate victory. Surrender may yield the battle to achieve success in the war.

Surrender offers the opportunity for humility, the chance to acknowledge and accept that we are not all-powerful; on our own, we do not have all the answers. Surrender presents a chance to seek understanding, guidance, and power from sources other than our self; it often breaches the armor of self-righteousness and opens the door to a spiritual path, the ultimate solution for life. We are beaten; we become willing to accept the transforming embrace of our inner spirit; we welcome the hope, security, love, and power that can lead us to ultimate victory.

Any time we feel turmoil, we haven't surrendered something; struggle and surrender cannot exist in the same time and place. We need to pause, ask for help, and release whatever is blocking our inner peace.

Prayer: I pray that I may surrender all my self-driven ways. Help me accept that I no longer want to struggle alone and become willing to accept divine help. Grant me the assurance of your love, mercy, and power.

Take three relaxing breaths; ask your inner spirit to guide your meditation; pause for a few minutes in silence.

June 8

Sharing problems decreases pain; sharing happiness increases joy.

Share*: to accord a portion in something to another or others.*

When we share something, we give away a portion of it to someone else. So it makes sense that sharing our pain decreases the amount of pain we have left. When we are hurting, simply talking about the source and depth of our pain with a friend seems to ease our anguish a little bit. Shedding tears, venting our frustration, or shouting our anger to the walls releases some discontent.

But sharing joy and happiness does not have the same results. Different rules seem to apply in these cases. Expressing these positive emotions, perhaps even communicating gratitude for them, does not diminish what remains in our heart and mind. In fact, the opposite occurs. As we share happiness and love, something expands inside of us; we are filled with more than what we gave away. The more we share, the more we have. Sharing love compels our divine source, our indwelling spirit, to open the floodgates of infinite love and we reap the benefits of the spiritual response flowing through us.

Prayer: My inner spirit, help me to find joy and happiness this day; increase my awareness of the blessings in my life; let me share my gratitude, hope, and love with others and reap the ever increasing rewards in my life.

Take three relaxing breaths; ask your inner spirit to guide your meditation; pause for a few minutes in silence.

June 9

**Strength and resilience often come from defeat.
Our best lessons come from the darkest, hardest times.**

Life may sometimes overwhelm us with tragedy or adversity; we may feel defeated and hopeless but these dark times provide the fire that forges our character. We can take something positive from any situation rather than brooding and whining about it. Defeat and despair offer the chance to gain:

Strength*: the ability to resist being moved or broken by a force; the quality that allows someone to deal with problems in a determined and effective way.* The strength of any muscle improves with use. Facing defeat and then moving forward builds an inner strength that is impossible to achieve any other way.

Resilience: *the process of adapting well in the face of adversity, trauma, tragedy, threats or significant sources of stress.* After suffering defeat and finding that it is not the end of the world, we have the knowledge, the certitude, that we can face anything, overcome it, and move on with our life.

Wisdom: *a reliable ability to decide with soundness, discernment, prudence, and intelligence; a sense tempered and refined by experience, training, and maturity.* Experience is a necessary part of wisdom; the worst defeats and mistakes offer the greatest opportunities to gain good judgment.

Prayer: Dear God, help me to see the positive aspects of defeat; let me not dwell and brood about my losses but to see my failures as necessary stepping stones to gain the attributes you desire in my life.

Take three relaxing breaths; ask your inner spirit to guide your meditation; pause for a few minutes in silence.

June 10

Today, let's be grateful for what we don't have.

Perhaps we no longer have hangovers, cold sweats, or fear of impending doom; perhaps a racing mind does not control our day with anxiety, fear, misery, heart-wrenching pain, or keep us from sleep night after night; perhaps the anger, guilt or worry that used to dominate our life has subsided for today. Perhaps we are no longer controlled by the magnetic pull of an addiction; we may have shed some old habits that used to cause us problems. Maybe we don't sink into those previous depths of hopelessness; we don't experience the loneliness and isolation that pervaded our body, mind, and soul before we discovered the peace and power of our indwelling spirit.

Sometimes being grateful for what we don't have is easier than being grateful for what we have and let's not forget: Gratitude is a mighty expulsive force. It's impossible for anger, fear, resentment, anxiety, jealousy and so on to dominate our thoughts and emotions when we feel grateful.

Today, let's pass the searchlight of honesty across our life and find gratitude for what we don't have. Truly consider the improvement in life since shedding each of these. Misery may visit but leaves without taking residence.

Prayer: Dear God, help me not forget where I came from and be always grateful for all your blessings of removal. Your love has blown away many of my leaves of misery as the autumn wind clears the branches of the tree. Thank you.

Take three relaxing breaths; ask your inner spirit to guide your meditation; pause for a few minutes in silence.

June 11

Bad and hurtful things will happen to us; we can either stay mired in misery or move forward.

All of us will experience disappointment, sadness, grief, frustration, and other hurtful emotions. Many of them may originate from our own shortcomings; we may have had unhealthy expectations, acted with wrong motives, or made a mistake. Sometimes other people may inflict genuine harm on us; accidents or natural adversities may afflict us. We may plunge into a deep emotional upset or may seem to have a weight holding us down, keeping us from happiness. We are where we are; now, what do we do about it? We can stay stuck in misery or we can move forward.

Whatever the source of the misery, the discomfort we feel is real. We utilize the thoughts and actions that propel us from the shadows into the light. We acknowledge that "I am a child of divinity; I am the offspring of a divine source that wants me to be happy, joyous, and free. I have people in my life that want the best for me; I also want the best for me and commit to act in ways that bring me the best life. I can see, walk, and speak; I can achieve great things."

Then, we look for someone that may need a smile, a hug, of just a "Thank you for being in my life."

Prayer: My divine inner spirit, guide my thoughts, words and actions to reflect your purpose in my life. Give me the strength to overcome all obstacles, the peace to act lovingly, and the wisdom to make wise choices.

Take three relaxing breaths; ask your inner spirit to guide your meditation; pause for a few minutes in silence.

June 12

Being selfish, self-centered, and self-righteous often affects us physically.

Does your chest get tight or do you get a lump in your throat making it difficult to swallow? Does your breathing get hurried and shallow? Do you feel a knot in your stomach? Or do you feel the warm, secure glow of peace and love throughout your body and enjoy those deep, lung-filling breaths? The area between our belly button and our throat is a physical barometer of our spiritual condition.

These physical warning signals indicate that our body-mind-spirit harmony is disrupted. Perhaps we're allowing our self-directed will to guide our mind instead of seeking spirit guidance; or, we may be making decisions that isolate us from our spiritual core, our powerful source of transforming energy. These discomforts may indicate a spiritual disconnection and the need for maintenance.

We pause, take a deep breath, pray, and regain contact with our inner reservoir of harmony. Actually slowing down and doing this brings order out of chaos, allows peace to replace tension, and releases courage to overcome anxiety and fear. Today, pay attention to these signals; respond immediately when the physical turmoil starts and avoid more misery.

Prayer: I pray that I may become more sensitive to the physical indicators that I am running on self-directed will. Let me remember that I enjoy peace when my inner spirit directs my mind.

Take three relaxing breaths; ask your inner spirit to guide your meditation; pause for a few minutes in silence.

June 13

Excessive focus on "ME" leads to being childish and overly sensitive.

Our frenzied world offers numerous opportunities to slide into the "It's all about me" attitude. Our previous life of functioning as the center of the universe coupled with being surrounded by people clamoring for worldly goals exerts a magnetic force that tries to pull us back into the morass of self-importance. Then, we get offended when no one takes our real or imagined problem as seriously as we do, when they don't give us the attention we crave and demand, or when they don't live up to our expectations. We cry "It's not fair" or "Why can't they be decent and loving?"

We must remember that our journey, our thoughts, words, actions, and feelings are totally our responsibility. We hope to enjoy the best life available on this planet; we know that this requires nurturing our body and spirit and progressively disciplining our mind to accept spiritual direction. When we temporarily allow situations to pull us back to our old behavior or become irritated, discontent, or anxious, we don't blame another person; we accept responsibility for our feelings and attitude and take action to change.

Prayer: My loving inner friend, elevate my thoughts, words, and actions to align with spiritual values; let me not find excuses for my shortcomings; give me the initiative to move forward and the strength to overcome all temporary obstacles to my progress.

Take three relaxing breaths; ask your inner spirit to guide your meditation; pause for a few minutes in silence.

June 14

A spiritual life is not required for living—only for enjoying the absolute best times while we make the journey.

We can find temporary satisfaction and even some happiness without a spiritual life; we can spend our life chasing what the world tells us is important and never give any real consideration to God, spirituality, or divine values. Belief or faith is not required to draw a breath, to be recognized as a success, or even envied or idolized by other people. But we absolutely cannot live up to our potential without an active, practical spiritual component in our life.

The spiritual element adds another dimension, another reservoir of power, guidance, and security that supports us when we meet the inevitable challenges. It offers strength in hard times, brings peace during turmoil, finds order out of chaos, enhances understanding when confusion reigns, elevates our thoughts, words, and actions to allow us to endure pain without falling prey to misery; it gives us the opportunity to access the most profound happiness and to enjoy extraordinary relationships. This transforming energy can overcome our harshest character challenges and replace them with attributes that improve our life.

Yes, we can exist without this power but life is much better when we access this divine gift. Connect with your inner spirit right now—this moment— and throughout the day.

Prayer: My Creator, please help me stay conscious of my birthright as a child of God. Help me to be kind, loving, tolerant, wise, and compassionate today; guide me to extend a helping hand, a smile, or an embrace to elevate another soul and demonstrate your love to every person.

Take three relaxing breaths; ask your inner spirit to guide your meditation; pause for a few minutes in silence.

June 15

Healthy expectations are based on facts; unhealthy expectations, on fantasy.

Expectations: *our certitude about what will or should happen.*

Unhealthy expectations are based on our opinions, fantasies, and desires, what we think "should" happen, or what is "fair" according to us. They may have little factual basis with only a small probability of actually happening; they often contribute to anger, guilt, resentments, jealousy, self-pity, worry, fear, anxiety, and other self-inflicted miseries. Healthy expectations are based on facts, information, and experience.

If a situation has resulted in the same outcome nine out of ten times, expecting a similar outcome the next time would be a healthy expectation. If someone has previously told the truth, even under difficult or embarrassing circumstances, we can have a healthy expectation that they will tell the truth now.

Contrast this to an unhealthy expectation: Here, previous outcomes had not consistently occurred as anticipated, but we are still confident of the result in spite of the evidence; there may be little real reason to expect a certain outcome but we believe it will occur simply because we want it to happen or think that it's only "right". This false certainty and attitude opens the door to a variety of misery. The existing evidence and experience do not support the conviction. Desire cannot make fantasies come true.

Prayer: My divine creator and indwelling spirit, help me not expect others to be perfect; grant me an enlightened perception. If disappointed, help me to examine and accept any part I may have had in this, accept it as a learning experience, and respond with tolerance, patience, and love.

Take three relaxing breaths; ask your inner spirit to guide your meditation; pause for a few minutes in silence.

June 16

We slide; we don't fall, into complacency.

We may have been blessed and joined the ranks of the fortunate few, that small group who has suffered the depths of adversity, who has surrendered and exchanged self-directed misery for a divinely guided life, and then enjoyed the fruits of enduring peace and deep happiness. Nevertheless, now is a time to be careful; we'll slide backwards if we become complacent.

Complacency doesn't start with the conscious decision that "I'm going to stop doing the things that really transformed my life." Complacency slowly erodes our peace and strength one drop at a time. We start finding excuses; we become a little lazy; we forsake a few actions that have contributed to our growth; we fail to start additional efforts that might help us improve.

One day, we don't take the time for prayer and meditation and lose a little piece of our serenity; we speak out in anger and then justify our reaction instead of apologizing; we feel discontent but fail to seek and eliminate the root cause; someone hurts our feelings and we indulge in self-pity instead self-examination; we take our great fortune for granted instead of feeling grateful. Complacency can overcome all progress and stifle our intentions and dreams; constant awareness, effort, and discipline are the only viable defenses against this quiet enemy.

Prayer: Dear God, thank you for inspiring me, giving me direction and strength and bringing me from the dark times into the light. Help me consistently and gratefully do all that is necessary to not slide into ways that detract from my life. I ask that your will be done in my life today.

Take three relaxing breaths; ask your inner spirit to guide your meditation; pause for a few minutes in silence.

June 17

Pray for values, not things and for growth, not gratification.

Mature prayer does not ask God to solve our difficulties buts seeks the wisdom and strength to guide and sustain us as we courageously deal with our challenges; it seeks spiritual balm to quiet our disturbing emotions and the power to purify our motives and direct our mind; it never seeks a selfish advantage over our fellowman. We might pray for

- knowledge of God's will and the willingness to grow;
- guidance and strength to find the best resolution for our problems;
- spiritual progress for our loved ones, humanity, and our self;
- aid in overcoming traits that impede our spiritual growth;
- help in directing our thinking and the ability to pause when in doubt or contention; we seek thoughts of:
    - love to replace our selfish motives;
    - helping others to offset our self-centeredness;
    - understanding and tolerance to dissolve our anger;
    - gratitude to erase our anxiety and self-pity;
    - mercy and forgiveness to remove our guilt and remorse; and
    - spiritual assurance to melt our fears.

Prayer: My spiritual guide let me know the direction, choices, thoughts, and actions that align with your values in all I face this day. inspire every mortal to seek and find your presence.

Take three relaxing breaths; ask your inner spirit to guide your meditation; pause for a few minutes in silence.

June 18

Our perception is our reality.
It may be correct or incorrect, biased or tolerant, loving or fearful, but it is the lens through which we see everything.

Perception: *how we regard, understand, or interpret the situation, its outcome, and its possible influences on our life.*

When we see mirrors in a funhouse that make us look shorter, skinnier, or fatter, we know that we don't really look like that so we enjoy a laugh and move on. But in our daily life, we can have a distorted perception that wreaks havoc in our life and not realize it. Anger, fear, jealousy, self-pity, past regrets or future fears can warp our view of situations and people; then, we act and react based on this false perception and cause problems.

We can avoid these skewed perceptions. If we are disturbed, we pause, access our inner power and seek calmness; we acknowledge that our reaction may stem from our perception, from how we see the situation. We share with a trusted friend and evaluate if we're allowing something unhealthy to influence our view:

- Is self-pity, anger, fear, resentment, grief, or anxiety distorting our view?
- Is our selfish, self-righteous, or self-centered nature determining how we see?
- Have preconceived ideas, bias, or opinions warped the way we see this situation?
- Will it have a long-term impact on our life or are we blowing it out of proportion? Are we making a big deal out of a trifle?

Prayer: My loving spirit, please remove any past burdens, entrenched bias and future anxiety that may distort my view of people and the world. Let me see with spiritual vision.

Take three relaxing breaths; ask your inner spirit to guide your meditation; pause for a few minutes in silence.

June 19

Prayer opens the conduit for transformation.

Imagine that we have a garden that we depend on to feed our family and it is dying from lack of moisture. Someone tells us of a large reservoir that can freely supply our need but we must erect a channel, a pipeline, to move the water from the reservoir to the garden. We desperately run a small hose, go back to our garden and find a dribble coming forth, barely enough for a few plants. Realizing our error and limitation, we replace our meager pipe with a large water line that supplies all that's needed for the garden to grow and flourish.

The wonderful and life-sustaining gifts of the spirit are always available to each of God's children; the reservoir of spiritual power simply needs an open path to freely flow from the source to the need. Prayer and meditation open the human end of this conduit. A conscious or unconscious cry for help can open the pathway and provide short-term nourishment but self-directed will can close the flow. Continuous, sincere, mature, and faithful prayer enlarges the channel and increases our capacity to receive the waiting benefits.

Prayer: My divine Creator, help me be more receptive to your guidance; increase my willingness to share my efforts, dreams, needs, and hopes with you. Open my heart, mind, and soul to your peace, your power, and your love for me.

Take three relaxing breaths; ask your inner spirit to guide your meditation; pause for a few minutes in silence.

June 20

Help me not stray into the evil bypaths of my imagination.

Some may say "What! I never think of really bad things—my imagination is not evil." Our understanding of the word *evil* often covers a broad spectrum of meanings—from something that is slightly wrong to the committing of murder, mayhem, or atrocities. Let's get specific and consider *evil* to denote any thought, word, or action that *unknowingly* deviates from God's will. So this short prayer asks for help in avoiding those thoughts that may conflict with what God would want us to think. This may include thoughts of

- anger: We think of getting even, coming up with that snappy reply or justify why we should be upset.
- self-pity*:* Our mind reviews real or imagined scenarios where other people don't treat us with respect or value; we re-live situations that did not unfold according to our expectations.
- blame: We mentally justify, rationalize, and find excuses to avoid accepting responsibility.
- the Yeabuts: We entertain excuses for self-driven thoughts: Yea but, it isn't fair; Yeabut ...
- self-aggrandizement: We picture our self as the hero, receiving the admiration and adulation of others.

Such similar mental excursions may not lead us into the darkest evil but keep us from finding love and inner peace.

Prayer: Help me not stray into the evil bypaths of my imagination. Make me aware when my fantasy thoughts drift to considerations that do not benefit me.

Take three relaxing breaths; ask your inner spirit to guide your meditation; pause for a few minutes in silence.

June 21

Spiritual power flows to the surrendered soul.
If we're struggling with anything, we haven't surrendered something.

We have a number of physical laws to describe the movement of energy. One of these states that the distribution of energy follows the path of least resistance—the higher the resistance, the less the flow; the lower the resistance, the higher the flow. A high resistance can block all movement of energy.

Spiritual energy works in a similar way. No physical barrier can slow or prevent the flow of this force but even this awesome power cannot overcome the resistance of self-driven will. The minimum resistance to spiritual energy occurs when we experience complete and total surrender. This spiritual law might be seen as:

Total surrender = zero resistance = maximum receptivity of energy.

Our inner life—our emotions, peace-of-mind, attitude and thoughts—are the barometer that reflect our degree of surrender. Any amount of struggle indicates that we haven't completely surrendered. We ask for help to completely release any remaining self-directed desires and allow the maximum flow of spiritual energy.

Prayer: Dear God, please melt my resistance and purge my slightest commitment to self-driven fallacies. Help me accept in the deepest fibers of my being, in my heart, mind and soul that "It is my will that your will be done in my life."

Take three relaxing breaths; ask your inner spirit to guide your meditation; pause for a few minutes in silence.

June 22

Most things that upset us are illusions.

We're sitting over morning coffee; something triggers the thought that we may face an upcoming problem. Then our mind starts looking at all the scenarios that might happen and we explore the additional problems each may bring. We breathe a little faster, our chest tightens a little, our groin and stomach start to contract; we start a whirlwind of thoughts. All based on the projection of fear-driven possibilities that started with a single thought that may or may not be true. This "maybe" problem is not yet real. Right now, we are sitting in our kitchen and drinking coffee.

We take action the instant the first thought intrudes. We know that our spiritual condition determines our peace and that our mind, if left uncontrolled, can take us into chaos and misery. We also know that we can exercise our will power and choose to invite our inner spiritual power to guide our thinking. Spiritual power consistently triumphs if we open the channel and allow it to flow into our mind and being.

So we do exactly that; we pause, breathe deeply, acknowledge our need, and ask for spiritual help to direct our thoughts and quiet our emotions. We repeat this until we regain our serenity. This always works.

Prayer: My infinite source and all-powerful center, I ask that your divine direction and purpose guide my thoughts today; keep them from succumbing to any form of fear; let me feel your presence in my soul.

Take three relaxing breaths; ask your inner spirit to guide your meditation; pause for a few minutes in silence.

June 23

We react much more than we act; our instantaneous and often unconscious reactions often determine the quality of our day.

To every action, there is a reaction. Every time friends, family, acquaintances, strangers, nature, or institutions ACT, we RE-ACT. We answer with a physical action, a mental evaluation, an emotional response, or some combination of these. This reaction then becomes an ACTION that triggers another response.

If we have the sense that we are loved, valued, and in harmony with God and others, our reaction is quite different than if we feel insecure, anxious, and fearful. Those who feel loved act lovingly—and acts of love have a better chance of sparking a beneficial response than do unloving acts of vengeance, anger, demeaning words, or self-righteousness. Such an elevated reaction requires that we have found our spiritual foundation and daily strive to maintain our spiritual center and power. Only the strong can withstand the assaults of the less fortunate or the immature.

If we engage in reactions that do not reflect what we want to be, we acknowledge the error, ask our inner spirit for help, and do better the next time.

Prayer: My loving friend, my divine guide who always wants the best for me, I pray for the insight, wisdom, power, and receptivity that moves me to feel and reflect your enhanced divine values. Help me be what you would have me be today.

Take three relaxing breaths; ask your inner spirit to guide your meditation; pause for a few minutes in silence.

June 24

Smothering can slowly kill a good relationship.

Smother: *to deprive of oxygen and prevent from breathing; to suffocate.*

We cherish close, intimate, loving relationships; we want to have that deep connection wherein another person is almost a part of us; they share our laughter, our hopes and dreams, our disappointments, our failures and rejections. We try to not to hold on too tightly; smothering can suffocate any loving relationship.

Extraordinary relationships are never stagnant but always growing, striving to improve and experience a higher level of enjoyment. Such a wonderful association is made up of individuals; its growth relies on the growth of each person.

Each may need some time alone or time with friends, selected privacy, or time to pursue personal growth. Having such times without conflict requires loving trust and that each person is secure in their own self-worth. Each knows that the other person can add to, but cannot create, their happiness and peace of mind; then, each can extend healthy love—the active and healthy concern for the well-being of another that recognizes the necessity of loving freedom.

Prayer: Dear God, help me reflect the love and freedom you extend to me as a beloved child to all my relationships. Let my love grant the freedom for others to grow; let me extend enlightened trust; help me release all fears and need for bondage.

Take three relaxing breaths; ask your inner spirit to guide your meditation; pause for a few minutes in silence.

June 25

Doing God's will is often as simple as doing
the right thing
at the right time
for the right reason.

We're living this new life and seeing wonderful results. Then, we encounter a situation where we don't know what to do. How do we move forward? We pause, take three relaxation breaths, open the pathway to our inner spirit, and ask for guidance to help us see:

- What is the right thing to do? Which choice follows the higher values and principles? Does one improve the growth of my soul more than the other? Does one cause unnecessary pain to anyone? Is one alternative more unselfish, loving, or kind than the other? Do I have a "gut feeling" that one option is wrong?
- What is the right time? We don't use this as an excuse to procrastinate but ask ourselves: Do I have to make this decision right now? Do I need more information to make the best choice? Will it be a catastrophe if I do nothing?
- What is my motive for choosing the different options? Does it reflect divine values or self-driven will? Actions driven by less-than-righteous motives always cause problems.

Prayer: Dear God, I try to do my best. I ask that you keep me from evil; let me not cause any unnecessary harm to any person or myself; open the eyes of my mind so that I may see your way; grant that I go forward with peace.

Take three relaxing breaths; ask your inner spirit to guide your meditation; pause for a few minutes in silence.

June 26

Understanding ethics is an essential anchor for our character and moral choices.

Ethics: *moral principles that govern a person's or group's behavior and determine the quality of human interactions.*

Question: What in the world does ethics have to do with my life?
Answer: Everything!

The Golden Rule summarizes the highest ethical principles: "Do unto others as you would have them do unto you." It's pretty simple; treating everyone the way we want to be treated yields a better life for us and those around us.

The minimum ethical code for an individual to achieve a satisfactory life—or for any group or civilization to stay viable—is the Silver Rule: "Do *not* do unto others what you would have them *not* do to you." Again, it's pretty simple: do not treat people in a manner that you would not like to be treated. This basic ethical code produces many principles in our culture including the Principle of Non-maleficence: "Do no harm to another person; however, if harm must be done, do the least harm."

We see guidelines based on this applied in medicine—the Hippocratic Oath ("first, do no harm..."), law enforcement—(minimum force to attain objective), and personal conduct—when faced with a decision, try to do no harm; if harm is unavoidable, always opt for the least harm that may be incurred for all concerned.

Prayer: I pray that I avoid harming any person this day and that I add no unnecessary misery to anyone's life; if pain cannot be avoided, help me act with understanding and discretion to cause the least pain.

Take three relaxing breaths; ask your inner spirit to guide your meditation; pause for a few minutes in silence.

June 27

"The wise can direct their thoughts, subtle and elusive, wherever they want." (Buddha, Opening of the Dhammapada)

According to this old saying, are we wise or not? Take a simple test: Sit in silence for three minutes and tell your mind not to think. How many seconds elapsed before one thought after another slipped across your mind? *Do you control your mind or does your mind control you?*

Practicing meditation helps us gain control over this mental machine but requires practice. Many want to find the stillness in meditation, try it a few times, get discouraged when the thoughts bombard their mind, and say "Forget it, I can't do that." But meditation is one of the few things that success is in the attempt.

Find a quiet place, sit comfortably, and take three or four deep relaxation breaths to still the body and mind. Select a word or short phrase that embodies peace—God, peace, love, "be still" or another.

Multiple mental interruptions are part of the process and we peacefully accept them; we don't engage them but let them simply float by; we mentally say our sacred word to bring us back to stillness and repeat the relaxation breaths if needed seeking seconds of silence between the interruptions.

After doing this for awhile, we notice that our body and mind are slightly more relaxed; our attitude and outlook are changing; we may not react as quickly; we start to pause during the day to find guidance and peace; we don't get upset as quickly as we used to. Increasing peace is inevitable if we keep trying.

Prayer: Dear God, help me find inner peace; quiet my mind and grant me a time of stillness. If thoughts interrupt, let me patiently return to the stillness and never cease spending this time in your presence.

Take three relaxing breaths; ask your inner spirit to guide your meditation; pause for a few minutes in silence.

June 28

Even correct facts are not always the same as truth.

Facts pertain to physical reality; truth reflects spiritual principles. Facts consist of information, data, and evidence that can be verified by an impartial investigation; opinion or motive has no influence on facts. Truth incorporates facts, the motive of the speaker, receptivity of the hearer, and the compassion of the communication.

If our six-year-old daughter asks us where babies come from, what do we tell her? If we tell her all the *facts* about conception, childbirth, and labor, we may risk psychologically harming this young child. She may not be ready to receive and process this information. As the older, wiser parent, we don't deny or hide the facts but select them carefully to give them to the child as she matures and becomes ready to receive them.

Suppose we are driving by a motel and see a friend's wife emerging from the motel with another man. Do we tell our friend or anyone else about what we saw? What is our true motive? Is it really any of our business? What if they were attending a conference or having lunch to plan a surprise birthday party for him? What harm may come from saying nothing right now? What is his state of mind—does he have a lot of other turmoil right now? Is this a loving, compassionate, and supporting action?

Imparting truth invokes more responsibility than relating facts. Truth can enhance both the giver and receiver; facts can help *or* harm the speaker, the hearer, and other people. We may know facts but want to communicate truth.

Prayer: Dear God, help me always to seek truth. Help my understanding, motive, and communication align with what you would have me do.

Take three relaxing breaths; ask your inner spirit to guide your meditation; pause for a few minutes in silence.

June 29

A cruel word cannot be unsaid.

We are human; we react to what other people say and do. Sometimes we allow the pressure of unresolved guilt, anxiety, fear, or stress to influence our words or actions; we lash out and say something that hurts, something that is cruel or mean. We rationalize and justify our deed but it remains totally inexcusable; we are responsible for our words and actions no matter how we feel.

Most of us cannot stay loving, tolerant, kind, gentle and respectful all the time; however, we can try to improve these attributes. Simply pausing for a moment to find an alternative message, remaining quiet and not saying a thing, or walking away can help us not speak cruel words that inflict pain.

Sometimes, we need help to do this. We may desire to change, to stop saying hurtful things but find that we still speak without thinking or caring. Here, when we are in our morning prayer, we acknowledge our shortcoming and our desire for improvement; we ask for the power and strength to let us pause before we speak and the guidance to control our tongue. With a righteous and sincere request, God will do for us what we cannot accomplish on our own; our indwelling spirit can help us pause, pray, and think before we speak.

Prayer: My wonderful and loving spirit, I pray that you help me to pause. Help me take a moment before I speak; let me consider if my intended words are necessary, if they reflect the loving person I want to be; and then let me speak with love, tolerance, and tact.

Take three relaxing breaths; ask your inner spirit to guide your meditation; pause for a few minutes in silence.

June 30

Worry originally meant "to choke or strangle."
Now, it's seen as "to afflict with mental distress."
Neither has anything to do with solving problems.

The thought enters our mind: Something bad or something we really don't want to happen *may* happen. We start to worry about it and the seed is planted; the anxiety and tension start to grow. If we're honest, we also know that this act of worrying does not contribute one iota to solving real or imagined problems. We cannot worry with sufficient force to emanate an energy that can go out into the cosmos, transcend time and space, and actually cause or prevent something from happening. We may understand that this is physically impossible but that does not stop the worry.

However, worrying does accomplish a few things: we lose our contact with our inner spirit; we suffer mental and emotional repercussions that devastate our peace of mind; we lose sleep; we are more likely to suffer health problems. The mental and emotional effort spent on worrying prevents us from finding real solutions to our problems—and can actually generate new problems (we forget something important or have an accident because of our pre-occupation with worry.)

Often our will-power does not have sufficient energy to stop our mind from worrying; our inner spiritual energy is the only power that can change these thoughts. We can pause and make contact with our inner spirit, ask for the strength and willingness to release the worry and then, make a gratitude list. We repeat this if the worry returns.

Prayer: Dear God, relieve me of this bondage of worry; guide my mind to discard thoughts that ignite or support this fallacy. Help me surrender and let your loving power cleanse my mind.

Take three relaxing breaths; ask your inner spirit to guide your meditation; pause for a few minutes in silence.

July 1

Impatience stretches time.
Five minutes become an hour; a day turns into a week.

It is amazing how our mind makes things grow. Now, most scientists are going to disagree and say that mental energy cannot really affect material reality; they have equations, formulas, and mathematical calculations to prove their point.

But some of us know better. We have actually experienced having a small problem and then start thinking about it; suddenly, it grows into a giant that dominates our mental-emotion stream. Our marvelous, magic, magnifying mind can make problems grow, actually create problems out of nothing, and—this is important—expand time.

When we get in a hurry, our mind seizes the opportunity to work it's time-expanding magic. Someone promises to be ready in five minutes; we patiently wait; we look at the clock and notice how slowly the second hand is moving; we try to shift our concentration to something else but our mind brings it back to the s-l-o-w dragging of time. We become aware of each passing second that seems to be taking longer than it should. Again, we shift our concentration only to realize that the ten minutes we think we've been waiting is really only two minutes.

It's all in our mind. Impatience is a spiritual wake-up call; it demonstrates that our minds are self-driven instead of spirit directed and provides the opportunity to allow our inner spirit to shift our thoughts to spiritual values, ideas, and actions.

Prayer: My loving inner spirit, please help me be patient today; thank you.

Take three relaxing breaths; ask your inner spirit to guide your meditation; pause for a few minutes in silence.

July 2

We can never receive the new while we are full of the old.

If we are full of knowing, we cannot learn.
If we are full of physical things, we cannot receive spiritual power.
If we are full of misery, we cannot accept happiness.
If we are full of our self, there is no room for God or others.
If we are full of anxiety, we have no capacity for peace.
If we are full of our opinions, the truth can never pierce the armor of self-righteousness.

We can be filled with knowledge but void of wisdom.
We can be filled with facts but not know truth.
We can be filled with action but empty of results.
We can be filled with doing and miss being.
We can be filled with tomorrow's dread and miss this moment's joy.

Let us recognize each self-imposed fullness that interferes with our growth, become willing to release it, pray for our indwelling spirit to dissolve all barriers, and embrace the grace and love so readily available.

Prayer: My loving inner spirit, empty my heart and mind so that I may receive the gifts of the spirit; remove all contention and turmoil so your peace may fill my soul; eliminate my preconceived ideas and judgments that block reception of truth.

Take three relaxing breaths; ask your inner spirit to guide your meditation; pause for a few minutes in silence.

July 3

Tell God the truth; he already knows it.

We may reach a point in our spiritual journey where a less-than-holy emotion dominates our life; every time we think of the situation, our mind refuses to let go. Perhaps it's a resentment that triggers a devastating rage or a bitter hurt that controls our mind and feelings; perhaps a disappointment or regret seizes power over us.

When that happens, we can go on our knees and tell God the truth. We share the good, the bad, and the ugly; we tell the thoughts and emotions that are hidden within.

God already knows; he won't hit us with a lightning bolt or have demons tear us apart but we'll start to change. Sharing our true feelings and shortcomings with our creator opens the door to a new life. He truly knows our every thought and feeling every second of our lives—and loves us anyway.

Telling God how we feel never surprises him but the honesty and openness offer real relief for us. A weight lifts from our body, mind, and soul; we feel a new freedom. Our access to spiritual power is in direct proportion to our honesty with our creator and our self.

Prayer: Dear God, I am so grateful that even with my frailties and errors, you accept me as your child. Instill a willingness to grow in my heart, mind, and soul.

Take three relaxing breaths; ask your inner spirit to guide your meditation; pause for a few minutes in silence.

July 4

You can't push a rope.

Many things have a certain function and perform that task well. A rope may tie things together, pull a tied object, or form a temporary barrier. But if we want to tie the rope to an object that's twenty feet away, we either pull the end of the rope or pick it up and take it there; WE CAN'T PUSH A ROPE from point A to point B. It bends and gets kinky; the harder and longer we push, the worse the mess gets—similar to the results we get when we try to push things and people to get them to respond the way we want.

Sometimes people and situations resist our self-directed determination; we cannot always make things happen—although, *in our minds* it should be obvious that the result we desire is best for all concerned or it's just the way it should be. Here, we need to pause, relax, let it go, and accept the fact that we are not God; we don't always know the right answer nor can we make things happen according to our plan (which is sometimes a blessing). Trying to make things happen in a certain time, force specific results, or make people do what we want produces frustration and unintended consequences.

We might remember that pushing a rope doesn't work.

Prayer: I pray that I may know when to quit pushing; help me accept that I am not God and cannot always make things happen my way and in my time. Let me release everything and find peace.

Take three relaxing breaths; ask your inner spirit to guide your meditation; pause for a few minutes in silence.

July 5

We see the world through our eyes but interpret the world through our attitude.

Attitude: *a tendency or predisposition to think, feel, or behave in a certain manner.*

Poor attitude is more difficult to recognize and correct than poor eyesight. We have obvious warning signs if our vision starts to fail and do something about it. We may not respond the same way if our attitude causes us problems. We can suffer havoc, pain, and chaos in our life and never consider that our attitude may be the cause of our problems.

The most beneficial attitude recognizes that reality of the world and the reality of the spirit are different; accidents of time, misfortunes of nature, poor choices by our self or others may hurt us but these temporary setbacks only affect our outer world.

In our inner world, we can live every moment with unshakeable confidence in our future: we see hope in the darkest times; we feast upon uncertainty, fatten upon disappointment, and enthuse over apparent defeat; we welcome difficulties, exhibit indomitable courage in the face of distress, and exercise unconquerable faith when confronted with doubts of the world. The certainty that we are children of the divine overshadows every aspect of our life.

Prayer: Dear God grant me an attitude of love, peace, and hope that comes from your presence in my life; let me feel the security and certainty of my destiny as your child.

Take three relaxing breaths; ask your inner spirit to guide your meditation; pause for a few minutes in silence.

July 6

Humility is simply recognizing our proper relationship with God and other people.

God alone is all-powerful and all-knowing—we're not; he exhibits perfect love, compassion, and wisdom—we don't. Despite our achievements, successes, mistakes or failures, we are a child of God and so is everyone else. We are all children; we will make mistakes; we will have good days, bad days, and times we simply want to survive.

Being humble does not require a self-loathing "I am a piece of sewage" attitude, but does require honest recognition of our failures and shortcomings plus our making apologies and restitution if appropriate; humility rejects selfishness, self-centeredness, self-righteousness, and self-justification; it carries the conscious, constant, and consistent awareness that the power and direction for the best life comes from the divine source and not from our limited human capabilities; humility is the bedrock that supports tolerance, patience, acceptance, forgiveness, love, and compassion to shape our attitude toward all other people and our self.

With humility, we accept that we are not God but one of his many children; we do not see people as being above us or below us, better than us or worse than us; we are open and teachable.

Prayer: My loving divine parent who always wants the best for me, I ask this day to be aware of your power and place in my life; remove any vestige of self-driven desires and actions that separates me from your love or prevents me from bestowing love to anyone I meet.

Take three relaxing breaths; ask your inner spirit to guide your meditation; pause for a few minutes in silence.

July 7

"We first make our habits, and then our habits make us."
(—John Dryden)

Habit*: an acquired behavior pattern regularly followed until it has become subconscious and involuntary.*

Most of us have some good habits and some harmful ones. Since these are subconscious responses, we may not even be aware of some that hurt us. Someone inflicts a real or imagined wrong and we automatically react with "justifiable" anger, resentment, guilt, or self-righteousness without *conscious* considerations. We add an emotional weight to our day and wonder why we don't feel peace.

Today, let us be more aware of our reactions. Anytime we feel disturbed, lash out at another person, allow someone to control our feelings, or fall into the sewer of unhealthy thoughts, let us pause, breathe deeply, and quietly examine our response: Does this response benefit or harm my well-being and relationships? Did I make a *conscious* choice to do this or did I just react? If I did not consciously choose to get angry, feel guilty, worry, or whatever, then this emotional habit hurts me.

We cannot solve any problem until we know we have a problem; we must identify these involuntary behaviors before we can eliminate their inflicted burden. Once recognized, we summon our physical, mental, and spiritual resources to replace them with habits that benefit us.

Prayer: Dear God, make me aware of those thoughts, words, and actions that I need to change. Help me to see their destructive impact on my life; grant me the wisdom, guidance, and power to overcome any barrier that prevents me from living the life you want for me.

Take three relaxing breaths; ask your inner spirit to guide your meditation; pause for a few minutes in silence.

July 8

What I know that ain't so causes me problems and limits my life.

John was working as a temporary employee when he made a mistake that cost his employer a lot of money. Later he noticed coldness from his boss that he hadn't seen previously; he saw that he wasn't invited to participate in group discussions as before; he came to the conclusion that he would be terminated; fear drove him to accept a less attractive position. As he was leaving, his supervisor told him that the company hated to see him go, that his work was excellent except for that one mistake and they were preparing to offer him a permanent position.

Do we have those places in our life where we interpret negative (or positive) meaning into innocent gestures? Are we convinced that we know how an individual will act or think because they belong to a specific group or have a certain appearance? Do we allow fear, bias, or pre-conceived ideas to affect our opinions, words, and actions?

Common sense and prudence dictate that we evaluate other people's actions but we must be careful not to allow our own shortcomings to distort our conclusion. We should always consider the possibility that "What we know ain't so."

Prayer: My inner guide and strength help me be open-minded to new people and ideas; remove any bias, un-healthy preconceptions, and blinding self-righteousness.

Take three relaxing breaths; ask your inner spirit to guide your meditation; pause for a few minutes in silence.

July 9

Nature does not have a heart or show compassion; bad things can happen to anyone and God didn't cause it.

Let's quit blaming God for things he doesn't do. God created nature but nature is not God; it is the mechanical, material part of his creation. He established universal laws and is the source of the energy that activates nature but does not micro-manage it.

Other people's choices, accidents, and random misfortune can visit pain and suffering on us. One person's bad choice can cause an accident that impacts another person's life. Natural disasters such as earthquakes, floods, hurricanes and other events are adjustments of the physical forces of our young and unstable planet; disease originates in nature; bad things sometimes happen to good people but God doesn't cause it.

He doesn't pick where disasters or misfortune hits but does supply the needed resources to endure the pain inflicted by nature or other people's actions; he offers direction for thoughts, words, and actions that lead to the best outcome; he provides the strength that enables us to triumph over hardship and grants an inner peace while we meet the challenges. He may not be the cause of the problem but is the source of our solutions.

Prayer: Dear God, help me to see the world as it is and you as you are. Grant me the peace, hope, love, and faith of your presence within me; bestow all the power I need and the wisdom to know and follow your will.

Take three relaxing breaths; ask your inner spirit to guide your meditation; pause for a few minutes in silence.

July 10

Establish and maintain a conscious, continuous, and consistent contact with God.

Everybody wants the secret to the happiest, fullest, most rewarding life on this planet; millions buy books, seek gurus and experts; they seek the hidden answer that may ease their struggle and bring joy. Today, the secret is given to you: Establish and maintain a conscious, continuous, and consistent contact with God; activate your "kingdom of heaven" within.

Conscious: Stay aware of your relationship with divinity—you are a child of God; your birthright grants you an indwelling spiritual power that can fill you with knowledge, peace, love, strength, hope, purpose, and a view of your long-distance destiny.

Continuous: Keep your spiritual connection open. Seek spiritual sustenance as desperately as you seek physical food.

Consistent: Open communication throughout every day to give thanks; open it at the onset of any physical, mental, or emotional disturbance. Do not limit this infinite life-expanding power.

Contact: Within each of us lies a reservoir of divine spiritual energy but we must open the channel; a phone conversation is impossible if only one end is communicating.

Prayer: My loving inner spirit, open my mind, heart, and soul to your outflowing love; help me know you as the most vital part of my life; strengthen me to acknowledge and accept your power and love as I accept the very air I breathe.

Take three relaxing breaths; ask your inner spirit to guide your meditation; pause for a few minutes in silence.

July 11

Secrets can keep us sick.

We may have some hidden obsessions that add burdens to our life. We may suffer past regrets or indulge in mental fantasies which cause us to feel shame if revealed; we bury these deep so that no one can know the real us; we live with a fear that weighs on our body, mind, and soul. No, we don't want to tell everyone everything about our life; that would be insane. But if we want to be the best version of our self, we must find freedom from the inner weights and barriers caused by keeping secrets.

If we do not already have someone we trust with our secrets, we pray for guidance to find that person; we look at friends, spiritual companions, counselors, and therapists until we find that special person who we can allow to truly know us and see what we consider our dark side.

We again pray and ask our inner spirit for strength and courage; then, we honestly share our secrets. Often, what we saw as a terrible thing that might demean or destroy us shrivels and dies under the light of sharing; it is seldom as bad as we thought when held captive in our fear-driven mind; we may discover that others are known to suffer with similar thoughts and that we are not alone. We are free.

Prayer: Dear God, give me the courage to share any secret that keeps me from feeling the full power of your love and the love of others; grant me insight to find the right person to trust and share all of me.

Take three relaxing breaths; ask your inner spirit to guide your meditation; pause for a few minutes in silence.

July 12

Be thankful today. We often take our most valuable blessings for granted.

If you can see,
if you can walk,
if you have a roof over your head,
if you slept in a bed last night,
if you have a family,
if you have hope,
if someone loves you,
if you love another, or
if you have a relationship with God, GIVE THANKS.

We can become so immersed in our hectic life, in our dreams, our expectations, what we want, what we think we "must" have that we never find peace or happiness; it is impossible to be content when we focus on what we want but don't have. But it is also impossible to stay miserable when we focus on our unrecognized blessings—those things that, if eliminated from our life, would make our world much darker. Our blessings do not have to consist of mountains of money or magnificent mansions; true happiness and peace always start within. We acknowledge the gifts that are really important, the gifts that we often take for granted because they have always been there.

Prayer: I pray that I stay aware of the many blessings in my life; help me to see and appreciate the gifts I have received that make my life better; help me not take any gift for granted but feel and express my gratitude.

Take three relaxing breaths; ask your inner spirit to guide your meditation; pause for a few minutes in silence.

July 13

If I am "up to my butt in alligators," I raised every one of them from a baby until they were big enough to bite.

We can become overwhelmed—problem after problem keeps hitting us until we can't breathe. But each of these had a beginning, an incubation period, and a time of growing into the current status; it was not always a ten foot long attacking alligator. Avoiding chaos requires that we not allow the problems to grow so large—or even better, we avoid hatching the eggs of "alligator problems."

We adopt practices that help us do this: 1) We take responsibility for our life—we cease allowing other people to control our feelings and reactions; 2) We become more sensitive to disturbances in our feelings, thoughts, motives, and actions that can breed future discontent and misery; 3) We adopt a nightly review to diligently root out these harmful patterns and ask our self:

- What upset me today? Did I bury the feeling or release it?
- Did I lower my pride and discuss this with someone I trust?
- Were my motives selfish, self-righteous, and self-centered, or loving and altruistic?
- Did I indulge in self-pity?
- Did I pause and pray before I reacted?
- What could I have done better?

We identify the potential problem while it's still small and take steps to handle it—we don't let it grow.

Prayer: I pray that I stay aware of the many blessings that make my life better; help me not take any gift for granted but feel and express my gratitude for all that I have.

Take three relaxing breaths; ask your inner spirit to guide your meditation; pause for a few minutes in silence.

July 14

Both material success and failure are temporary manifestations; they are often illusions that have little long-term effect on our lives.

Materialism, acquiring things, and looking out for number one are the primary motivations for many people; to them, these indicate a successful life or a failure; they are elated when victorious and downcast with real or perceived failure. But success and failure are always temporary—they only last a short while.

Material success can add to our comfort and enjoyment and make our life easier; however, it is our inner life that truly determines our happiness, satisfaction, and peace-of-mind. Even here, we may be tempted to rate our performance and achievement as a "success" or a "failure"; we may think we fall short of our ideals or should do much better. But this spiritual life is different. It is a never-ending pursuit; we may do things right today and achieve a short-term goal but we always know that this is only a stepping-stone—that more effort, growth, and expansion always lie ahead.

We may make a mistake today but we learn not to see these as failures; we accept them as an inevitable part of our growth. Every mistake brings an opportunity to learn, change, and grow.

Prayer: I ask that you grant me spiritual vision to see what is truly important in my life. Help me accept success with humility and defeat and disappointment with courage and hope; let me not attach too much importance to either and to keep my faith in the spirit.

Take three relaxing breaths; ask your inner spirit to guide your meditation; pause for a few minutes in silence.

July 15

You can keep going long after you can't.
Call on your inner spiritual power for strength.

Working hard? Exhausted? Do you feel like giving up and quitting? Perhaps consider: Is what you're attempting important? Is it necessary or is it a self-imposed priority? What are the consequences of quitting—will there be serious long-term repercussions or only ripples of inconvenience? If this is one of those things that must be done, then believe that you can keep going; you can overcome tremendous obstacles.

If the desire is strong, the goal righteous, and the need great, we can go way beyond our perceived limits. Each of us possesses physical, mental, and spiritual reservoirs of energy; however, we may tend to overlook the true potential of our inner spiritual power. This inner resource can direct our mind to work more efficiently, to become more aware of potential solutions, and to strive toward beneficial goals. This additional power can strengthen and reinforce our physical abilities and help us push beyond what seems possible; it can fortify our resolve and desire.

With prayer, faith, and hope we quietly open the channel to release this awesome energy and allow it to make us stronger, more resilient, and certain.

Prayer: Dear God, I am tired. I pray that my efforts be in line with your desires for me; Let your life force fortify my body, your power guide my mind with wisdom, and your strength reinforce my commitment. I ask that your will be done in my life.

Take three relaxing breaths; ask your inner spirit to guide your meditation; pause for a few minutes in silence.

July 16

Spreading love is like lighting candles: we can light a hundred candles from a single flame and never diminish the light of our own candle.

Acts of love are even better than this! Our own candle gets warmer and brighter with each act of love we give away; the rewards are great and the cost is small.

Becoming an active lover removes us from being the center of the universe; our attitude and outlook shift to a higher level; we act for the benefit of another without seeking anything for our self. Acting lovingly enhances our relationship with God, with our self, and with other people. Our actions reflect the grace given to us by our divine parent; we freely give another person the unearned or unmerited act of love, favor, or kindness.

We may not feel loving; we may be buried in selfishness, self-pity, and self-centeredness but something wonderful happens when we bestow love. Bringing light to another person illuminates our heart, mind, and soul; the heat of love melts our inner barriers. Small acts of caring change the lives of both the recipient and the giver. Today, demonstrate love to one person in need of love.

Prayer: My inner spirit, help me receive your love for me this day; help me to let it flow through me to all I meet. Make me aware of the small acts of love that I can offer and let me freely give and ask for nothing in return.

Take three relaxing breaths; ask your inner spirit to guide your meditation; pause for a few minutes in silence.

July 17

Are you an optimist, a pessimist, or a spiritual realist?

The optimist sees the glass as half-full, the pessimist as half-empty; the spiritual realist sees exactly what is there and knows that it's enough to quench the thirst—and that it can always be re-filled.

Something happens; we categorize it as good or bad based on our belief that it is beneficial or harmful. If we later follow-up to compare the actual results with our initial opinion, we'll find that we're often wrong. As a spiritual realist, we know that events and people can affect our life but we also know that

- pain can be the touchstone of spiritual growth;
- character is forged between the hammer of pain and the anvil of adversity;
- disappointment and seeming failure often spur great achievements;
- the brightest stars of the heavens are best viewed in the darkest night; and that
- we are a child of divinity and we have an ultimate destiny of joy and happiness—no matter how dismal, painful, or unpleasant the current situation.

Viewing situations, events, and people with spiritual reality helps us see things exactly as they are right now and accepting that future events may determine if they are beneficial or not—and that even if these outward manifestations appear harmful to us, we have a spiritual shield to protect us.

Prayer: Dear God, help me to have a true and long-distance view of my value as your child. Let me feel the assurance of your love, peace, and strength.

Take three relaxing breaths; ask your inner spirit to guide your meditation; pause for a few minutes in silence.

July 18

**Our outer life concerns people, places, and things;
Our inner life determines our peace, courage, and hope.**

Whether we know it or not, each of us experiences two versions of life simultaneously: the outer life and the inner life. If we want the best life on this planet, we must develop and integrate these sometimes opposing views. We have very little (or no) control over the people, places, and things of the outer world but can control our inner world.

This inner world determines our true quality of life; it is the source and home for our peace, hope, and love; our mind, willpower, personality, characteristics, and inner divine spark shape this existence. This is where we re-live thoughts and experiences, dwell on future hope or anxiety, indulge in destructive self-pity, anger, resentment, and fear or discover that we can open a channel to our internal divine presence and seek our personal transformation. We can access the healing energy that leads us to the "peace that passes all human understanding," gives us the courage to face any adversity, and the strength to overcome all obstacles.

Then, this wonderful re-birth changes our outer world: We treat people with love, respect, and kindness. Our outlook on wealth, prestige, and material things changes—we know that all these can add to our enjoyment of life but can never create it. Any disturbance in our peace comes from a disturbance in our inner life—never from the situations that are causing challenges in the outer world.

Prayer: I pray that I may have the insight to see the truth: the value and quality of my life depends on my relationship with you and with other people more than anything that happens in the outer life.

Take three relaxing breaths; ask your inner spirit to guide your meditation; pause for a few minutes in silence.

July 19

"God ever responds to the *faintest flicker* of faith."
(Urantia Book)

I was riding my favorite mare and leading two pack mules deep in a Wyoming wilderness area. I pitched camp in an aspen grove; the river, valley and mountains stretched for miles. Deepening clouds threatened a thunderstorm before morning. I went to sleep but was jolted awake by an awesome light-and-sound show; thunder bounced off the mountains and rolled across the valley; lightning, brighter than any fireworks, illuminated everything and let me see that the horses were a little nervous but holding steady. After the storm passed, I went to them and calmed them down. Walking back to my tent, I switched off my light and observed the absolute blackness. Solid darkness that revealed nothing—not even shadows hinting at the separation of the valley, the mountains, and the sky.

Then I remembered a phrase that said, *God ever responds to the faintest flicker of faith.* Standing there completely alone, I scratched a match to flame. Seeing this little bitty flame in the vast darkness gave that saying a deeper meaning. I held in my hand the only source of light for miles.

This practical demonstration gave depth to this simple statement: I was not only looking for God, he was searching for my glimmer of faith at the same time; if I had even the slightest flicker of faith—even as small as this tiny match—and the entire universe was in darkness, he would find and respond to that.

Prayer: I pray that the winds of love, grace, and compassion fan my small faith into the light of transformation. Let me feel your power and strength infuse my heart, soul and mind.

Take three relaxing breaths; ask your inner spirit to guide your meditation; pause for a few minutes in silence.

July 20

**We may not always know what God's will is,
but we generally know what it ain't.**

Ok, we want to try this spiritual path but get confused about what God's will is for us. We think we should be loving, compassionate, and serve other people but find it difficult to apply this to the practical decisions in life. We face situations where we cannot clearly see what God's will is; we want to do it but are perplexed.

We can be pretty certain that God's will does not guide us to act with selfish, self-centered, self-righteous, or fearful motives; our experience proves that these lead us into dishonesty, untruthfulness, anger, resentments, lack of caring and compassion and a variety of misery. If we can avoid those motives, we have a good chance of walking the path that our God wants for us.

We know that if our thoughts, words, and actions focus solely on what's in it for us, we're probably not aligned with divine values and principles. We know that acting with anger, belittling someone, gossiping, blaming, avoiding responsibility, and plotting revenge do not reflect our status as a child of God who is trying to do our best. If we pause and ask, we generally know what God's will ain't.

Prayer: My Higher Power, help me to walk the path of your choosing this day; let me feel your guidance and protection; guide me to avoid selfish, self-centered, self-righteous, and fearful thoughts words and actions. Help me be loving.

Take three relaxing breaths; ask your inner spirit to guide your meditation; pause for a few minutes in silence.

July 21

There is not enough time to hurry; slow down —breathe and enjoy this moment.

Do you ever have to hurry, hurry, hurry? Do you scurry here and there running to get something done? We all have those times when we must rush, but we often hurry because it has become a habit. Our pace is programmed for fast, faster, and hectic; we go so fast that we miss the moment. Let's make an effort to slow down today.

We set our phone or an alarm to remind us to pause five times today for two minutes each time. This ten minute investment can transform an entire day. Don't accept any excuses.

In this exercise: We pause, take three deep relaxations breaths, release them very, very slowly while saying "Peace, harmony, relax, relax." We allow our breathing, our body, and our mind to slow down; we become aware of our inner stillness and peace; we say a quick "hello and thank you" to our inner spirit. We use the physical side of our life to ease the mind and let the spirit function. Constant hurrying prevents peace.

Prayer: I pray that I may slow down this day. Help me to pause, find my inner peace, and be grateful for my recognized and unrecognized blessings.

Take three relaxing breaths; ask your inner spirit to guide your meditation; pause for a few minutes in silence.

July 22

God doesn't have any grandchildren. Our children are his children.
Every person on this planet is his child.

Being a parent is one the most rewarding and joyful tasks in life; it can also be one of the most frustrating, challenging, and fearful—a massive threat to our serenity. We want the best for our children and sometimes cannot understand why they insist on doing things that limit their potential, cause harm, actually put them in danger, or devastate their lives. Free-will choice—our children's and other people's—is generally at the root of their problems; we can't blame God for people's decisions, actions, or accidents of time and misfortunes of nature.

Remember, our children are also the offspring of divinity—they have the same direct, personal connection to our divine parent that we do; this wonderful source is ever ready to bestow bountiful spiritual gifts to all his children, gifts that can transform every aspect of their lives. When they reach out, the spirit always responds; when they seek relief and guidance, the floodgates open.

We cannot—and God will not—force any person to receive the abundant life. We can demonstrate the effects of spiritual power in our own life; we can stand ready to help, but not enable; we can love without judgment or condemnation always remembering that God doesn't have any grandchildren.

Prayer: Dear God, help me release my children and others to your protection and care; I ask that each of them reach out to you and find the wonder of your love.

Take three relaxing breaths; ask your inner spirit to guide your meditation; pause for a few minutes in silence.

July 23

We cannot use being human as an excuse for bad behavior.

We're all human. No one can feel positive, happy, and hopeful all the time. We have great days, okay days, and times of contentions or outright despair. It's a challenge to be kind, loving, and gentle when we're not centered or are in turmoil; but even then, we are responsible for our actions. We cannot use our feelings to excuse unloving behavior.

First, we stay aware of our attitude. The practice of pausing five times each day for two minutes and connecting with our spiritual foundation also gives us a chance to take a quick on-the-spot look at our feelings and attitude—and to do something about it if we are not peaceful, positive, and spirit-centered. Then, we'll have less chance of saying or doing something that leads to regret or unnecessary harm.

Secondly, in those times when we do react and say or do something that is less than we want be, we do not hesitate to repair the slightest damage; we apologize or make restitution if necessary and eliminate any associated burden; we ask our inner guide to relieve our contentious feelings, re-direct our thoughts, and help us do better as we go through the day; we direct our thoughts and actions to someone we can help.

Prayer: Dear God, help me act with kindness, peace, and love this day; help me not allow any turmoil to overly influence my thoughts, words, and deeds. Let my actions and reactions reflect the true value I have for others.

Take three relaxing breaths; ask your inner spirit to guide your meditation; pause for a few minutes in silence.

July 24

Valuing differences in people is a key to successful relationships.

People are inherently as different as their fingerprints. Whether we choose to ignore, appreciate, or denigrate these differences often determines the success or failure of our relationships—and our own happiness. The person facing us at this moment is a complex amalgam of his or her experiences, expectations, outlook, hope, and dreams—and everyone is unique.

Let us value the divine nature of each person, accept their humanness, and lovingly extend the right to be different without getting upset; we can disagree without being disagreeable. We don't compromise our core values but simply allow the other person the freedom to be themselves without denigrating them or feeling rancor.

As we develop healthy self-love, we have less cause to prove our self or our ideas "right"; we learn to truly value the differences in people and see where our considering a new perspective or idea, appreciating a different background, or giving value to diverse experiences might actually improve our life. Today let us seek peaceful acceptance instead of contention and honestly seek the value of differences in people.

Prayer: I pray that I may move beyond tolerance to love; help me see the worth of different opinions, ideas, and values; make me aware that unity is more important than uniformity.

Take three relaxing breaths; ask your inner spirit to guide your meditation; pause for a few minutes in silence.

July 25

Spiritual progress requires humility.

Defeat, humiliation, and extreme disappointment are often the origin of humility. A heart-felt defeat may move us to accept that we are not all-powerful or all-knowing and accept that we cannot experience peace and happiness when we place our self above God or other people; then, we may experience and realize the value of humility.

We might even rise to the point that we see this wonderful attribute as absolutely necessary if we want to enhance our spiritual life; we may discover that we do not have to be beaten into humility but can seek it for its own rewards. Maintaining humility requires discipline.

Every day, we acknowledge that we are a child of God and that our true power and direction flow from this infinite source; we express gratitude for the seen and unseen blessings. We stay aware that each person we meet is also a child of God; we might judge their actions but always acknowledge their divine value. We ask our inner spiritual power to sever the hold of our self-driven will—those thoughts and acts based on selfishness, self-centeredness, and self-righteousness; we seek periods of quiet prayer and meditation to access the power for transformation; we consciously commit to practice patience, good judgment, tolerance, and compassion.

Prayer: Dear God, help me not confuse humility with humiliation and to accept in my deepest heart that I am a child of divinity. Guide me to stay aware of my value and give all people that same consideration.

Take three relaxing breaths; ask your inner spirit to guide your meditation; pause for a few minutes in silence.

July 26

The spirit seeks entrance into our hearts but we must open the door.

"Behold, I stand at the door and knock. If anyone hears my voice and opens the door, I will come in to him..." (Revelation 3:20 NKJV)

We may experience confusion and doubt; we may endure defeat and disappointment; the world may appear in chaos and turmoil; but the citadel of the spirit is the inner bastion against all suffering. God does not magically evaporate our problems but provides the direction, strength, and peace to traverse them and find the best solution. We are the only ones that can choose to activate this potential power; we must invite our inner spirit to transform our life.

- Morning: We begin each day with a few minutes' quiet prayer and meditation; then, we invite our inner spiritual power to guide our thoughts, words, and actions this day.
- Throughout the day: We pause five times for two minutes each just to breathe, acknowledge our inner spirit, and say "Thank you" and "Please help me the rest of this day."
- At night: We review our day: Did we pause? We acknowledge where we could have better demonstrated love, compassion, tolerance, and patience; then we recognize our growth.

We can spend our day driven by self-will and reap the well-known results or we can invest twenty minutes into transforming our life; we must answer the knock and invite the spirit to join us.

Prayer: Help me respond to the ever-present power; I choose and invite my divine friend and guide to share this day with me. Let me stay aware of your presence this day.

Take three relaxing breaths; ask your inner spirit to guide your meditation; pause for a few minutes in silence.

July 27

What we falsely see as justifiable anger will definitely harm us and can cause injury to others.

"Holding on to anger is like grasping a hot coal with the intent of throwing it at someone else; you are the one who gets burned." (Paraphrased from Visuddhimagga IX 23)

We live in an imperfect world; people and institutions can cause us pain or harm. This may be done on purpose or inadvertently. Or it may result from misunderstanding or our misguided expectations and perceptions. Is not our anger justified when we're taken advantage of, lied to, or betrayed? Buddha's description of anger accurately portrays that this emotion always burns us; it matters not if the feeling is *seemingly* justified.

When many of us feel that initial spark of anger, we are absolutely certain that it is justified. Someone has wronged us and we have a "right" to feel this way. Perhaps they were wrong, but so what? We are the one with the feeling burning inside of us, controlling our mind, upsetting our peace, and waiting to ignite even more misery. The object of this hot wrath may be completely unaware of our state, totally uncaring, fully innocent, or even gleeful.

If we understand that anger is "a physical and emotional manifestation of spiritual immaturity," can justifying our own immature behavior ever benefit us? Or is it our responsibility, as a child of the divine who seeks a better life, to find an alternative response that maintains our value, dignity, and self-respect?

Prayer: Dear God, please save me from being angry. Help me see that my perceptions, expectations, or understanding of this situation may not be exactly true. If someone has truly wronged me, melt the burning anger and help me respond according to your way.

Take three relaxing breaths; ask your inner spirit to guide your meditation; pause for a few minutes in silence.

July 28

The problems of this moment are my only real problems; tomorrow's worries and yesterday's regrets are illusions.

It's impossible to stay peaceful and make the best decisions when our mind is dominated with regrets of yesterday or apprehension of tomorrow. Contention from either is an illusion—they are not real at this point in time; however, the inner turmoil can prevent us from finding the best solutions for the real problems of this moment.

Living in the NOW, in this very moment, is difficult and requires discipline. We strive to control our mental giant and ease the contentious feelings so we can make better decisions today. When thoughts of the past or future overwhelm us, we take steps to bring us back to the moment:

- We accept that our mind is the only part of us that is time-traveling; our body is in the moment.
- Our inner spirit can guide our thoughts; we pause and ask for help to quiet our emotions and direct our mind.
- We systematically and honestly evaluate what we're really facing—how important is it really? We isolate the decisions that we must make in this moment; if necessary, we assign a priority to handle most important tasks first; we ensure that we do not neglect unappealing but important duties but subject them to our best problem-solving skills.

Prayer: My inner spirit, help me release all regrets from yesterday and fears of tomorrow; ease my mind and soothe my troubled feelings; guide my thoughts, words, and deeds to find the best solutions for my real challenges.

Take three relaxing breaths; ask your inner spirit to guide your meditation; pause for a few minutes in silence.

July 29

Everyone gets into a rut at times.
Some set up housekeeping and live there; others move on.

Our rut can be at the bottom of addiction, alcoholism, or overwhelming loss or it may be just an "okay" existence with a lack of initiative or willingness to change. The devastating loneliness and despair resulting from the deep rut may move us to find solutions; however, a less-than-desperate rut may let us settle for a mediocre life.

Do you ever consider "Is this the best I can do? Is this really all that I hope to get or give in this life? Is it possible to live and not allow other people or events control my attitude and feelings? Must I always worry about the future or dwell on the mistakes and failures of the past? Do I have to settle for whatever life throws at me or can I do something about it? I wish life was better than this."

Practical spirituality offers the direction and power to get out of any rut, transform our attitude and actions, and grasp the wonder of a better life. It offers the tools to face success, failure, and disappointment with equanimity, peace, and poise. We can trade those "okay" days or times of just getting by for days with laughter, hope, peace, and joy. We don't have to settle for mediocrity.

Prayer: I pray that I may not slide into complacency and accept wherever I am because I believe it is the best I can do. Ignite the fires of hope and the desire to change within me and move me to act according to your will.

Take three relaxing breaths; ask your inner spirit to guide your meditation; pause for a few minutes in silence.

July 30

**Reading minds should be left to psychics.
Actual communication is more effective than mindsight.**

Has anyone ever told you—or have you told anyone "Well, you should have known what I meant... what I wanted ... what I needed?" Of course there are some things in a relationship that may be self-evident but communication—actually expressing important desires, needs, and expectations—can often prevent unnecessary hurt feelings and misunderstandings.

Each of us brings our history, experience, personality, hopes, values, beliefs, expectations, and perceptions into every relationship we have. Some may be similar to those brought by the other person and others may be quite different. Sometimes, it's hard enough to know our selves—why we think, feel, act, and react the way we do, why something that may appear insignificant to others is important to us, or why it may not have been important yesterday but something happened today that made it so. It's even more difficult to always anticipate these things about another person.

It's our responsibility to be clear when we feel something is important even if we believe that it "should" be obvious to anyone; words and understanding eliminate the need for reading minds. Today, let us make an effort to communicate clearly in all our relationships and not expect someone to read our mind.

Prayer: My loving inner spirit let me clearly speak and hear with love this day; help me be receptive to the needs and dreams of others; guide my thoughts, words, and actions to demonstrate caring, tolerance, empathy, and compassion.

Take three relaxing breaths; ask your inner spirit to guide your meditation; pause for a few minutes in silence.

July 31

Wrong expectations can corrode and destroy our relationship with God.

Most of us do not believe that God will help us win the lottery; however, we may entertain other expectations about this spiritual life that set us up for disappointment.

If we want consistent, reliable, and repeatable results, we need to align our expectations with what produces these results—the truth. Our *spiritual* parent is interested in our *spiritua*l growth and maturity and not overly concerned with our materialistic success. God is not Santa Claus to fill a wish list of gifts; he does not suspend natural laws to compensate for our poor choices; he never interferes with anyone's free will to make them choose according to what we see as right, fair, or compassionate.

God does provide us with strength to break the chains of addiction and alcoholism; he offers the power to guide our mind to beneficial thoughts instead of misery. He grants us love to melt resentments, vigor to rise above the storms of self-will, and understanding to make good choices. He offers insight to find elusive answers, courage to overcome fear, and balance to administer mercy with justice and compassion with wisdom; he leads us to love in the face of condemnation and to forgive the unforgivable. He grants the peace that passes all human understanding; he fills our body, mind, and soul with the security of divine over-care and the unshakeable trust in our eternal destiny.

Prayer: My loving spiritual parent, help me to understand our relationship more deeply; let my prayer that "It is my will that your will be done in my life" be seared into every fiber of my being and all my spiritual nature.

Take three relaxing breaths; ask your inner spirit to guide your meditation; pause for a few minutes in silence.

August 1

Forgive but never forget. Release all emotional bonds to past actions but remember the event to avoid repeating it.

Following the old adage of "Forgive and forget" causes problems; we must forgive but only a fool forgets. When someone does us a real or imagined wrong, we *must* forgive that person if we want peace within our self. However, forgetting what happened—wiping the event, our faults, and the other person's contribution from our memory—will make us susceptible to repeating that hurt. We must totally let go of the *feeling* associated with the event but retain the factual memory of what happened.

We cannot reach such an elevated perspective on our own will power and desire; this requires the intervention of spiritual power. Prayer and meditation can bring enlightened forgiveness—that state of mind and emotions that lets us remember past hurts with forgiveness (we feel no negative emotional response) while we use the experience to gain wisdom (learn not to repeat the mistake.) Our deepest hurts and disappointments can serve as the springboard for our greatest growth when we achieve such a release.

Prayer: Dear God, help me release all emotional bondage to my past. Grant me your power and wisdom to see all past hurts and shortcomings as building blocks that can make me a better person.

Take three relaxing breaths; ask your inner spirit to guide your meditation; pause for a few minutes in silence.

August 2

Saying or thinking "I don't have enough time" reveals opportunities for growth.

Each day has twenty-four hours. This is not flexible; it cannot expand to fit our needs, wants, lack of planning, trying to cram more into a day than it's possible to accomplish, or tackling low priority or unnecessary tasks. The amount of time is fixed; we have to adjust our "must be dones" to fit within that time.

We will have those days where we have a lot that must get done or at least a lot that we believe must be done. This presents an opportunity to combine the spiritual with the practical; we can use the "POP" method of planning, organizing, and prioritizing to use our time more effectively. We eliminate or minimize time wasted on trifles or less important tasks.

For each undertaking, we pause, find our spiritual center, and then make the best choice. We ask: "Is this absolutely necessary—what happens if it doesn't get done? Does it have to be done now—what would happen if I delay a little? What is the most effective order to accomplish what I need to do? Can I ask someone to help me?"

Many of these tasks concern our outer world; yes, they may be important but we must stay spiritually centered while we take care of them. We should not allow a false sense of "Hurry, it must be done" nor people, places, and things to control our happiness and peace.

Prayer: My inner spirit, help me feel your presence, strength and guidance; spread your peace within me this day. Clarify my thoughts, direct my efforts, and let me walk this day according to your will.

Take three relaxing breaths; ask your inner spirit to guide your meditation; pause for a few minutes in silence.

August 3

Faith does not prevent adversity; it provides the power and direction to navigate obstacles with assurance, dignity, and love.

Do I have healthy expectations about the results of a spiritually-directed life? We live in an imperfect world with other imperfect people; accidents, misfortunes of nature, and other people's choices/actions impact our lives and God does not micro-manage any of these.

Adversity, disappointment, and loss are part of life but practical faith gives us a choice on how we will make the journey. It helps us utilize the two greatest gifts in our life: free-will choice and the inner divine spark, the "kingdom of heaven within".

When hard times or just complacency and mediocrity hit, we must choose: Do I suffer from decisions directed by self-driven will or do I acknowledge my limitations and seek the help so readily available? Do I call on my inner spirit to guide me out of the muck and misery to a sublime peace or do I choose to keep suffering? Do I rely on my limited strength or do I seek additional power? Strength, courage, peace, and hope are only a prayer away.

Prayer: Dear God, please guide my faith to align with your desires; grant me the humility to seek your guidance, strength, and love; elevate my mind to partake of your wisdom; shower me with grace that I may find peace in the midst of turmoil, tolerance in tribulation, and love in any hardships I face.

Take three relaxing breaths; ask your inner spirit to guide your meditation; pause for a few minutes in silence.

August 4

If we're receptive, surprising things can enhance our awareness of God.

We live off-grid in the high mountains of Colorado and were having a recurring problem with the satellite internet connection. A satellite orbiting 22,300 miles above the earth transmits the signal to a dish on our house. Severe weather conditions or physical clutter on the receiving dish can interfere with the signal but the weather was crystal clear and the dish was clean. A technician found that the receptivity of our home signal would be very strong and then suddenly decrease and break the connection. *The measured signal from the source stayed consistently strong.* The modem was faulty and a new one immediately eliminated the problem.

Our connection with God is similar. He constantly "beams" love, power, and peace toward us. Sometimes we allow outer conditions (the clutter of people, places, and things) to interfere but the real challenge is maintaining our inner receptivity. It falters when we fail to pause and pray, slow down and give thanks, or recognize the beauty, love, and absolute wonder of his creation. We get distracted by trifles and become immersed with "doing" instead of simply "being."

But his signal is always there—strong, consistent, and powerful. We simply have to open our hearts, minds, and soul to receive it.

Prayer: My loving inner spirit, help me be receptive. Elevate my thoughts; purify my motives; guide my words and actions so they reflect your will and I may find peace.

Take three relaxing breaths; ask your inner spirit to guide your meditation; pause for a few minutes in silence.

August 5

Accepting things we don't like isn't easy and often happens in three stages.

If I keep running headfirst into a brick wall and it always bloodies my head, I can deny that I'm hitting the wall or that it's hurting me (denying the *fact* of reality); but this leads to repeating the same action and suffering the same result. If I want to quit hurting, I face three progressive levels of acceptance:

1. Resistive acceptance: I understand that the reality does exist (I accept the *fact* of reality—it is what is); I bear up resignedly and believe that it's wrong or unfair. (I don't want that wall to be here; it's not fair or right but if I want to stop hurting, I'd better quit running into it).
2. Neutral acceptance: I am at peace with the facts; I cease struggling; although I still don't like or appreciate what has happened, I calmly accept it and move forward with my life. (I don't agree with this wall being there; I don't like it or understand it, but it must serve some purpose.)
3. Total acceptance: I enhance my understanding; something makes me see how the reality I face can actually benefit me and I start to appreciate it. (I had the opportunity to view what's on the other side of the wall and it's keeping a pride of lions from attacking me! I would be insane to tear it down. I'm grateful for that wall.)

Prayer: God, grant me the serenity to accept the things I cannot change, the courage to change the things I can, and the wisdom to know the difference.

Take three relaxing breaths; ask your inner spirit to guide your meditation; pause for a few minutes in silence.

August 6

One moment of anger can yield a lifetime of regret.

Sometimes the words and actions that fly when we are angry can wound another person so deeply that healing takes months or even years; some deeds done in a flash of rage oft bear life-altering consequences—both for other people and for our self. Learning not to react in anger definitely gives us and those around us a better life.

We have tools that help us mature spiritually and eliminate much of the need for, and indulgence in, these bursts of emotions. We strive to be free of anger but unless we're a saint, we'll sometimes find our self immersed in that flash of emotion. At all costs, we must avoid words and acts which we might regret. When anger overwhelms us, it is easy to justify responses that do not reflect the type of person we want to be.

We must insert a time interval between the feeling and the reaction to slow down our response. We pause, take a deep breath and ask our inner spirit "God save me from being angry; help me not react while this feeling is controlling me. Melt this anger and help me find peace." We keep repeating this until we can find an appropriate (not angry) answer.

Prayer: I pray that all feelings of anger may melt away. Fill my heart, mind, and soul with love, tolerance, patience, and compassion. Grant me that ten second hesitation and guide me to ask for your help before I respond.

Take three relaxing breaths; ask your inner spirit to guide your meditation; pause for a few minutes in silence.

August 7

"Resting on our laurels" creates the breeding ground for discontent and misery.

This old phrase refers to being satisfied with one's past success and to consider further effort unnecessary. This doesn't work; we always go backwards if we rest too long. Science explains this as "entropy", a universal law that says that when left alone, any system tends to deteriorate, to degrade from order to disorder.

We clean the house until it's spotless, leave it alone, and later see stuff lying all around and the dirt is back; we lose weight, feel good about it, relax, and then later notice the ten pounds we put back on. This is entropy. Work is the only thing that can stop this deterioration.

Entropy tells us that not only can we not grow without work, but we will actually slide backwards if we do not work. Our spiritual life, our peace-of-mind, and our relationships will deteriorate if we do nothing! Work—expending effort—is required but we also must learn to put our energy into effort that produces the desired results. Having a process that helps us connect with our inner spiritual power, guides us to unleash this power to solve practical living problems, and offers a path to unending daily growth can overcome personal entropy—if we consistently do the work.

Prayer: My loving divine spirit, let me see any contention or irritation as an opportunity for growth; instill the initiative to move off the dead center of complacency and lethargy; let me not find satisfaction in mediocrity.

Take three relaxing breaths; ask your inner spirit to guide your meditation; pause for a few minutes in silence.

August 8

God loved us as much when we were mean, nasty, and un-loving as he does on our best days.

He loves the homeless as much as the pope, the death row prisoner as much as the preacher, and the drunk as much as the charitable. His love is not based on our actions or success.

Everyone has had bad days—those times when we do things that are so much less than what we want to be—and it's important to remember that our mistakes, poor decisions, being mired in self-pity, anger, blame, or resentment, even our participation in meanness or outright evil never cause our loving parent to love us less. We are children of the divine; the devotion and love flowing from our spiritual parent to us does not depend on our beliefs, desires, or acts; it is natural outpouring from a loving parent to any child.

To feel that love, to experience it in the deepest places of our being, it has to flow through us to others.

Each day, we try to do a little better than yesterday; we strive to understand; we try to be patient, kind, forgiving, tolerant, and compassionate; we acknowledge our errors and try to learn from them, always staying aware of "the kingdom of heaven within", our indwelling spirit that connects us to the infinite.

Prayer: Dear God, thank you for loving me; thank you for your forgiveness, mercy and grace; thank you for loving me when I am unlovable, sheltering me when afraid, giving me strength when weak.

Take three relaxing breaths; ask your inner spirit to guide your meditation; pause for a few minutes in silence.

August 9

Expect to get dirty when you wrestle with pigs.

Few question the accuracy of such a simple statement; yet, we may fail to see how often we wallow in the pigpen area of our mind—that dirty little corner that contains selfishness, self-centeredness, self-pity, and self-righteousness. Hopefully, we want to be clean but if we've spent a lot time in the pigpen, it's hard to resist the urge to crawl back in. It's easier to stay clean than to get filthy again and have to go through the work of cleaning up, but the pigs keep tempting us.

We can get out of the pigpen at any time; we don't have to allow the dirt and crap to become ingrained in our skin; we don't have to allow the stench to permeate our body, mind, and soul until we stink so bad no one wants to be around us. We can leave the pigs behind, walk to the shower of the spirit, scrub with honesty, sincerity and humility, dry with prayer and meditation, hold our head high, and go into the fellowship with the rest of God's children.

Today—this minute and every minute throughout this day—we can choose to let our mind wrestle with pigs or stay clean. Let us honestly evaluate where our thoughts, words, and actions still reek of self-driven will.

Prayer: I pray that I may not yield to the temptation to return to my old ways. Grant that my motives stay clean and pure and that my thoughts are not soiled by self-driven desires and actions. Let the vision of your pristine love guide my attitude.

Take three relaxing breaths; ask your inner spirit to guide your meditation; pause for a few minutes in silence.

August 10

We rush to accomplish unimportant things; hurry breeds inner tension.

Our life gets faster and faster. From opening our eyes in the morning to closing them at night, we are a whirlwind of activity. We're accustomed to the pressure in our chest, the lack of deeply satisfying breaths, and the inability to peacefully sit and relax. We barter our time and serenity for the prizes we're told we must have; we volunteer for the rat race and then wonder why we're always rushing. Some things we scurry to achieve this day may have little effect on the real quality of our life; they are midgets made into "must have" and "must do now" giants by our mind and the world around us.

Each morning let us honestly evaluate the deadlines that challenge us. We pause, find our spirit-center, and remind our self that: We are children of the divine and we seek to keep our inner peace while functioning effectively in the world.

As we preview what "must" be done, we ask: "Is this a self-imposed deadline? (If so, we need not allow it to cause tension or hurry); How important is this really? Will my world collapse or be severely damaged if it isn't done—and done today? Is it truly my responsibility? Does my motive include pride, fear, unhealthy care-taking, or people-pleasing?" Then, we ask for help to accomplish what needs done with grace, poise, and peace.

Prayer: Dear God, let me not be troubled or rushed; help me to pause, breathe, and talk to you as I face the challenges of this day.

Take three relaxing breaths; ask your inner spirit to guide your meditation; pause for a few minutes in silence.

August 11

Self-pity is a quicksand that mires us in misery and prevents growth.

At some time, we may face events that appear wrong or unjust; our mind spews thoughts of "It isn't fair; it isn't right; they should not have done this; I don't deserve this; or, why is this happening to me?" Any or all of these may be true but so what? The quicksand of self-pity can pull us deeper and deeper into a muck of emotions and keep us mired in mediocrity and misery. There we face the question: Do I choose to stay here or do I move forward?

Self-pity breeds unhappiness, resentment, and victimhood; it always begets blame which automatically eliminates any possibility of overcoming the challenge; plus it always brings a host of other self-defeating miseries. However, if we choose to advance and take action, we can break free.

We use our physical, mental, and spiritual energies. Physical: we make a gratitude list, take a walk and look for beauty, and listen to uplifting spiritual messages, or do volunteer work. Mental: we make the conscious decision to elevate our thoughts, increase our awareness of "I" centered thinking, and then try to eliminate or minimize this self-centered tendency; we meditate to seek the quiet that redirects and refreshes our mind. Spiritual: we access our infinite inner spirit energy to provide the strength, direction, commitment, and perseverance we need to move beyond the mire and stagnation.

Prayer: Dear God, help me not wallow in this muck of self-pity. Give me the strength I need to pull free from this darkness and move into your light. As your child, I ask for your help.

Take three relaxing breaths; ask your inner spirit to guide your meditation; pause for a few minutes in silence.

August 12

Immediately classifying an experience as "great" or "terrible" often proves wrong.

Most of us have experienced events that we thought would devastate our life and were later proven wrong. In truth, some of these may have slipped into non-problems and quietly disappeared; a few may have actually impacted us but not as badly as we feared; others may have yielded positive benefits if we honestly looked for them. On the other hand, many of us have experienced things we thought wonderful at the time but later proved toxic and harmful. If we are dominated by self-driven will, we are not always a good judge of what is good or bad for us when we are in the middle of the experience.

If what is happening appears to be really awful, we ask: "Why am I reacting this way? Is my reaction fear-based? What am I afraid of? Am I overreacting because this may interfere with something I desperately want or something I am making too important? Am I being overly sensitive? Does my reaction reflect my spiritual values?"

Likewise, if we think that what is happening is the best thing since apple pie, we might reflect on "Does this advance my spiritual nature? Does it contribute to my soul growth or only to my finances and ego? Does it enhance my long-term destiny or merely satisfy a short-term desire?"

Success and failure are temporary; time always modifies our current view of any situation.

Prayer: Dear God, help me not over-react today; let me not too quickly judge the long-term value of any disappointments, adversity, or success; help me to think, speak, and act in line with your will.

Take three relaxing breaths; ask your inner spirit to guide your meditation; pause for a few minutes in silence.

August 13

Serenity: ***the ability to experience deep inner peace and calmness even if facing unresolved problems.***

Even if we try to live a spiritually based life, we'll face times when we lose our peace-of-mind. We are human; we'll allow our spiritual connection to slip; external problems—real or imagined—can dominate our mind; our emotions may sometimes descend into turmoil. This disconnect may linger for hours or days; we may feel really bad or merely like something is missing from our life. We must take action to return to that peace and tranquility.

If we face true problems (situations that immediately threaten our well-being): 1) We honestly look for any part we contributed to this and correct it; 2) If outside forces have control over the material outcome, we effectively work to minimize their effect on us and 3) Having done all that's within our power to do, we release the results to God, knowing that these cannot affect our inner peace unless we allow it.

Then, we re-establish our serenity. We know that peace flows from our inner spirit; we devote consistent time and effort to enlarge our connection to our divine friend and resource; we expand our morning prayers and meditation, pause throughout the day and make contact, and repeat this at night. God never leaves us; he is always there, awaiting our return.

Prayer: My loving inner spirit, if I face unresolved problems, grant me the peace of heart, clarity of mind, desire, and willingness to find answers that align with what you want for me. Let me feel your loving embrace and guidance as I walk through this day.

Take three relaxing breaths; ask your inner spirit to guide your meditation; pause for a few minutes in silence.

August 14

"Do not give your attention to what others do or fail to do; give it to what you do or fail to do." (Buddha, Dhammapada 4:50)

We are not perfect and neither is any one on this planet. Situations, events, and other people can adversely affect our life. When this happens, it's our choice whether we offer condemnation and blame or acceptance and fortitude. From over 2500 years ago until today, some things are relatively unchanged: people are people and we are responsible for our own thoughts, feelings, words, and actions.

Spirit-led people have tapped an additional inner resource that may not eliminate misfortune but does offer power, guidance, and strength to traverse it with the least harm.

When something undesirable happens, how long and how deeply do we allow it to dominate our life? Does our mind automatically rush to find the defects in others, find excuses for our behavior, or to quickly place blame? Can we shift our thoughts to a higher level or does our mind stay bogged down in the muck? Do we focus on the problem or the solution?

We might ask our self: "Did I do something in the past or present that contributed to this? Am I making a "big deal" out of a trifle? What must I do to avoid a recurrence or to move beyond this turmoil? Am I spiritually-centered; do I truly trust and depend on my inner spirit or are these merely words; why am I allowing this to upset me?"

Prayer: My dear friend and spiritual helper, help me to focus this day on my motives, acts, thoughts, and words; let me not give power to other people's success or failure.

Take three relaxing breaths; ask your inner spirit to guide your meditation; pause for a few minutes in silence.

August 15

Change occurs with or without our consent; we can resist and struggle or "go with the flow."

Change is inevitable—we are powerless to stop it—but we can choose how we make the transition. Do we go kicking and screaming, resisting every aspect of change? Or are we able to find consolation, peace, and growth in change we don't like?

Our *attitude, expectations, perceptions, and motives* determine our response to change and also influence the outcome. We can allow our self-driven will to skew these and fight the change; then, we spend time and an effort trying to control things "our way" and suffer much more than is necessary.

Or, we can use spiritual principles to aid us in experiencing the change: We commit to relying on our spiritual foundation; we follow through with action, not just intention. Then, we let the change carry us as a river carries a canoe; we "go with the flow"; our spiritual values guide our progress to steer clear of the rocks and rapids; we appreciate the beauty around us; if we hit a barrier that holds us, we simply accept it and allow additional change to unfold; we take everything beneficial that we can wring from this transition and float by the rest.

Prayer: Dear God, help me to align my will with your desires; remove all struggle from within me; let me cease resisting change. Guide my journey and help me wisely overcome any obstacles I face.

Take three relaxing breaths; ask your inner spirit to guide your meditation; pause for a few minutes in silence.

August 16

Last week's bath doesn't make us clean today.

We've experienced the benefits of following this spiritual path but then life happens: The world, people, and situations demand our attention; complacency and rationalization slowly erode our commitment and we start skipping the spiritual exercises that gave us our results. We get tense, perhaps experience a little anger or frustration or simply not at peace; we react, our mind starts racing and we find the world and people controlling our day.

We are no different than many but are simply validating a truism discovered and tested thousands of times before: If we want to constantly and consistently partake of serenity, strength, hope, and security, we must constantly and consistently practice the spiritual life to keep the connection to our spiritual power. Or in our more simple terms, "Taking a bath last week doesn't make us clean today."

Every day is the day we must acknowledge our birthright as a child of God, as member of this human family; every day is the day we try to align our will with God's will in all we do; every day is the day we commune with our inner spiritual power; every day is the day that we start with prayer and meditation and then seek opportunities to serve our brothers and sisters. No exceptions and no excuses.

Prayer: Dear God, give me the commitment and strength to seek your presence every day; help me never take for granted the blessings you so freely bestow.

Take three relaxing breaths; ask your inner spirit to guide your meditation; pause for a few minutes in silence.

August 17

Whose fault is it if we ignore resources readily available to us?

We may defiantly choose not to turn on the light when we enter a dark room. If we stumble and get hurt, should we blame the darkness or our decision?

We can allow worry and anxiety to keep us awake; we can rush through the day overwhelmed with stress; we can react to words and actions of other people and feel irritated, angry, and "less than"; we can let a real or imagined unfairness devastate our life and fall prey to self-pity. Or we can use readily available spiritual resources to avoid much of the difficulties and disappointments. It's our choice. Each of us possesses the resources needed to secure a life of peace, harmony, and happiness. Whose fault is it if we volunteer for misery?

We are children of the divine and blessed with an indwelling spiritual presence that has the power to transform our life. It matters not if we are addicts, homeless, poor, suffering illness, or in good health and sitting in a mansion. Each of us has the same birthright; we are a child of God. Each day we must surrender and ask this inner spirit to guide our thoughts, words, and actions; we request the power to overcome any obstacle we face and the guidance to align our choices with God's desired direction; we seek the ability to pause when faced with contention and to pray before we act.

We choose not to dwell in darkness and misery but to take full advantage of the wonderful resources so readily available.

Prayer: I acknowledge that I am a child of the divine; I ask that I am always aware of the reservoir of spiritual power, direction, and strength available to me and that I access this wonderful gift today.

Take three relaxing breaths; ask your inner spirit to guide your meditation; pause for a few minutes in silence.

August 18

When we pray, let us eliminate all unhealthy expectations and do our part.

Effective prayer recognizes that God supports our spiritual growth and suggests: 1) He will do for us what we cannot do for our self and 2) that the central focus of prayer should concern our *spiritual* life while recognizing that this directly affects everything else. We must

- courageously face the inevitable challenges of life. Prayer is not an escape mechanism but opens the conduit to receive additional strength, courage, and insight;
- exhaust our human capacity to solve the problem;
- recognize that we cannot solve the problem by ourselves and need additional help; and
- progress in spiritual maturity and seek to align our will with God's rather than ask him to align his will with our desires.

Then, as a young child seeking parental help, we present our needs to our father/mother God confident of receiving aid. With these guiding principles, the results will correlate directly to the spiritual maturity and wisdom of our petition.

For example, if we have severe economic problems, prayer does not help us hit the lottery but can quiet our emotions and bring clarity to our mind so we can find the best solutions; if we are heartbroken from a relationship, prayer does not force the other person to love us but can give us the insight to change so that we form relationships based on love rather than on need.

Prayer: Dear God, source of the divine spark that lives within me, grant me the strength, insight, and peace to face the challenges of this day; help my mind, will, and abilities to conform to your way.

Take three relaxing breaths; ask your inner spirit to guide your meditation; pause for a few minutes in silence.

August 19

Spiritual practices can "brain wash" us.

Someone may warn us that religion or spiritual people can "brain wash" us. This may prove to be true; perhaps our mind needs cleaning. The filth of misery—resentment, anger, worry, fear, jealousy, envy, low self-worth, and a myriad of others—may stain and soil most of our thoughts; this mental dirt eliminates any chance for peace or happiness. Our mind has to be cleansed before we can hope for a better life.

An act of surrender starts this cleaning cycle: we must fully accept that we have problems and cannot solve these without help.

Action follows: We start the day with prayer and meditation as we sit in silence and feel the presence of divinity; we seek guidance, strength, and understanding. Then, we pause for a few minutes throughout the day to stay consciously aware of our divine birthright; we strive to be loving, tolerant, and gentle. We spend a few minutes in quiet review each night to see what we could have done better and acknowledge the growth and blessing of this day.

New filth can stain our lives each day so we must make this a daily practice; we need a continuous cycle of "brain washing." Do you have any thoughts that need cleansed today?

Prayer: My loving spirit, my self-driven ways have polluted my mind. Please cleanse it. Wash away my pride, prejudice, anger, fear, and all misery; purify my thoughts and sanctify my motives.

Take three relaxing breaths; ask your inner spirit to guide your meditation; pause for a few minutes in silence.

August 20

Balance mercy with justice; bestow compassion with wisdom.

Only a divine being can demonstrate perfection in these attributes; we must do our best in each situation; we seek spiritual and worldly maturity to enhance the lives of others and our self.
Mercy: *kind or forgiving treatment of someone who could be treated harshly.*
Justice: *being righteous or fair in dispensing rewards or punishment.*

We live in an imperfect world with other imperfect people; we have laws for society and should also have guidelines for our self that reflect our desires, values, and ideals. If we only extend mercy, the evil and lawless may prevail; if we mete out only justice, we leave no room for forgiveness, kindness, or love. In society and in our personal life, we seek the blend of mercy and justice that yields the righteous result.

Compassion: *sympathetic consciousness of others' distress together with a desire to alleviate it.*
Wisdom: *a reliable ability to decide with soundness, discernment, prudence, and intelligence; a sense tempered and refined by experience, training, and maturity.*

Progressive spiritual maturity increases our consciousness of other people's distress and leads to the desire that they share the love, peace, and hope that infuse our life but we cannot alleviate all misery. Compassion devoid of wisdom can lead to enabling instead of helping, to supporting evil instead of seeking righteousness, and yield problems for everyone.

Prayer: My divine source and upholder, grant me the ability to demonstrate your love today. Help me be sensitive to each person's need for mercy; guide me to evaluate actions but not value or destiny.

Take three relaxing breaths; ask your inner spirit to guide your meditation; pause for a few minutes in silence.

August 21

Ignorance, disagreement, or opinion cannot alter truth.

We can't see it, touch it, or taste it but gravity really exists. Our belief, understanding, and acceptance—or lack of any of these—cannot alter the effects of gravity. Believing and shouting that "There is no such thing as gravity" as we jump off the cliff does not change the consequences.

Likewise, we can't see, touch, or taste the spiritual component of life but it also really exists; our disbelief or disagreement cannot alter its effect on our life. Violating the principles of honesty, humility, unselfishness, tolerance, patience, compassion, and love inevitably yields misery.

If we believe in God or a spiritual life and tell a lie, we likely feel guilt and regret. Hopefully, we recognize our shortcoming, make necessary amends, and try to do better.

If we don't believe in a spiritual part of life, we still pay a price. We may avoid the feelings of guilt and regret but another piece of our self-value erodes leaving us less than before; we have an underlying fear that our lie may be discovered and revealed; we add another "rock" to the weight of our inner burden. The consequences lessen our happiness and peace, impair our relationships, and limit our potential to grow and enjoy life. It is the nature of the universe that there are consequences for violating physical or spiritual laws.

Today, let us be aware of spiritual principles and live according to their guidelines.

Prayer: Dear God, lift the veil so that I may see the beauty of your truth; let your guidance penetrate the clutter in my mind; help me to feel the truth when heard. If my pride erects a barrier to belief, please help me be willing to be willing.

Take three relaxing breaths; ask your inner spirit to guide your meditation; pause for a few minutes in silence.

August 22

Don't wait for a burning bush or the thunderous revelation. Listen now.

Our communication with our spiritual parent does not have to cross the boundaries of space; we do not have to throw our prayers into the heavens to be heard; nor do we have to depend on an intermediary to intercede on our behalf. A fragment of our creator lives inside each of us, waiting for our communication; he knows immediately everything we think and feel and wants to help us but we must "be still and listen."

Our inner spirit communicates with us through inspired thoughts, superior feelings, enlightened understanding, and convicted knowing. We may face a decision, pray, and asked for help but nothing happens—and then we have a thought—an inspiration that clarifies the decision, that opens new possibilities, or gives an obvious solution seemingly out of nowhere. We may hear or read a statement of truth and feel a resonance—a KNOWING that this is true and is meant for us; something simply clicks and feels right—like a tuning fork vibrating at a sympathetic frequency. We may be struggling, in the darkness of complacency, lethargy, or self-pity and something—a word from someone, a song on the radio, a recurring thought—finally pierces the gloom with the light of hope.

Today, let us be aware and respond to spirit communication.

Prayer: Indwelling lover of my soul, quiet my mind that I may hear; still my emotions that I may feel; open my eyes that I may see; enlarge my heart that I may accept. Let me receive you in any and all forms this day.

Take three relaxing breaths; ask your inner spirit to guide your meditation; pause for a few minutes in silence.

August 23

Worry and anxiety indicate that we are still trying to control events. Do we trust God or not?

Releasing the desire to control the outcome of events and relationships is not easy; it requires surrender, dedicated practice, and commitment. We have physical and emotional indicators of our lack of success in releasing control of the future: Unhealthy fear and its myriad forms invade our mind and emotions; we forsake peace, security, hope, and love; we speak the words of trusting God but fall short of doing it.

"To a God-knowing kingdom believer, what does it matter if all things earthly crash?" Temporal securities are vulnerable, but spiritual sureties are impregnable. When the flood tides of human adversity, selfishness, cruelty, hate, malice, and jealousy beat about the mortal soul, you may rest in the assurance that there is one inner bastion, the citadel of the spirit, which is absolutely unassailable; at least this is true of every human being who has dedicated the keeping of his soul to the indwelling spirit of the eternal God. (p. 1096. Urantia Book)

Prayer: My loving spirit, help me to relinquish the idea that I can control anything in the future. Let me act and speak with righteousness, do what I must do, and trust the future to your loving overcare.

Take three relaxing breaths; ask your inner spirit to guide your meditation; pause for a few minutes in silence.

August 24

Sufficient to the moment are the troubles thereof.

A Zen story:

> A senior monk and a junior monk were traveling together. One day, they came to a deep river. At the edge of the river, a young woman sat weeping, because she was afraid to cross the river without help. She begged the two monks to help her. The younger monk turned his back. The members of their order were forbidden to touch a woman. Then, without a word, the older monk picked up the woman, carried her across the river, placed her gently on the other side, and continued his journey.
>
> The younger monk couldn't believe what had happened. After rejoining his companion, he was speechless, and an hour passed without a word between them. Two more hours passed, then three, finally the younger monk could not contain himself any longer, and blurted out "As monks, if we are not permitted to touch a woman, how can we then carry that woman on our shoulders?" The older monk looked at him and replied, "Brother, I set her down on the other side of the river, why are you still carrying her?"

We can carry the weight of our past mistakes, regrets, and erroneous beliefs or we can leave them. Sometimes we must call upon the mighty expulsive energy of our indwelling spiritual force to break the mental and emotional bonds.

Prayer: My indwelling spirit, please let the flow of your spiritual power purge all regret, remorse, disappointments, guilt, and resentment from me. Help me live in and for this moment.

Take three relaxing breaths; ask your inner spirit to guide your meditation; pause for a few minutes in silence.

August 25

Let us strive to be less self-centered today.

Self-centeredness: *when my attention is on "me" and how all other people, external situations, and actions affect any aspect of my life, desires, or opinions.*

This leads to being overly sensitive, insecure, and fearful plus a loss of humility, tolerance, compassion, patience, and love. Our thoughts, words, and actions are either 1) "me-centered" or 2) "spirit-centered" or 3) a shifting combination of both. Self-centeredness stands as one of our greatest barriers to inner peace and our serenity directly reflects which "centering" we have chosen. Let's try to be less "me-centered" and more "god-centered."

- *In the morning*: We ask that our thoughts focus on what we can do for others and how we may align our will with Gods' will; we request that we be immediately made aware anytime we exhibit the slightest degree of self-centeredness.
- *Throughout the day*: We pause anytime we are disturbed and ask if, in any way, "Is self-centeredness at the root of our disturbance?" We ask for strength to break these bonds and for the spirit to guide our thoughts, words, and actions.
- *At night:* We include a specific look at this trait when we review our day, searching for the less obvious participations and then ask our inner spirit to relieve us of this obsession and grant us improvement tomorrow.

Prayer: I pray that I may be vigilant and aware of any self-centeredness today; let me seek your guidance and help to eradicate the slightest occurrence.

Take three relaxing breaths; ask your inner spirit to guide your meditation; pause for a few minutes in silence.

August 26

What do we mean by "doing God's will" or "turning our will over to God?"

We may use words or phrases for years and not stop to consider what they mean. What are we really talking about when we speak of our "will" or "God's will"? In this context, our *will* simply is the *ability to make a choice and initiate action.*

Our experience shows that self-directed will (choices and actions centered on self enhancement) doesn't really benefit us. Our values, desires, and motives don't lead to great decisions; we act/react without thinking or, our choices hurt us.

"Turning our will over to God" means that *we use our power of choice* to choose to align our decisions and actions with an elevated (divine) way of doing things. We opt to exchange our values, desires, and motives for better ones; we seek improved ability to use our mind clearly and intelligently.

The very act of making this choice is an exercise of our will and we must use our will this way many times throughout the day as we face decisions and choose to follow spiritual direction. This choice augments our knowledge, wisdom, and direction that improve the outcome of our actions.

Prayer: Dear God, doing things my way is not working out real well; I choose something different. It is my will that your will be done in my life today.

Take three relaxing breaths; ask your inner spirit to guide your meditation; pause for a few minutes in silence.

August 27

The faith of one solider can defeat an army of fear.

Fear is a state of mind; it may be based on a true threat or totally fictitious. Whether the object of fear is real or imagined, the disturbance—the gut wrenching, mind-dominating reaction—is very real. Fear may be camouflaged as anxiety, worry, anger, self-pity, depression, jealousy, or another form of misery. This malady directly causes or supports many of our internal contentions.

Faith is the solvent that dissolves fear. But it must be an active, vibrant faith grounded in the understanding that we are a child of a loving creator who is ever ready to shower us with grace and power.

Faith functions through action. If fear or any of its myriad variations attack our peace of mind, we pause and pray; we assert our birthright—we are a child of divinity and know that this grants us access to tremendous spiritual power; we ask God to remove this disturbance and grant us the understanding that nothing can truly harm us, nothing can separate us from his love; we request guidance to see any action necessary to obliterate this contention and the strength to carry that out. If another person is involved, we pray for that person to be blessed with peace, happiness, and prosperity.

Then, we simply release the fear, the outcome, and the future to our loving creator. We trust that God will answer our prayers in the time and manner that yields the most beneficial results.

Prayer: My infinite source, grant me a strong and abiding faith this day. Fill me with the certainty of your love and overcare; let me not be troubled by trifles and grant me the strength and initiative to act according to your will.

Take three relaxing breaths; ask your inner spirit to guide your meditation; pause for a few minutes in silence.

August 28

Is something irritating you? Either let the irritations continue or be an oyster and make a pearl. It's your choice.

A grain of sand finds its way inside the oyster's shell. In order to protect itself from irritation, the oyster covers it with layer upon layer of nacre until it becomes smooth and round; a beautiful iridescent pearl replaces the irritant.

We may have those times where we allow people or events to irritate us; our spiritual maturity influences the frequency, depth, and length of our turmoil.

Like the oyster, our best results occur if we start the healing as soon as we notice the irritation. Our spiritual tools not only dissolve the irritant but can transform it into a pearl of wisdom or a gem of spiritual growth. Resentment can become an insight that changes our future reactions and behaviors; a vanquished fear can emerge as a bastion that strengthens our faith and our surety of the spiritual response; a contentious individual might be the tool that teaches us a superior level of patience and tolerance; an uncomfortable truth might reveal our tendency toward self-righteousness.

Like the oyster, we can make a precious gem out of the irritants but we have two great advantages: 1) Our spiritual power works much faster than the oyster's application of layer upon layer of nacre and 2) It works every time.

Prayer: My loving Higher Power, help me not allow irritations to find a place in my mind or heart. But if I do allow them entry, I ask that expulsive power of a mighty spiritual affection transform these contaminants into the pearls of spiritual growth.

Take three relaxing breaths; ask your inner spirit to guide your meditation; pause for a few minutes in silence.

August 29

Compromising our core values always causes misery.

Compromise is essential to any successful relationship. Any peaceful and rewarding association in a marriage, partnership, family, or with friends, acquaintances, and strangers must include compromise. However, compromising our core values can lead to problems.

Love—the active and healthy concern for another person's well-being—enters into many relationships and this attribute leads us to sometimes forfeit our desires or dreams for the good of the union or even for the direct benefit of the other person. Releasing worldly things, learning to hold our words to avoid contention, doing loving acts without expecting anything in return are the epitome of love and a hallmark of great relationships.

However, these selfless loving acts do not require that we relinquish our core values. We need to be careful about sacrificing our honesty, integrity, dignity, truth, faith, and self-respect to get along or because someone demands this. Repeatedly compromising our core values erodes our peace and happiness, affects our ability to be the best version of our self, and limits the relationship.

Prayer: My inner spiritual guide and power, grant me the tolerance, patience, and love so that I am willing to give more than I take from any relationship while I demonstrate truth, honesty, love, dignity, and compassion as one of your children.

Take three relaxing breaths; ask your inner spirit to guide your meditation; pause for a few minutes in silence.

August 30

Motive determines the right or wrong of many acts.
Motive: *why we act as we do; causing or being the reason for acting*

Let's say that someone at the office is collecting money for a charity. You think the cause is righteous and give twenty dollars. A week later, a similar situation arises. A colleague starts collecting money for another charity but you don't believe that this one is as worthy as the one last week and you're short on cash. Nevertheless, as your colleague comes around, you contribute another twenty dollars. You don't want people to think you are a tightwad, that you can't afford it, or that you don't support a good cause.

The *act* is identical but the different motives yield different emotional repercussions. Wanting to help someone is laudable; giving from fear or coercion erodes our integrity and leaves us feeling empty and wondering, "Why did I do that? I should have..."

Going beyond the actual deed and looking at our motive opens up new territory for many of us. We find that an act may be beneficial for one person but harmful for another; an act may induce growth one time but may retard growth another time. Much depends on motive. We ask: Is my motive selfish, self-righteous, self-centered, or fearful or is it based on love, compassion, and service? Does this choice advance or retard my spiritual growth?

Prayer: My loving spirit, help me be aware of my motive for acting. Grant me the insight to see my true motives and not justify errors; give me courage to act in line with my values.

Take three relaxing breaths; ask your inner spirit to guide your meditation; pause for a few minutes in silence.

August 31

We often over-react when we are not at peace.

Any thought, word, or deed that moves us from our place of inner peace adds a weight to our inner life. This inner dis-ease makes us more sensitive to real or imagined wrongs done by those around us. We react quicker with words and deeds that, if we felt peaceful and loving, would go unsaid and undone. Recognizing our discontent *before* we react can benefit us and everyone around us; we strive to be more aware at the onset of any inner turmoil or irritation.

When we feel this way, we can prevent additional problems if we pause, close our eyes for a moment, and breathe deeply a number of times until we physically and mentally slow down. We seek our inner spirit power to transform our attitude; we say a quick prayer that we cease any form of judgment, fear, or blame. We acknowledge that we do not want to give anyone the power to "push our buttons," to control our feelings and actions. We remind our self that feeling peaceful is one of the most important accomplishments of our day and that we can enjoy a better day(s) when we act from peace rather than react from turmoil.

Prayer: I pray that I can become more aware when I lose my spiritual center and peace of mind. Help me to recognize the small disturbances before they grow; give me the strength to pause and pray; restrain my words and acts until I regain my serenity.

Take three relaxing breaths; ask your inner spirit to guide your meditation; pause for a few minutes in silence.

September 1

Immaturity leads us to us rush to accomplish goals of limited value.

We're caught in the hectic, bumper-to-bumper traffic jams, always rushing here and there to do something vitally important; throughout the day, we're always in a hurry so we can later have time to relax, watch mind-numbing TV and discuss totally worthless topics—the latest reality show, computer game, or the status of some celebrity that we envy. Then, we go to bed with a whirling mind, take some medication or substance to sleep, wake up, and do it all over again.

This is a life?

Spiritual and emotional maturity changes us; we cease blindly following the ways of the world that do not truly benefit us; we accept that we live and function in a secular, materialistic world but we do not have to allow this outside turmoil overly affect our inner life. Maturity brings that knowledge of superior values, the certainty of divine love and presence, and the inner peace that quietly slows our life; maturity severs the need for approval of others, the need to always acquire "more" possessions, to be number one and at the head of the pack, and the pushing urge to hurry.

How much do we really need to hurry?

Prayer: Help me to slow down and enjoy this day; guide my thoughts to focus on objects of lasting value instead of the temporary possessions. Let my heart, mind, and soul enjoy peace and quiet.

Take three relaxing breaths; ask your inner spirit to guide your meditation; pause for a few minutes in silence.

September 2

Impatience often leads to wrong decisions
and unintended consequences.
What I must do can stand no delay!
Don't slow me down; just get out of my way.

Impatience takes root in selfishness and self-centeredness. We elevate our "wants" above the needs and aspirations of other people; things have to happen on our time schedule; we get frustrated if our smallest desires are delayed. This starts an inner conflict that pushes us to do "something" and this hurried action often leads to more problems. Impatience often creates problems where none existed.

A few practices that may help us overcome impatience include:

- We examine our past to see how often impatience has caused us to make a mistake.
- We accept that our self-imposed timetables often contribute little to our peace of mind or happiness—or to our material well-being; in fact, they are a repeated source of frustration, anxiety, and mistakes.
- We try to become more aware of every occurrence of impatience and ask our self "How important is it really?"
- We seek spiritual help in subduing this source of contention; we acknowledge this specific shortcoming in our meditation and prayers, recognize how it harms other people and our self, and ask that this trait be replaced with tolerance, patience, and love.

Prayer: I pray that I be immediately aware of the slightest impatience today; help me to pause in that moment, make contact with my divine source, release all self-imposed timetables, and find the peace that helps me accept the natural flow of time and events.

Take three relaxing breaths; ask your inner spirit to guide your meditation; pause for a few minutes in silence.

September 3

**We harvest what we sow;
if we plant corn, it's impossible to harvest beans;
if we plant fear, it's impossible to harvest happiness and peace.**

We'll always harvest misery when our life is based on self-driven will. Our focus on self makes us overly sensitive and vulnerable to everything and everyone around us; we see and evaluate everything based on our perception of how it affects us—how it impacts our wants, needs, dreams, and fears. Peace is impossible when driven by selfish, self-centered, self-righteous, and self-pitying motives.

If we want a harvest of peace and happiness, we must plant the seeds that yield it; we must resign as controller of the universe.

We devote time to build and maintain our spiritual connection; we pray and meditate each morning and include a request that our inner spirit help us not succumb to self-driven will this day and to make us immediately aware of any time we indulge in this practice; we acquire the discipline to pause before we act, especially if we are upset. We make a conscious effort to be loving, kind, tolerant, and patient; we try to stay aware of any person we can help, anyone that a smile or cheerful greeting might lift up.

Instead of aiming the spotlight at our self, we focus on other people and how we might help them.

Prayer: My loving source and divine inner spirit, this day let me plant seeds with my thoughts, words, and action that mature into peace, happiness, and love.

Take three relaxing breaths; ask your inner spirit to guide your meditation; pause for a few minutes in silence.

September 4

Do not be discouraged by the discovery you are human.

We will make mistakes but hopefully learn from them. "The mistakes which you fail to forget in time will be forgotten in eternity." (P.1739 Urantia Book)

The only way to avoid mistakes is to do absolutely nothing—and that is a mistake of its own. Our mistakes range from small ones to possible life-altering mishaps. Evolving spiritual maturity results in fewer mistakes but we'll not be mistake-free in this life. Our reaction may be more important than the actual mishap; it can keep us in misery or it can provide a gateway to transformation. We'll find long-term benefits if we

- own it: Accept responsibility if we caused the mistake; never blame another person or rationalize our actions.
- evaluate it: Identify our emotional response; self-condemnation, fear, and self-pity can distort the true effects of any error. We pause and pray to settle our mind and emotions; we take an honest look at the repercussions of this error. We identify the exact fault on our part that led to this mistake: Had we done our spiritual maintenance? Were our motives and actions based on self-driven will? Did we have enough and correct information? What could we have done differently that would have prevented this?
- embed it: We commit this event, the outcome, and our learning to memory to avoid repeating the mistake.
- release it: We release all emotional attachment and after effects.

Prayer: Dear God, help me accept that I make mistakes and that these do not affect my value as your child; let me accept, learn and grow from any mistake I make; help me not take myself too seriously.

Take three relaxing breaths; ask your inner spirit to guide your meditation; pause for a few minutes in silence.

September 5

Move a muscle and change a thought; add prayer and change a life.

Our thoughts and feelings may overwhelm us at times. Perhaps we've missed our morning prayers and meditation or forgot to pause during the day to seek strength and guidance. Or maybe wave after wave of misfortune and hardship have beat us down before we've had a chance to call for spiritual reinforcement. We may find it's difficult to stop and pray—or we don't even want to. This is a time in which we have to "act our way into right thinking" or move a muscle to change a thought.

We force our self to take a walk; we express gratitude (even if unfelt) for our legs, the fresh air, and the freedom to take this excursion. We consciously scan for a flower or anything from nature that might appeal to us; we listen for a bird or the trickle of water from a brook or the waves of the surf; we smile at a passerby; we breathe deeply and slowly, aware of the breath and stillness. We stop at the gym or yoga class; we exercise; we sweat. At home, we listen to inspirational music, read a spiritual message, or call a friend; we write (actually write—not think about) five things for which we are grateful.

We allow our physical actions to quiet our mind and emotions; then we access that wonderful reservoir of inner spiritual energy to transform our day.

Prayer: To my loving inner spirit: I sometimes neglect or forget you; I find myself hurting, disappointed, or afraid and ask again for your ministry. Grant me peace.

Take three relaxing breaths; ask your inner spirit to guide your meditation; pause for a few minutes in silence.

September 6

**Stay open-minded and humble;
we can never learn if we think we already know.**

This is the time of science, great accomplishments, vast education, material wealth, and the strength of the individual. Pride, self-confidence, and arrogance form the mosaic of the age; we see many who say "Oh yes, we are tolerant and open-minded (as long as you agree with us.)" This is also the age of unhappiness, insecurity, anxiety, broken and mediocre relationships, and a dependence on things and chemicals to make us feel worthwhile and happy.

We do not have to follow the misled majority; we can answer the call of the spirit, the leading of our heart and soul.

This day, let us strive to be truly open-minded, tolerant, and humble; we can shed the know-it-all attitude and admit that we really don't have all the answers. As we progressively practice these spiritual principles, we realize that we are embarking on a life-long, even an eternal, adventure.

We are the finite mind and embryonic spirit that has comprehended a small but wondrous sliver of the unlimited; the wisest, most dedicated among us may only scratch the surface of this infinite and eternal unfolding. But even the little amount we see, understand, and practice transforms our life; it raises us from a struggling human, mired and tired in the ways of the world, to a child of divinity that has received solutions for living that actually grant us an elevated life. Let us humbly give thanks and praise for our great fortune.

Prayer: I pray that I may always realize that I know but little and that I anticipate the joy of learning more. Thank you for all that I have; let me delight in my blessings.

Take three relaxing breaths; ask your inner spirit to guide your meditation; pause for a few minutes in silence.

September 7

Congruency teaches us to help but not enable other people.

Someone we love, or an acquaintance, or even a stranger falls on hard times and seeks our help. We want to help them but realize that sometimes our efforts may assist in a short-term solution but contribute to a long-term problem. Here, we try to help but not enable; we lend a hand but do not interfere with their growth, their freewill choice, or the consequences of those choices.

We try to determine:

- *How* did the person get into this position? Was it an accident or a misfortune of nature that brought disease and suffering? Or did their choice and action produce the problem? Is this a one-time occurrence—a mistake—or has this happened before and reflects a pattern of behavior?
- *What* do I expect from the person in return? Will my action lead to eliminating the problem or contribute to more problems? Am I interfering in their personal growth? Will this let them avoid the consequences of their own choices?
- *Why* will I do this? Are my motives selfish? Am I trying to make myself feel better? Am I acting so that they will not think badly of me?

Life happens; everyone makes mistakes and may need a helping hand. However, enabling hurts the person we want to help; it allows them to avoid the consequences of their own repeated mistakes and stifles the opportunity for growth. Today, let us seek spiritual guidance to apply congruency.

Prayer: Dear God, grant me wisdom in my compassion; guide me to truly help and not harm anyone.

Take three relaxing breaths; ask your inner spirit to guide your meditation; pause for a few minutes in silence.

September 8

Gossip may be factual but is never truthful.

Gossip: *idle talk or rumor, especially about the personal or private affairs of others, typically involving details that are not confirmed as being true.*

The accepted definitions of gossip illustrate a common limitation: the failure to differentiate between truth and fact. Facts pertain to physical reality supported with data and evidence; truth relates to spiritual principles. Idle talk or rumor may be factually correct (or it may not) but this is not the same as being true (that it is factually correct plus it benefits someone, is communicated with love and compassion, and is necessary.)

Gossip is an insidious evil that can unnecessarily injure the person being discussed plus render the speaker and hearer of the conversation less than they were before; it cannot meet the standards of truth and always decreases everyone involved.

We strive to be loving, kind, and compassionate to all of God's children. The world, other people, our own shortcomings, and wanting to "fit in" often present opportunities to choose whether we respond with elevated values or regress to self-driven ways. Today, let us choose the way that is best for us and beneficial to everyone.

Prayer: I pray that my thoughts and words may be true. Make me aware of the idle talk I hear and speak and guide me not to participate in gossip today.

Take three relaxing breaths; ask your inner spirit to guide your meditation; pause for a few minutes in silence.

September 9

Five factors are necessary for long-lasting change.

We must:

- accept that we have a problem;
- want to solve the problem;
- identify a solution that works;
- implement this solution–do the work; and
- perform the necessary maintenance.

All of these factors must be in place before any long-lasting change can occur in anyone. For our self, we must honestly assess the problem and acknowledge the full repercussions it causes in our life; then we must develop a sincere desire to change. This acceptance and "want to" are great starting points but must be followed with proper action. We find a solution that has been proven to solve this specific problem and do the work necessary to implement that solution. And there is always maintenance; the old habits that caused the original problem are deeply rooted and do not simply disappear; we only acquire the more desirable traits with conscious, persistent practice.

These five factors also clarify why we cannot make another person change. When facing a true problem, the person with the problem must accept the reality of the problem and develop a genuine desire for change. If we recognize a problem affecting the life of a person we love, we examine our motives to see if it is really any of our business. If so, we pray for guidance and offer help but always realize that each person must find his or her own acceptance of the problem and the desire to find a solution. We cannot do it for them or make them do it.

Prayer: Dear God, help me to clearly see what I must change so that I can live the life you want for me. Grant me the strength and guidance to make these changes.

Take three relaxing breaths; ask your inner spirit to guide your meditation; pause for a few minutes in silence.

September 10

Our ego is a misery magnet.

Our ego nurtures a selfish, self-centered, self-righteous, it's-all-about-me attitude. We're skipping along feeling good; then that negative thought that appears out of nowhere, or we notice another person's way of looking at us, or we encounter a situation that doesn't go according to our plans. That starts the little feeling of anger, fear, guilt, resentment, jealousy, or anxiety; our mental magnet activates and starts attracting other negative thoughts; our mind obsesses with the problem and we can't get out of the misery cycle.

We are children of the divine; however, our ego can erect impenetrable barriers that repel the grace and love emanating from our source. Self-driven will inevitably brings disaster, discontent, humiliation, and defeat; these can bring us to our knees in recognition that we do not have the power to change. We know that we must get rid of our ego but make little progress using only our mind and determination. Only a great spiritual force can rip out the deep-rooted tentacles of self-driven will; only spiritual power can heal and open our heart, mind, and soul to make us receptive to the truth, beauty, and goodness of the universe.

We simply have to give up, ask for help, and follow a few simple spiritual guidelines. Today, let our spiritual power overcome our ego's misery magnet.

Prayer: I pray that I be made aware of my ego today. Let me hear the ringing of an angel's bell in my mind if I engage in any thought, word, or action that emanates from my self-driven will.

Take three relaxing breaths; ask your inner spirit to guide your meditation; pause for a few minutes in silence.

September 11

Rehearsal of tomorrow's fear
Ruins this day we need hold dear;
Thoughts bring anguish to our mind
Breeding others of like kind;
Fear of real or imagined cause
Destroy this moment if we not pause
Seek and find
Our spirit bastion that can repel
And grant us peace instead of hell.

This moment—this instant of time of which we are aware right now—is the only thing that is real. The next hour, day, or year are only possibilities and all the yesterdays only memories in our mind. We must choose how we spend this moment. Will we allow it to be tarnished and destroyed or will we seek the best moment?

This instant, it's our choice: Do we permit fear to dominate us; do we allow the whirlwind in our mind to overwhelm us; or do we access our inner spiritual power to find peace? No matter what is happening or what may happen, we will go through it—either with peace or in turmoil. Moment by moment we build the next hour, the next day, the next year, and our entire life; each moment we choose our happiness and our destiny. How do we start our day? Do we connect with our spiritual source? As we pass through today's moments, do we pause to find peace, guidance, and power? Or do we continue on self-will?

Prayer: My loving inner spirit, help me to pause and find peace in your presence and your power. Quiet my mind; replace fear and dread with strength and equanimity.

Take three relaxing breaths; ask your inner spirit to guide your meditation; pause for a few minutes in silence.

September 12

The magnificence of the starry heavens is best seen on the darkest night; the most important lessons often come from the worst problems.

We cannot see the stars while the sun is shining; likewise we often fail to see blessings in our life when we're doing well. But then life happens—adversity overwhelms us, people and events thwart our hopes and dreams. We may feel hurt, alone, anxious, or threatened. We are human and live in world that constantly tests us, that provides opportunities to grow. stay uncomfortable, or downright miserable. It's our choice: we can remain in fear and mediocrity or we can move forward.

Wisdom comes with experience and much of it comes from making mistakes, surmounting challenges, or working our way out of mediocrity. We gain perseverance—that ability that overcomes failure and disappointment with a commitment to keep trying and to pursue the righteous cause—as we face and overcome repeated frustration. Strength—whether of character, physical ability, or spiritual commitment—builds only when we push onward in spite of deep weariness.

Our indwelling spirit can shift our perspective in times of darkness; it can bring clarity of mind to find the best solutions, strength to endure and prevail, and help us see the hidden values in hurting.

Prayer: I pray that I may see the concealed blessings of adversity. Grant me the strength I need and the discernment to make the right choices.

Take three relaxing breaths; ask your inner spirit to guide your meditation; pause for a few minutes in silence.

September 13

If we desire one virtue, let it be humility.

Humility: *the quality of having a low or modest view of one's importance.*

Humility is not an abject, groveling attitude; it is simply accepting our self as no more or less important than anyone else but always less than God; it includes the awareness that we know little and are open for knowledge and understanding; it is an attitude that each person has value and is important. Humility influences all virtues and shapes our character; it is the basis for true ethics—the moral principles that govern a person's behavior and relationships with other people. Humility reflects quiet strength, not weakness or humiliation.

If we desire to be a better person, to actually experience the best life we can, we must practice humility. Without it, we live with varying degrees of self-righteousness and pride that block real growth. Daily prayer and meditation followed by service to others help us acquire and keep this valuable asset; these acknowledge and affirm our relationship with our divine source and with our family of humanity. Sincere and overflowing gratitude keeps us in the grace of humility.

Prayer: I ask that I find humility in all my thoughts, words, and deeds this day. Help me to not think of myself or my desires as more important than anyone else's and make me aware of all opportunities for serving or helping another child of our divine creator.

Take three relaxing breaths; ask your inner spirit to guide your meditation; pause for a few minutes in silence.

September 14

We may have great intentions but sometimes react un-lovingly.

Even in our intimate close relationships, we may not always exude love, tolerance, and patience. We may suffer those brief moments where we respond with anger, an unkind word, or petty self-pity. A simple tool may help remind us that we just might be wrong:

Attitude Adjustment Coupon

The undersigned person recognizes that he (she) may temporarily act in a manner that is not loving, kind, or caring. This person acknowledges that there may be brief intervals when his (her) thinking and reactions may be *slightly* wrong. To minimize the turmoil caused by this rare condition, this coupon gives the bearer the right to require that the undersigned person:

1. Pause, remain quiet for five minutes, and try to pray.
2. Consider the *very slight* possibility that he (she) might be wrong.
3. Think about how the bearer of this coupon actually demonstrates his (her) love.

Following this, both parties agree that any following conversation must start by sharing a prayer together and then "I love you because..." stating three reasons why each of them loves the other person.

If I do not immediately complete the above actions, I agree to be the total slave of the bearer of this coupon for one (1) full week. This coupon automatically renews with each use.

______________________________ Signature

Like all tools, this yields results only if it's used.

Prayer: Ok God, I'm trying to do the right thing but I do make mistakes. Help me to recognize my shortcomings and grant me the strength to swallow my pride and make appropriate amends.

Take three relaxing breaths; ask your inner spirit to guide your meditation; pause for a few minutes in silence.

September 15

Divine love can heal broken relationships.

God is love; the essence of the universe is love. We are meant to love but human frailties can shatter the loving bond in any relationship. In our deepest heart, we yearn to have this bond restored, to have loving, caring, respectful, communication with that person. Sometimes, the repair of this association may not seem to be possible but we should never doubt the healing power of divine love.

We pray, trust, act with love, and release. We talk to our divine parent withholding nothing; we tell him (her) of our pain, our problem, and our desires; we ask for help in this reconciliation and ask for guidance so that we do nothing to undermine the chances of healing. We acknowledge that we are not all-knowing and that we may not be the best judge of exactly what should happen or when it should occur. Then we release and we trust.

These daily prayers are essential to help us find peace and take positive and beneficial action. We keep an open line of communication with loved ones but never push an agenda—we want to demonstrate open receptivity and a love that asks for nothing in return; we acknowledge those special days with a card or a short loving note—never expecting a reply or acknowledgement. And we continue to pray, trust and act.

Prayer: Dear God, let me turn this broken relationship over to you. Heal my heart; help me to see all that I must do so that I fulfill my part in this restoration. It is my will that your will—and your time—be done in all my life.

Take three relaxing breaths; ask your inner spirit to guide your meditation; pause for a few minutes in silence.

September 16

Relationships are the primary breeding ground for spiritual maturity.

Relationships—those personality associations that cause a physical, mental, emotional, or spiritual response in us—are the most challenging, perplexing, frustrating, rewarding, fulfilling, and important events in life. Our desire for spiritual attributes is but theory until tested, proven, and solidified in relationships. Yes, we need our quiet, alone time but relationships are absolutely essential for the culling, nourishing, and watering that yields growth.

If in contention, we want to immediately see this as an opportunity for growth. We ask: "Why am I reacting like this? Why am I allowing another person to control my feelings and my thoughts? How important is it really? What spiritual attribute am I failing to demonstrate? What can I learn from this—what lesson is this teacher trying to impart to me?" We especially try to be aware of contributions from unloving sources—those gifts of contention that grant us opportunities to be loving, tolerant, and patient.

If experiencing love and serenity, we recognize the blessing and give thanks: "I am blessed to have this person in my life—and for this experience of love. My heart is overflowing with love; tears of gratitude flow quietly from my eyes. I know I sometimes fail to show my appreciation but I will change that today—I will tell them exactly how much he or she contributes to my life."

Relationships are everything.

Prayer: I pray that I may not have unhealthy expectations in any relationship; let truth, honesty, open-mindedness and love guide my perception.

Take three relaxing breaths; ask your inner spirit to guide your meditation; pause for a few minutes in silence.

September 17

"He will know perfect peace whose mind is stayed on God. "
(Isaiah 26:3 NKJV)

If I am upset, my mind shifted; God didn't move.

Our mind, that constant stream of thoughts into our consciousness, determines the quality of our moment, our day, and our life.

We may find it difficult to feel our spiritual connection as we experience the trials of life. Distress and disappointment may temporarily overwhelm; the world may strike blow after blow to chip away at our worldly possessions and image; we may feel misery, anxiety, or despair. We may lose a love; our pain may bring us to question how God could love us and let this happen.

Then we remember that life happens; our attitude, actions, and reactions are the only things we can control. We've accepted that "Everything depends on our thinking. Our mind determines our life."

We persevere and take action to shift our thinking; we listen to an uplifting message or an inspirational gospel song or simply pause and pray; we seek the comfort and fellowship of like-minded friends; we look for someone less fortunate to help; we seek opportunity to be of service in any way. We take spiritual actions and our thoughts slowly return to the only power that really works: the power and love of God. We find peace.

Prayer: Let me see the power and outworking of the spirit in all I encounter this day. Help me to stay aware of your presence in my life and of all that you add to my life.

Take three relaxing breaths; ask your inner spirit to guide your meditation; pause for a few minutes in silence.

September 18

We are responsible for what we do and say, no matter how we feel.

We all have those days. Perhaps we're sick or in pain; maybe someone hurt or irritated us; we may have resentment about past wrongs or a dread of impending doom. Or, we're down and miserable for no apparent reason. Someone does something and we react; we say or do something inappropriate and then we justify our action: "Well, I wouldn't have said that but I was feeling bad." We offer excuses for our behavior but must remember that we are responsible for our actions no matter how we feel.

We make it right; we apologize without excuses. Then, we have a choice: Do we allow the outer world, past regrets, or fears of the future determine our inner world in this moment—and for the rest of our day? If we want a better day, we pause, take our relaxation breaths, and connect to our inner spirit. We think gratitude—we mentally review at least five things for which we are grateful and are important in our life; we claim our divine birthright for spiritual guidance, peace, love, and tolerance and ask our inner power to help us change our attitude; we look for the opportunity to spread an act of kindness.

Starting or re-starting our day with these small efforts improves the chance that we'll avoid the inappropriate actions and subsequent amends.

Prayer: My inner divine spark, help me accept responsibility for all my words and actions. Grant that I stay aware of your presence, power, guidance, and love throughout this day. If I err, move me to immediately correct my mistake and rejoin you.

Take three relaxing breaths; ask your inner spirit to guide your meditation; pause for a few minutes in silence.

September 19

Any person can join the Phoenix People—the apex of humanity.

The Phoenix People are those who have suffered, undergone a profound inner experience, and emerged to a better life. They symbolize the story of the beautiful avian creature that would sense its approaching death and burn itself in a cleansing and purifying fire. From the ashes, a new, stronger phoenix would arise.

In the spiritual relationship, Phoenix People

- recognize a spiritual aspect to life but have varying views of details;
- have full tolerance for other spiritual beliefs and non-beliefs;
- believe in the overall friendliness of the universe; and
- have faith, *based on results,* that an inner spiritual energy can transform the individual.

In the self-relationship, they

- strive for physical, mental, and spiritual integration (allowing the inner spirit to direct the mind);
- differentiate between pain and misery and avoid misery;
- approach living challenges as an opportunity for growth;
- demonstrate a gentle sense of humor; and
- live fully in the present moment.

In relationships with other people, they

- form relationships to augment but not create happiness;
- do not allow other people or the environment to unduly influence their feelings;
- love with wisdom; and
- exhibit healthy expectations and perceptions.

Prayer: My loving inner spirit, please direct my thinking and divorce it from all self-driven will that may interfere with your plans.

Take three relaxing breaths; ask your inner spirit to guide your meditation; pause for a few minutes in silence.

September 20

Life can interfere with our serenity.

But it is often our fault when we allow this to happen. Our spiritual connection becomes weak; we act/react without pausing; we allow another person or situation to control our feelings and thoughts; we make a wrong choice; we make a "big deal" out of a trifle; we rush to meet self-imposed schedules, blindly scurrying to accomplish nothing of real value; our mind succumbs to an obsessive thought that dominates our time.

Our serenity is proportional to our spiritual condition. If we want to maintain that wonderful feeling of peace, security, and contentment, we must actively pursue our spiritual path. We start the day with prayer and meditation. We make a commitment and stop a number of times throughout the day to establish our inner connection and say "Thank you; please let me be aware of your presence this day; guide my thoughts, words and actions to align with your will; help me to be aware of all opportunities for service."

At the slightest onset of contention, we pause and repeat this short but powerful contact with our inner spirit; we never allow the turmoil to gain momentum. Life happens but we have the tools to walk peacefully through each day—if we use them.

Prayer: I pray that I may start this day with total peace; let me stay aware of your presence, power, and love every step I take.

Take three relaxing breaths; ask your inner spirit to guide your meditation; pause for a few minutes in silence.

September 21

Don't get stuck on stupid.

Making mistakes is part of life and results from actually doing things instead of sitting around and watching the world drift by. But in living this spiritual life, we will find times when we revert back to our old behaviors—we may get angry and justify our actions; we may allow anxiety or fear to control our mind; we may keep repeating the same errors. This is different than a mistake; we know better but do it anyway.

Stupid happens; we have to be careful and not get stuck in it.

We have better days if we can get out of this mindset as quickly as possible. We don't have to stay in turmoil or contention. We invest a few minutes to regain our peace as soon as we feel tense, nervous, discontent, anxious, or keep encountering people who we allow to "push our buttons." We acknowledge that we might sometimes over-react, be too sensitive, become obsessive, or make things or people too important.

We pause, take some deep breaths, connect with our inner spirit and ask for help to change our thinking and relieve our feelings; we mentally review (and truly consider) five things for which we are very grateful; we reflect on the peace, hope, and security that we have lost and want to recover; we become willing to change our thoughts, words, and actions to enjoy a better day.

Prayer: Dear God, I want to live a better life, to feel close to you and do what you want me to do. But I make mistakes and sometimes get distracted from what is really important. If I make an error, help me quickly acknowledge my fault and seek your guidance.

Take three relaxing breaths; ask your inner spirit to guide your meditation; pause for a few minutes in silence.

September 22

Working on the symptom never solves the problem.

A man replaced the old roofing on his porch; he tore off the old shingles and threw them to the gravel driveway. When the repair was completed, he meticulously cleaned the area, removing all the shingles, roofing, and debris he could find. Over the next weeks, his truck had a series of flat tires—all caused by old roofing nails. Each time, he changed the tire, got it repaired, and again went back over the driveway to search for additional nails. After the fourth flat tire, he ran a large magnet over the driveway and found dozens of hidden nails; he kept working until he removed all the nails in the area—and had no more flat tires.

Symptoms keep occurring until we eliminate the basic problem.

Misery—those feelings of anger, resentment, jealousy, self-pity, anxiety, fear, guilt, the need for chemicals to alter our moods, the need to acquire "things" or people to feel good, and other self-focused emotions—are always symptoms. The underlying problem, the one thing that we must repair, always lies within us; we must develop a healthy self-love; we must see, accept, and love our self exactly as we are—not the way we want to be. Doing this requires that we build a vibrant, living relationship with our indwelling spirit, the inner guide that reflects the direction, values, and power of the universal deity. Today, let us allow our spirit to conquer our problems and not live in the symptoms.

Prayer: My loving inner spirit, guide me so that I may see hard times as a challenge, defeat as opportunity, and disappointment as a learning experience. Awaken the yearning in my heart to enlarge our relationship and accept more of you into my life.

Take three relaxing breaths; ask your inner spirit to guide your meditation; pause for a few minutes in silence.

September 23

Sometimes, we want to run the world from our playpen.

As much as we'd like to, many of us cannot always stay positive, spiritual, and emotionally mature. We may sometimes start the day feeling irksome, a little discontent or irritated with no obvious reason; or we notice that people are not doing things the way they obviously should do them or that they are not showing us the respect and attention we think we deserve. We may try to correct the situation by giving directions or offering suggestions or keep cataloging everything in our mind, building a mental inventory of all that is wrong. Or we can accept that we might be a little immature at this point and that trying to rule the world from our playpen doesn't produce a happy, peaceful day.

We are gifted with physical and emotional indicators that gauge our spiritual well-being. We may have a slight tightness in our chest; our mind may be a whirlwind of negative or judgmental thoughts; we may feel a little discontent or irritable. We'll have better moments and days when we recognize these early warning signals and take corrective action before we are stuck in the swamp of restlessness. We pause, practice our deep relaxation breathing, and connect with our inner spirit. We acknowledge our discontent, ask for help to restore our peace and do not proceed until our serenity returns.

We may have to repeat this throughout the day if we truly desire the best day; we remember that action, not intention or desire, produces results.

Prayer: My loving creator let me be aware when I drift from the peace and serenity that you offer to me. Grant that I pause and seek your presence throughout this day.

Take three relaxing breaths; ask your inner spirit to guide your meditation; pause for a few minutes in silence.

September 24

We suffer misery when we follow fools or are distracted by the immature.

Each day we are inundated with images and information that want us to buy, to believe, or to become concerned or enraged. Some may shun or ridicule a spiritual life or may simply have a different value system than ours; others may break our trust, lie to us, or abuse us. We observe the drive for material gain, power, and prestige that dominates people's lives—and may see what appears to be "success" for their efforts. Fools and the immature inundate the world.

We must live in the world but set our own course. We hear the fools but know the transforming embrace of spiritual power; our experience has verified this reality; we have witnessed the change in other people's lives' and in our life; we choose to allow our inner spirit to direct our mind and provide us guidance, strength, security, and hope.

We are committed to live with honesty, integrity, love, compassion, loyalty, courage, and truthfulness; our performance may fall short of our ideals but we continue to strive for growth. We recognize that others may not have these values or may also fall short of living them. We do not allow this immaturity to distract us; it does not become the focus of our attention; we view our shortcomings and those of others as opportunities for growth and are grateful for them.

Prayer: I pray that I can live in the world but not be dominated by the world. Help me stay focused on my spiritual life; let me see all things from a spiritual perspective, to handle but not be overly concerned with material challenges.

Take three relaxing breaths; ask your inner spirit to guide your meditation; pause for a few minutes in silence.

September 25

We have less contention and conflict if we listen to God's gentle nudges and whispers.

God's direction is seldom delivered with lightning bolts and thunder; it is often only a mild tugging in our gut or a slight feeling of discontent that hits when we are considering, or taking, an action which may be telling us "Hey, this isn't a good idea." These may be so gentle that we ignore them, rationalize our actions, and do what we wanted to anyway. Quite often, we'll reap unpleasant or unwanted consequences and even in reflection may not recognize the early warning that could have avoided the action. Life (and our days and moments) are better when we recognize and listen to these gentle nudges and whispers.

Hopefully as we grow, we become more sensitive to the tender warnings and pay attention. We may be considering something that may be a small deviation from of our values—perhaps telling a small white lie that hurts no one, listening to a little gossip, fudging (barely a little) on our expense report and feel as if a small weight has entered our awareness, something inside of us has lost harmony, or have that flash of thought that "this is wrong."

These nudges warn us to pause and re-evaluate what we're doing. We honestly and sincerely examine how our proposed action aligns with our moral compass; we consider if something in our unconscious experience is raising a warning flag; we ask our self "What is causing this influx of negative energy or heaviness?" Life is easier when we respond to the gentle warnings.

Prayer: I pray that I may become more aware of the gentle warnings that could keep me from hurting others or myself. Help me to take that moment to pause instead of rushing blindly ahead on my self-will.

Take three relaxing breaths; ask your inner spirit to guide your meditation; pause for a few minutes in silence.

September 26

Releasing resentments to find peace of mind requires action—not wishes.

If an action gets the desired results, we don't have to agree, understand, or believe but must take the action if we want the results.

We may have suffered a real or imagined wrong in the past; every time we think of the person involved or of the event, an inner turmoil destroys our peace. The person against whom we hold this resentment is going on with life but we have given them control over us. Do we want to continue this way or do we want to change?

Following is a guaranteed process that will melt any resentment if done every day for twenty-one days:

> Ask God to give the offending person everything that you want in life—happiness, peace, love, great relationships, and so on. Always tell God the truth while you're doing this. If you don't believe in or are not sure of God or that he will respond—tell him; it's also ok to tell him that you really don't mean this prayer and you're doing this only so you'll feel better; you can even tell him that you hate this person but you don't want them to control how you feel. Don't worry, he won't hit you with a lightning bolt; he already knows exactly how you feel. We experience great freedom in telling him the truth. The power of the resentment will fade; light always dispels the darkness.

Getting rid of the resentment depends solely on our action, honesty, and willingness—not on our belief, pureness, or deep religious ties.

Prayer: Dear God, help me to be willing to be willing to come to you with all my burdens. Let me surrender all and open my heart to you.

Take three relaxing breaths; ask your inner spirit to guide your meditation; pause for a few minutes in silence.

September 27

A brick house is built one brick at a time;
our life, one day at a time;
our day, one act at a time.

We cannot change the world nor can we change anything about the past. All we can do is simply try to build the best life we can from where we are right now. How do we build a solid structure that can withstand the winds of pain and adversity and emerge to bask in the warm sunlight that always follows the storm? Like the brick house that stands strong and beautiful for decades, we start with a firm foundation and build one brick at a time.

Our relationship with our God, our inner divine spirit, is the firmest foundation possible; we must build and nurture this intimate connection if we are to erect anything that will stand the test of time.

On this strong base, we build our house, our life. We focus on every brick—each act—we place today:

- Are my motives pure; are they loving, kind, and altruistic or selfish and self-serving?
- Is my will self-directed or is it aligned with divine values?
- What is the purpose of this act? Does my goal advance the growth of my soul or the well-being of another person?
- Do my thoughts about this act reflect enhanced values of love, truth, and integrity or lesser ideals?

Each of us is responsible for placing our own bricks—and only our own bricks.

Prayer: My inner guide grant me peace in my thoughts, wisdom in my decisions, and love in my actions today. Help me to walk with you and align all I think, say, and do with your plans.

Take three relaxing breaths; ask your inner spirit to guide your meditation; pause for a few minutes in silence.

September 28

Embracing our failures and shortcomings gives us freedom.

Do we carry memories as scars that remind us of past wounds, mostly healed but always a reminder of old mistakes? Do we still have those memories which, if activated, upset our peace today? If so, we might erase even the scars. We seek an enlightened view that lets us embrace every step of the journey that resulted in our finding the ultimate gift in life, an intimate relationship with a God of our understanding.

Hopefully, we honestly face the dark side of our life and admit the part we played in our problems; this is reality and we face it without blame or excuses; we accept that we are human and made terrible mistakes that may still cause repercussions in our life. We try to see how each hurt, each failure, each humiliation contributed to the erosion of our self-reliance and arrogance, how each helped move us to the point that we were willing to try something different. Many of us had to be bludgeoned into surrender. If we had been ready to change earlier, we would have.

When we see how each hurt contributed to the life we now enjoy, we can embrace each one. The scar removal process becomes: admit, accept, and embrace every element that gave us new life.

Prayer: Dear God, I come to you as your child. I have made many mistakes and know that you have forgiven me. Let me see each error as stepping stone to your presence.

Take three relaxing breaths; ask your inner spirit to guide your meditation; pause for a few minutes in silence.

September 29

We need to shine, not preach.

We have been blessed to find this wonderful way of living. Life and its challenges still happen and we know that it's not all rainbows and sweetness; but we also know that we have real solutions for anything that life can throw at us; we also know that we are not alone, that we have found friends and companions on this same journey. We see the still suffering, those who are convinced that running their life on self-will is going to miraculously work out for them. Some of these may be family, loved ones, friends, or simply people we know. We have found the treasure and want to share with them—but they aren't receptive, they continue in their misery.

All we can do is try to shine, to make our light so bright that it draws the hurting to us as a moth to the flame. We strengthen our spiritual connection; we spend time in prayer and meditation seeking guidance for our lives and ideas on how we might help others. We demonstrate, not merely talk about, loving service; we are polite, caring, tender, and respectful to everyone. We meet misfortune with courage, disappointment with hope, and turmoil with peace. We let the brightness of our lamp prove that the brilliance of God's love and power can displace any darkness and illuminate a better path. Today let us offer a light of example rather than the whip of preaching.

Prayer: My inner guide and strength, grant me peace in all my thoughts, wisdom in all my decisions, and love in all my actions today. Help me to walk the path of your choosing and align all I think, say, and do with your plans.

Take three relaxing breaths; ask your inner spirit to guide your meditation; pause for a few minutes in silence.

September 30

If we truly believe we are all children of God, why do we expect anyone to be spiritually mature?

Who among us might declare "Oh yes, we are all God's children" and then later condemn someone for not living up to our expectations, perhaps saying or thinking "They should know better than that" or "Boy, are they childish"? And fail to see the hypocrisy in our words?

The world reinforces our driven, overly-sensitive, I-want-my-way attitude; each of us must work to become spiritually mature. This is a long process; we will not achieve perfection in this lifetime but can try to grow as a "child" of the divine.

We discovered that a personal relationship with God actually delivered the peace and happiness that we could not find in the self-driven secular world. We experienced a life-transformation; our attitude and outlook on life changed; we became more responsible and treated people as we would like to be treated.

Then, we realized that many do not choose to follow this path; they pursue worldly success with different priorities and sometimes interfere with our lives. Our great blessing to have found this new life does not make us better, only more fortunate than those who still chase the illusions of the world. They are children who have not found what we have, children deprived of our advantages, children who do not know the wonderful life of the spirit. But they are still God's children; we pray for them and try not to let their tantrums taint our day.

Prayer: Dear God, today let me see every person as one of your children. Guide me to be patient, tolerant, loving, and understanding as I would with any small child.

Take three relaxing breaths; ask your inner spirit to guide your meditation; pause for a few minutes in silence.

October 1

Claim your inheritance as a child of the divine.

We are grateful that we know that we are offspring of a divine source, that we truly are children of God. This realization does not make us better than anyone but does provide outlook, understanding, power, and resources that are available only to spirit seekers; we are more fortunate than many.

` Our physical genetics passed physical features to us; our spiritual genetics gave us a spiritual inheritance including the greatest gift we possess: our indwelling divine fragment, a direct connection to the power and wisdom of our spiritual parent. We have been given free will—the ability to choose and act—that we use to access and maintain a relationship with our inner divinity.

Tapping into this inner reservoir opens a multitude of life-changing powers: We find a new freedom—we do not depend on other things or people for happiness, joy, peace, or satisfaction; We are gifted courage that lets us face any situation with assurance, poise, and equanimity; We discover the ability to sever all emotional shackles that bound us to past regrets or mistakes; We enjoy peace that is not determined or significantly influenced by worldly success or accolades of others; We have hope—the certitude that although adversity may come, disappointment may envelop us, and pain may inflict us—nothing of this world can ever destroy our inner peace unless we allow the destruction.

Prayer: My inner spirit and guide, let me feel your presence in my deepest heart, mind, and soul; let all my resistance cease and peace pervade every fiber of my being. Fill me with the joy and gratitude of knowing that I am truly a child of God.

Take three relaxing breaths; ask your inner spirit to guide your meditation; pause for a few minutes in silence.

October 2

**No matter how hard and earnestly we pray,
God won't provide a parking place.**

We live in this world; we face financial, health, and relationship challenges; we may be afraid, anxious, or feel that we are constantly striving, butting our heads against a stone wall and wonder why God doesn't help us. We believe, we pray, we try to do good but still are hit with overwhelming difficulties.

It may help to understand that God is the parent of our spiritual nature, and as such, he is interested in our spiritual progress. However, the spiritual transformation he offers can also influence our material achievements. God does not solve all our earthly problems for us but does provide tools to solve our own.

Our life improves as we experience the spiritual transformation: We enjoy an inner peace; the constant cacophony of mental self-talk starts to subside; We have clarity of thought and a sense of purpose and direction; Our attitude becomes positive, less self-centered, and more interested in helping others; we find enhanced levels of power, integrity, ethics, courage, honesty, and truthfulness that help us see previously unseen solutions and opportunities.

God may not provide a parking place when we are in desperate need, but the peace and clearness he provides let us see the obvious place instead of blindly rushing by.

Today, let us try to do things his way instead of our way.

Prayer: My inner spirit, help me focus on my spiritual growth and not be overwhelmed by today's challenges. Grant me inner peace, strength, and vision to overcome any adversity and disappointment.

Take three relaxing breaths; ask your inner spirit to guide your meditation; pause for a few minutes in silence.

October 3

God won't make us do anything;
he'll even let us refuse the wonderful gifts he freely offers.

As the parent of our spiritual nature, God gives us a fragment of divinity, the "kingdom of heaven within" that offers each of us

- a new power to break addictions and cast aside all shackles of the past and fear of the future; this is the energy of spiritual transformation;
- divine guidance to help us pause and pray and
- an increasing awareness of the divine attributes of love, courage, forgiveness, truthfulness, honesty, compassion, mercy, and wisdom.

This power, guidance, and awareness can release us from loneliness, despair, and misery:

- We enjoy a sublime peace which surpasses all human understanding.
- We are infused with a sense of security and well-being.
- We are gifted an ability to conquer the vicissitudes of life and transcend the inevitable disappointments and pain with equanimity, peace, and love.
- Our feelings of isolation and loneliness vanish; we feel a connectedness with others;
- We are permeated with an altruistic desire to help and serve others; we want to share this awesome life with anyone who wants to experience it.

These are free gifts that we can accept or refuse. Today, let us pause and open our body, mind and soul to receive the divine presents.

Prayer: Let me open and receive the wonderful bounty that you so freely offer.

Take three relaxing breaths; ask your inner spirit to guide your meditation; pause for a few minutes in silence.

October 4

Every act has a consequence.

We get out of bed and start the day. We may pleasantly anticipate the day ahead or dread what we see coming. Our actions will determine whether we have a bad day, an "ok" day, or a great day. All acts have consequences. Establishing a connection with our inner spirit—whether we want to or not, whether we believe it or not—accesses another dimension of power that smooths our day.

Upon awakening, we say "Good morning" to our inner guide and give thanks before our feet hit the floor. We take time for prayer and meditation even if we think we cannot spare these moments. As we engage the day, we may encounter challenging people or circumstances or the world's hectic pace may try to overwhelm us. How do we respond?

If we are driven by self-will, we'll experience anger, anxiety, self-righteousness, fear, or other forms of misery; our actions will reflect these motives and yield consequences that prevent peace and serenity. Or, we can follow a different path; we can pause, take a few deep breaths, re-assert our divine connection and enjoy an elevated direction and power. We still face the same challenges but now we function with dignity, poise, confidence, and peace which result in different outcomes.

All acts have consequences; people and situations respond to our actions. Today let us choose peace instead of turmoil.

Prayer: My divine inner source, please guide me this day. Help me to feel your presence; direct my thoughts, words, and actions as I face the challenges of this world.

Take three relaxing breaths; ask your inner spirit to guide your meditation; pause for a few minutes in silence.

October 5

I am the master architect of my own chaos.

Inner chaos starts with self-driven motives and a clamoring mind.

God wants his children to be happy, joyous, and free and to feel at peace. Sometimes we may allow our selfishness, self-centeredness, and self-righteousness to interfere and separate us from this offered life. Our mind is in turmoil and we cause chaos. We don't have to continue down this path; we can work on our relationship with our divine source to access the transforming power.

Such a relationship is a two-way street. God, the universe, the infinite is always reaching out to us; we only have to open the circuit, establish the connection, and receive the rewards so freely offered.

A great relationship takes communication, time, patience, and effort. We take time to open our end of the communication; we pray and talk to God; we meditate, the quiet listening or reflecting on the divine to seek and enlarge our understanding of this wonderful power. We persist with consistent and continuous effort to open and widen the circuit for the flow of divine gifts knowing that sometimes we may not realize the transformation we are experiencing; others may see it in us before we do. Then, we suddenly or slowly recognize that the hold of other people, events in the outer world, the future, and the past is broken; we are free.

Let us start this moment to trade chaos for serenity, anxiety for security, and a clamoring mind for peace.

Prayer: I want to release all that harms me; I pray that I can open the door and allow divine peace, power, and direction to enter my life.

Take three relaxing breaths; ask your inner spirit to guide your meditation; pause for a few minutes in silence.

October 6

Lack of attention often produces mistakes and regrets.

We're driving and our mind wanders to what someone said or did; we become immersed in the mental images and then, the accident happens. Or—we're doing a task; our mind spins off to something else; then, we make a mistake that ruins the project or makes us have to do everything over again. Or—we have a good relationship or job; we take it for granted and fail to give it the attention required; then, our self-made problems threaten something very important to us.

From relationships to accidents to the mundane, lack of attention causes preventable problems. Our actual version of living in the moment may be a little closer to "Oh yes, living in the moment is a great idea! But I'm too busy to pay attention to the details!"

Combining a little hindsight with a smidgen of insight makes it obvious that we'll make fewer mistakes if we concentrate on the details of each task as we do it. As we engage in any activity, we train our self to become aware of, and to avoid physical, mental, and emotional distractions; we discipline our mind, forcing it to concentrate on the task at hand even if we have to constantly make it return to where it should be. We give appropriate attention to those things that are important to us or those whose failure might have highly undesirable consequences—our relationships, our career, driving a car, and others. Such moment-by-moment awareness avoids preventable problems, saves us from a lot of hurtful consequences, and helps us gain control of our mind so that we can appreciate and live every moment.

Today, let us be aware of mental detours and bring our mind back to the activity in front of us and the moment at hand.

Prayer: My inner spirit, help me be aware anytime my thoughts try to avoid the moment; give me the strength to discipline my mind and make it return to the task at hand.

Take three relaxing breaths; ask your inner spirit to guide your meditation; pause for a few minutes in silence.

October 7

Prayer moves us toward divine values.

The world and our animalistic nature draw us to live by self-driven will; prayer gradually but unfailingly changes our motives, thoughts, and actions to a higher level. We enjoy

- *peace of mind, the feeling that all is well.* We discover the ability to match calamity with calmness and feel the certainty that everything will work out;
- *enhanced mental clarity.* We become able to see answers that previously eluded us. Our mind becomes more focused; our mental efficiency increases. We experience fewer problems and find easier resolution to challenges and conflict;
- *increased awareness that certain habits create much of our misery.* This often leads to a commitment to replace them with higher levels of behavior;
- *a new consciousness of being able to choose an alternative way of acting or reacting.* We don't have to allow other people to dictate our feelings; we have a choice plus the tools to implement our decisions; and
- *a sense of direction that aligns with our purpose in life.* When facing a decision, we may experience an intuitive feeling that one direction is better than the alternative; we may see an underlying motive that helps us honestly evaluate our options and discern a better way.

Prayer: Dear God, bring peace to my mind and cleanse my motives; let me feel your divine presence flood my mind and my very being with values and attributes that reflect the worth of your child. By your grace, guide my mind to be a blessing instead of a barrier.

Take three relaxing breaths; ask your inner spirit to guide your meditation; pause for a few minutes in silence.

October 8

All relationships can benefit from spiritual influence.

Our associations with people may include those that live a spiritual life, some that acknowledge a universal deity but do not bring this into worldly affairs, and some that do not want anything to do with this thing called God. And their thoughts, words, and acts reflect their active faith and belief or lack thereof. We cannot always choose the other person in every relationship in our life. So we'll likely encounter a broad range of attractive traits with a mix of unattractive ones. This is the world in which we live; thankfully, we are only responsible for our self; we'll realize the best potential from each relationship if we stay aware of our divine inheritance.

We are responsible for including God in every relationship no matter what the other person does. We ask for guidance, strength, and help in our morning devotionals; we remind our self that every person we'll meet today is a child of God; they may reflect mature attitudes or act as selfish, self-centered toddlers. We seek to balance justice with mercy, compassion with wisdom, and contention with dignity, poise, and equanimity.

We use our spiritual tools as we go through the day: If we face a challenge or start to react, we pause and pray before the lightning strikes; we take a moment to relax and find a few minutes of quiet to acknowledge our inner spirit and breathe peacefully.

Feeling the presence of the spirit simply offers the opportunity for the best day we can have.

Prayer: Help me feel your spirit presence and accept that each person I meet today is also a child of God. I pray that my thoughts, words, and actions today reflect my birthright. It is my will that your will be done.

Take three relaxing breaths; ask your inner spirit to guide your meditation; pause for a few minutes in silence.

October 9

Sometimes the best way to solve entangled problems is to forsake them for a time.

We may still hit those times in life where real or imagined problems overwhelm us; we try to sort things out but become imbedded in the problem; we pray, but peace and real solutions elude us. Sometimes, walking away and taking time off often yields new answers.

This removal treatment might require a few hours or a few days depending on how deep our disturbance; our goal is to break the ingrained thought-feeling pattern that dominates our mind.

We utilize physical, mental, and spiritual resources to attain rest, relaxation, and diversion. If possible, we change our environment: We might opt for a nature activity and take an afternoon or weekend for camping, hiking, rafting, or taking a photography excursion; we might go to a movie and dinner, go to the park and read an interesting book, visit family or a friend we haven't seen for some time. We might decide we need a short vacation or enjoy some silence at a retreat. Whatever we do, we spend some quiet time reviewing our blessings and do not allow our mind to drift and engage the original chaos.

We'll go back with a clearer head and steadier hand. Many times an obvious solution that we previously overlooked suddenly appears; or, we may realize that the pressing problems were really creations of exaggerated fear or false "big deals" that were not really important.

Prayer: I pray that I know when I need to remove myself from entangled problems; grant me the insight, strength, and courage to walk off, become engaged in another activity, seek and find inner peace, and then return.

Take three relaxing breaths; ask your inner spirit to guide your meditation; pause for a few minutes in silence.

October 10

Pray before you act—not after.

If we decide to commit suicide, we can go to the roof of a ten-story building and jump off. Then, on the way down as we pass the eighth floor, we realize that this was a terrible idea and change our mind; we can have tremendous faith and pray as hard as we can, but we're going to splatter on the ground. God will not suspend the law of gravity to save us from our poor choices and stupid actions.

However, if we sincerely ask for help when making our decision to jump—*before taking the action*—God definitely responds. He'll provide an opportunity to make a wiser decision. The turmoil inside lessens; a thought suddenly flashes into our mind that offers a different perspective, provides an opportunity for hope, or supplies an obvious solution; we notice the beauty and peace in a previously unnoticed sunset and our inner uproar starts to quiet; or someone suddenly appears out of nowhere to talk with us—and say the exact thing we need to hear at that moment. *Something* will occur that presents an opportunity to see things from a different perspective.

God often does not always give us the burning bush or hit us with a lightning bolt but quietly offers us better alternatives if we pray before we act. Then it's our choice which option we take.

Prayer: Dear God, help me not to hurt anyone or myself with rash actions; grant me that moment of clarity so I pause and pray before I act. Let me not make any unnecessary choices when I am suffering pain or misery; help me be willing to turn to you for the help you so freely offer.

Take three relaxing breaths; ask your inner spirit to guide your meditation; pause for a few minutes in silence.

October 11

Selfish, self-centered, and self-righteous motives cause most of our misery.

- *Selfishness* occurs when I seek something for my own advantage, pleasure, or well-being without regard for others. It includes all thoughts, words, or actions that focus on obtaining my own desires without consideration of others.
- *Self-centeredness* searches all events that impinge on my life and focuses on how they impact *me*—what is their relationship to what I want, what I need, what I think should happen? Everything is judged by its potential effect on the heart and soul of my universe–me. Self-pity is a variation of this.
- *Self-righteousness* refers to overconfidence in my rightness, or being smugly moralistic and intolerant of the opinions of others. I think I'm right and pay little attention to other peoples' ideas; I don't need to follow directions; I believe that I either know the best answer or can figure it out. This prideful attitude sheds constructive criticism and limits opportunities for growth.

We harm ourselves any time we engage in even a smidgen of these traits but much of what we see, hear, or experience seems to support that these are a normal part of the modern world. However, we have chosen a different path and it's our responsibility to avoid them like a plague. We want to stay aware of anytime they enter our life and take action to insure that they do not take root and grow.

Prayer: My inner spirit, my guide and power, help me recognize any time I indulge in self-directed will. Grant me the power to stop immediately and seek your presence and guidance.

Take three relaxing breaths; ask your inner spirit to guide your meditation; pause for a few minutes in silence.

October 12

**If I think my partner should never impose on me,
I may be better off with a pet than a human.**

Whether in an intimate relationship or a casual one, we may sometimes feel like the other person is imposing on us. We pause and remember "Whenever I am upset, there is something wrong with me" and realize that we may be succumbing to unhealthy expectations, self-pity, or over-sensitivity. Or, someone may actually be imposing beyond what is acceptable. Now what do we do about it?

If this is an intimate relationship, we accept that we are both human; no one is perfect. Both of us will make mistakes; acknowledging and correcting these is part of building a wonderful union; we view the intermittent upsets as speed bumps, not barricades. We acknowledge everything that this person does for us, the little gifts that they contribute to our life.

In all relationships, we pause and take positive action when we first feel the discomfort. We determine if unhealthy expectations, our state-of-mind, or over-sensitivity contribute to our reaction; were we tired, anxious, hectic, or already carrying an emotional burden? Or did we have plans and find it difficult to fit this in? We pause and pray for tolerance, patience, compassion, and love. But we must also honestly evaluate: Is this truly an unacceptable imposition? If so, we need to find ways to respond with dignity, love, and poise.

Prayer: Dear God, if I feel that someone is imposing on me, help me first to see any shortcomings of mine that contribute to this feeling and become willing to change. Guide me to act with love, tolerance, and patience in all I do.

Take three relaxing breaths; ask your inner spirit to guide your meditation; pause for a few minutes in silence.

October 13

If we're headed in the wrong direction, God allows "U-turns".
Actually, he'll even stop traffic to give us the opportunity to turn.

"Heading the wrong direction" can apply to anything from living a totally destructive life-style to enjoying some actions that limit our potential or cause subtle harm; neither allows us to live our best life. We may have to repeatedly suffer before we are ready to give up what is hurting us and try something different.

This act of surrendering and becoming willing sets in motion a response from God (the universe, spiritual forces) that opens doors and provides opportunities to accomplish that change.

Suddenly, we meet that right person who shares a perspective that guides us in our new direction; we hear a song that sings the exact words we need to hear at exactly the right time; we see or hear a phrase repeated that has a special meaning, that guides us into new ideas or actions. We get news of unexpected surprises that offer solutions to some of our problems; something happens, we experience a slight change in circumstances or in our attitude that lets us see solutions to previously unresolved challenges.

As we pray or merely deeply breathe in gratitude of our new direction, we feel an overwhelming sense of peace, security, and love that reassures us that we are on the right path.

God responds to our desire to change direction anytime.

Prayer: My loving creator parent and indwelling spirit, help me release anything in my life that separates me from you, that prevents me from doing your will and enjoying the best life I can live.

Take three relaxing breaths; ask your inner spirit to guide your meditation; pause for a few minutes in silence.

October 14

Don't get trapped in mental turmoil.

Disappointed? Hurt? Betrayed? Experience the pain, ask God for help, and move forward. Never dwell on mental turmoil.

If you were hiking in the mountains and tripped and fell in the trail, would you stay for a day to examine the place you fell, repeatedly cursing the branch that tripped you? Would you hike five miles further, think about the fall, turn around, and go back to brood over this spot again? Would you let two weeks pass and then go back to re-visit the place and branch so you could once again feel the pain and frustration? Or would you simply hurt a little and move on while being more careful not to trip again?

If we love the outdoors, a few trips and bruises won't stop us from enjoying something that contributes so much to our life. Of course, if we choose to hike this trail again to enjoy the scenery and challenge it offers, common sense dictates exercising caution as we approach that treacherous branch.

Likewise, we do not have to dredge up past emotional hurts and mistakes for agonizing review; nor do we avoid stepping out and living because we fear being hurt again. We are gifted our inner spirit that can sever the bonds of past pain and guide us along a safer path. We stay aware of the source of previous pain so we don't repeat that error but do not allow it to control our current actions.

Prayer: My loving God, help me not deny the hurts I feel in life but acknowledge them, identify the true cause, accept any part I had in their creation, forgive wherever necessary, and move forward confident in your love, guidance, and protection.

Take three relaxing breaths; ask your inner spirit to guide your meditation; pause for a few minutes in silence.

October 15

**Each day, each moment,
we are either the master of time or its servant.**

Fact: Each year has 365 days (plus one day for leap year); each day has twenty-four hours or 1440 minutes. There's absolutely nothing we can do to change this. The question we face is how do we best use this thing called time? How will we use the minutes we have today?

We live and function in the outer world; here, we have our job, home, possessions, relationships, and all the garments and trappings that many people consider to be everything in life. Family, education, peers, and much of what we see and hear every day set the priorities and the pace of this outer world. They try to define what is important, what we "should" accomplish, how fast we should scurry to do this, and what is deemed "success" or "failure." If we accept all that we are told, we inevitably become the servant of time.

Making inner peace, security, and growth our highest priorities changes our usage of time. We do what is necessary in the outer world but quit believing the lies about success and failures; we feel less stress, anxiety, insecurity, and need to hurry; we function in this outer world but are not controlled by it. We invest our time in practices that actually produce the results we seek; we stay aware of our inner spiritual power; we practice our spiritual exercises to stay strong and directed and walk each day with love, patience, and tolerance. We use time wisely rather than being its' slave.

Prayer: Grant that I may spend time with you, my inner spirit, this day and use each moment wisely. Help me to pause, pray, and see what is truly important.

Take three relaxing breaths; ask your inner spirit to guide your meditation; pause for a few minutes in silence.

October 16

The apocalypse is imminent!

Apocalypse: *to uncover or reveal, a disclosure of knowledge or "lifting of the veil"; colloquial meaning—an event involving destruction or damage on an awesome or catastrophic scale.*

The statement "The apocalypse is imminent" may trigger certain feelings but perhaps these often shift when the full meaning is offered. Hearing "An event involving destruction on a catastrophic scale is imminent" produces quite different reaction than hearing "A disclosure of knowledge is imminent."

Consider: If a simple word can yield this type of misunderstanding, how much does our understanding of the world or our relationships with people suffer because of similar misconceptions? Do we not limit both when we think we already know, believe others' opinions without proof, or base our acts and attitude on hazy, ill-defined, or incomplete information?

In this case, knowing the precise meaning may lead us to agree that we are participating in an apocalypse; we are experiencing a "lifting of the veil," developing an ability to see what was previously hidden. Coming to understand that our divine parent has bestowed a very fragment of his divinity, the kingdom of heaven within, to live and dwell within each person lifts the veil of guilt, shame, fear, and remorse; the disclosure uncovers a potential of love, hope, peace, and never-ending service that depends solely on our free-will choice and subsequent actions. Knowing that each of us can have a direct and personal connection to God clarifies our relationship with the divine and with every person.

Prayer: I pray that I may be open-minded and not chained to my pre-conceived ideas; open my heart, mind, and soul so that I may welcome the truth.

Take three relaxing breaths; ask your inner spirit to guide your meditation; pause for a few minutes in silence.

October 17

Where does your mind spend its spare time?
Our daydreams reflect and affect our attitude.

Many of us have a mind that just keeps pushing thoughts into our awareness; these mental excursions may wander into the "what if..." or the "If only ..." categories and initiate worry or anxiety; they may include thoughts about hitting the lottery, receiving recognition and acclaim, getting even or plotting revenge, sexual encounters, or 1000 other variations. These daydreams reflect our attitude and are a barometer of our spiritual and emotional maturity.

We accept that our thoughts can trigger corresponding feelings; thoughts of "It's not fair" or "It's not right" can initiate anger, self-pity, guilt, or shame.

This cause/effect sequence also applies to our daydreams. Our inner peace and attitude suffer if self-driven determination is the prime driving force for our musings. Consistent thoughts that reinforce selfishness, self-centeredness, or self-righteousness distort the direction and retard the speed of our growth. Will we not, even unknowingly, lean toward fulfilling these thoughts?

Let's try for progress in this fantasy world. Let us replace these harmful, limiting thoughts with loving, altruistic daydreams; we can see our self serving others, doing good for someone, or holding our peace under provocation; we can envision and feel the joy that comes from bravely standing for a value, anonymously giving a needed gift, or simply listening and sharing someone's tribulation. Then, when we retire at night, we can review where our daydreams played and ask for help to guide them to align with divine purpose and ideals.

Prayer: Dear God, help my daydreams reflect what is important to me; guide all my thoughts to align with your will.

Take three relaxing breaths; ask your inner spirit to guide your meditation; pause for a few minutes in silence.

October 18

Trying to do God's will is like walking a mountain trail in the dark and God has the flashlight; he illuminates the next step, not the whole trail.

We may sometimes pray for knowledge of God's will and think we receive no answer. We want to know for certain what God would have us do, but often all we receive is a glimmer of illumination that shines on a simple step that is obvious and right in front of us, nothing very spirit-revealing. It's not what we're looking for; we anticipated seeing something that would reveal the infinite plan for us leaving no doubt about what our actions should be.

However, if we are walking in darkness and God has the flashlight, he only shines the light on the very next step, the one single thing we need to do, the one place we can safely place our foot and step; the light is often a very subtle, dim glow and not a spotlight.

Spiritual maturity and receptivity help us discern the light; faith guides us to take the step and know that the next one shall be revealed when we're ready. His will is often to simply do what is directly in front of us, doing it for the right reason and with the right heart, and trusting that he will illuminate the next step.

We just have to go where the light shines.

Prayer: Our Father, help me wait for you to light my path; grant me the vision to see; let me trust you to dispel any darkness I face and to provide me with the safe, loving direction I need.

Take three relaxing breaths; ask your inner spirit to guide your meditation; pause for a few minutes in silence.

October 19

**God does provide food for the sparrows,
but they have to leave their nest to find it; he doesn't deliver.**

We live in a world that provides abundant opportunities for growth; it constantly challenges us to forsake a spiritual life and offers endless opportunities for conflict and contention. No matter how strong our faith or how close our beliefs approach the real truth, God does not provide a life of ease and comfort, free of conflict and difficulty.

Our parent supplies his children with the power, strength, purpose, and direction to overcome any obstacle and fulfill our divine destiny. But we have to use our free will and abilities; we must choose to accept our inheritance and claim what is rightfully ours.

Each day we must keep our vision of the spiritual life; we cannot let the secular sights and sounds that dominate the world overwhelm us; we cannot succumb to living, acting, and reacting from the self-centered stage that delights much of humanity.

We go in search of our spiritual sustenance; we seek our spiritual food. We start our day with prayer and meditation; we ask for and receive an influx of spiritual power, guidance, and wisdom; we feel the love and overcare of our creator and the fellowship of our brothers and sisters. When the world intrudes and erodes our peace, we pause and connect with our inner guide to receive serenity and strength. We share this life with any one we can; we shine but do not preach; we offer, but do not demand.

Prayer: Let me seek spiritual food throughout this day. Nourish my heart, mind, and soul with the power of the almighty; sustain me with your love that I may feed others; quench my thirst and longing that I may demonstrate fulfillment of your spiritual promises.

Take three relaxing breaths; ask your inner spirit to guide your meditation; pause for a few minutes in silence.

October 20

Neither physical nor emotional wounds heal if we jab the injury to see if it still hurts.

If we get cut, we clean and disinfect the wound to prevent infection; our body increases the protection by forming a scab over the injury. We don't poke and tear at this protective coating; we don't constantly push on it to see if the pain is gone; we give it time to heal. The best treatment for emotional wounds is similar.

They also require first aid. First we quickly acknowledge that we have been hurt; we do not blame the other person for our feelings; the wound is ours and it is our responsibility to treat it. We pause, pray, and seek inner peace; we review this situation with a trusted friend or advisor and look for any part that we may have in this:

- Were we overly sensitive? Did we over-react?
- Did we have unhealthy expectations, perceptions, or motives?
- Did we do anything in the past that contributed to this?

If yes, we take appropriate action to clear our side of the street. If no and we have been truly wronged, we minimize the damage; we separate our self from the situation for awhile; we pray for the offending person until no emotional scar remains. When a thought tries to re-open the wound, we again pause, seek our inner peace, ask God to grant us relief, and repeat our prayers of love; we do not keep jabbing the wound with thoughts that prevent healing.

Prayer: Dear God, I am human and am trying my best to walk the path of your choosing; help me accept any pain I feel and move toward healing. Please release your curing love and cleanse me.

Take three relaxing breaths; ask your inner spirit to guide your meditation; pause for a few minutes in silence.

October 21

Our integrity, dignity, and self-respect can erode one particle at a time until only a hole remains.

We will not enjoy undying bliss when we adopt this spiritual path. This is a process of growth; our previous patterns did not miraculously disappear but must be replaced by new, healthier habits; this requires time and repeated effort.

The world and its people remain the same: Secular, materialistic outlooks dominate many people; Selfishness, self-centeredness, and self-righteousness infect the moral stream of our age. However, we have tapped into a living reservoir of additional power, guidance, security, and intelligence that offers us the best life available on this planet. But we must maintain vigilance lest constant exposure to the misguided ways of the world erode our spiritual principles.

It's not always a momentous problem or catastrophe that causes us to slip from the great life; retrogression often occurs a little at a time. We skip our prayer and meditation one time without drastic consequences; we sacrifice our values because we're afraid of repercussions or want to gain selfish advantage; we entertain so-called justifiable anger; we blame another person for the way we feel; we feel a little self-pity and relish it instead of immediately recognizing the potential harm and letting it go.

Every day is the day we must make conscious contact with our inner spirit; every moment is the moment we stay aware of our inner peace; every decision is the one we must measure against our scale of right or wrong. Each day is filled with choices ranging from the mundane to the important; in each decision, we must try to do the right thing for the right reason.

Prayer: My inner spirit, make me aware any time I slip in following your intention for me. Help me to pause and align my thoughts, words, and actions with God's will.

Take three relaxing breaths; ask your inner spirit to guide your meditation; pause for a few minutes in silence.

October 22

Do I have areas in my life that I isolate from God?

Sometimes living a spiritual life is progressive: we surrender and ask for help to overcome a major problem and find relief; we start trusting God to help with other problems. We notice some improvement—we aren't experiencing the depths of despair, the paralyzing fear or hopelessness, and actually feel some peace at times. But we still have those flashes of anger or inexplicable loneliness, allow people to "push our buttons", or suffer periods of discontent and anxiety.

We wonder, "Why do I still feel this way? Why hasn't God changed everything?" Perhaps the answer is that we still hold onto to some areas; we keep them for our self and don't want God to know about them or interfere with them.

We cannot keep secrets from God; he knows everything we think, feel, say, or do—the good, bad, ugly and even the unmentionables—and loves us anyway; he does not force us to accept anything nor does he break down the spiritual barricades we erect. We may have what we consider a dark sexual secret, still want to cut corners with our financial integrity to gain an upper hand, enjoy a small resentment that is not burning away at our soul but simply lies there smoldering, or engage in mental fantasies that see us as the superhero or Casanova.

If we only acknowledge the flaw and invite him to help us, he will provide the power to change.

Prayer: I pray that I can truly surrender and release anything and everything that separates me from the all-powerful, all forgiving, all fulfilling love of the spirit.

Take three relaxing breaths; ask your inner spirit to guide your meditation; pause for a few minutes in silence.

October 23

Discontent often originates in the fear soil of human nature.

Fear does not always appear as a paralyzing emotion but often masquerades as anger, self-pity, anxiety, loneliness, guilt, or other self-directed feelings. Sometimes these start when a subtle negative thought enters our mind uninvited; we feel a slight discontent, a feeling of unease that matures into a knot of misery.

For much of this, the root problem is fear. Fear is inevitable when we consciously or unconsciously separate our self from our spiritual core. Fear originates when self-driven will determines our attitude; this automatically allows other people and the outer world to dominate our mind. Fear will continue to build until it finds an outlet or is expelled by the expulsive power of divine love.

Let's not accept the slightest disturbance in our inner peace without taking precautions. We pause and examine the whisper of discontent; we consider: "Why do I feel this way? What is pulling me away from peace? Whatever symptom I am feeling or un-spiritual thoughts I am thinking, help me to see how separation from my divine source allowed this to happen."

Then we re-gain our serenity: We blame no one or any situation; we pause, pray, connect with our inner spirit, and claim our peace.

Prayer: I pray that I may strengthen my faith to drive away all fear and all children of fear. Any time I feel disturbed today, help me to pause and contact you, my inner spirit for power and direction.

Take three relaxing breaths; ask your inner spirit to guide your meditation; pause for a few minutes in silence.

October 24

Do not go naked into the day.

As we start our day, many of us spend effort preparing an outward image that we hope meets the approval of the world; others may be little concerned with such approval and get ready for the day as easily as possible; but everyone goes clothed into the day. No one would seriously consider brushing their teeth, combing their hair and walking out the door totally naked. But how many of us will start this day with spiritual and emotional nakedness that leaves us exposed and unprotected?

Our spiritual armor shields us from the winds of adversity; it helps to minimize or even eliminate the unpleasant effects of disappointments, upheavals, and contention. This protective garment keeps us from succumbing to self-pity, being overly sensitive, or allowing others to control our feelings; it provides guidance, purpose, strength, power, and direction in all that we may encounter throughout the day.

These defensive coverings supply the power that helps us pause before we react, look for the positive and the spiritual value in all situations, walk away from gossip, and recognize the value of serving and helping others. We don our spiritual protection when we express our gratitude as we start the day, take time to pray, and sit in quiet, receptive meditation.

Prayer: Dear God help me gird myself with spiritual armor as I start this day. Help me feel your presence as I go into the world; grant me the strength, security, and purpose that can only come from you.

Take three relaxing breaths; ask your inner spirit to guide your meditation; pause for a few minutes in silence

October 25

Being loving and spiritual does not eliminate the need for boundaries.

We want to enjoy the best life possible and know that this requires spiritual growth. If someone repeatedly abuses us, denigrates our value, takes advantage of us, must we stand for more only because we are trying to be spiritual? No! As a child of God, there are times when each of us must stand and assert our dignity and value but we must learn to do this with love, tolerance, and courage.

We pause, pray, and ask for spiritual help to take an honest, sincere, and objective look at what is happening; we ask for the insight to see why we feel as we do; we thoroughly review our motives because we know that any act based on fear, guilt, anger, and other forms of misery never produces the best results. If we avoid setting boundaries because of our fear of confrontation or fear of displeasing another, we will pay a heavy future price.

We confide in a trusted friend or advisor, baring all that we have uncovered, knowing that we are not always the best judge of our actions and reactions when we are in the middle of turmoil.

Being spiritual does not mean that we must be fools or doormats; we must learn to establish boundaries and stand for our dignity while we stay loving, kind, and tolerant; we try to help but not enable.

Prayer: I pray for guidance as I engage in all my relationships today. Help me to balance my love, patience and tolerance with wisdom, courage, and strength. Help me to see the actions that truly align with your will.

Take three relaxing breaths; ask your inner spirit to guide your meditation; pause for a few minutes in silence.

October 26

When we make a mistake, we accept the responsibility and consequences; blaming others stifles growth.

Everyone makes mistakes. We must honestly and objectively evaluate who is responsible but not become mired in the emotions that often result from an error. If the fault is ours, we face the consequences and take responsibility but do not allow regrets, shame, remorse, and guilt to burden us. We focus on healing and growth; we make amends, learn from the experience, and move forward.

If someone else made a mistake that affected us, we separate the responsibility/consequences from the emotions. They made the mistake and must accept the responsibility; however, the feelings about how it affected *us* belong to *us*. We must avoid blame, anger, resentment, shame, self-pity, or other miseries. We practice enlightened forgiveness (releasing any negative feeling but retaining memory of the experience to avoid repeating it); we evaluate any non-loving responses we feel; we honestly admit and accept these feelings exactly as they are, asking our inner spirit to cleanse these and replace them with love, patience, and tolerance.

Our feelings, actions, and personal growth need not depend on other people's words, thoughts, or deeds.

Prayer: Dear God, help me accept that we all make mistakes. Grant that I may see my errors and those of others as opportunities to learn and practice responses that lead me to a higher life; help me view all mistakes as a gateway to growth. Help me judge the errors of actions but not the value of people.

Take three relaxing breaths; ask your inner spirit to guide your meditation; pause for a few minutes in silence.

October 27

Disappointment can lead to discouragement.

Disappointment: *feeling of sadness or displeasure caused by non-fulfillment of expectations.*
Discouragement: *losing confidence or enthusiasm; without hope.*

Most of us encounter disappointments; things aren't going to go the way we want all the time. Any disappointment can form an open wound that can turn into discouragement or resentment and create an additional burden.

Disappointment is always associated with an expectation. We examine the associated expectation: Was it healthy or unhealthy? Was it based on evidence, data, and experience or merely on fantasy, stemming from our dreams, "wants," or what we thought "should" happen? If from unhealthy expectations, we accept that our desired outcome was unlikely and perhaps childish or immature; we know that we need to align our expectations with reality to avoid unnecessary misery.

If our expectation was healthy, if we had done everything right and still suffer disappointment, we use our inner spiritual power to shift our thoughts, re-align our priorities, and help us find a new perspective. We make a conscious effort to remember that we still have many blessings; we still have hope—we know that this is a temporary setback and that we can overcome all challenges with the help of our spiritual nature. Is there a lesson we can learn? We remember "How important is it really?" and move on.

Prayer: My loving creator and source, I know that I will face disappointment in this life. Help me to always know that your help, guidance, and strength are available for my asking.

Take three relaxing breaths; ask your inner spirit to guide your meditation; pause for a few minutes in silence.

October 28

The easy answer is not always the best answer.

Our human, animalistic tendencies are often slothful and lazy; we want the rewards of a great life without working to get it.

Sometimes pain is the only thing that can make us move off the dead center of comfortable complacency: we get tired of hurting and do something to relieve the pain. The immature do as little as possible; they seek the easiest way to relieve the immediate symptom and this often results in more upsets. Moving beyond this adolescent animalistic response requires some work but is well worth the effort.

As we mature, we discover that we have an innate spiritual power, an energy that can transform our lives, break the shackles of our defects, and inspire and guide us to enhanced values and performance. We try to stay in a conscious constant contact with our inner spirit; we daily review our efforts, searching for where we might have fallen short; we make a conscious effort to be loving, kind, gentle, patient, and tolerant, looking for any way that we might help a fellow traveler.

These actions require time and effort; however, our experience has proven that only our own choices and actions can move us out of the mire of self-centered will to the elevated life we are meant to live.

Today, will you take the easy answers or strive to be the best version of yourself?

Prayer: Dear God, help me move from my complacency and lethargy; grant me the willingness to work and do what is necessary for a better life. Help me claim my divine inheritance as your child.

Take three relaxing breaths; ask your inner spirit to guide your meditation; pause for a few minutes in silence.

October 29

Our morning pattern is one of our most important habits.

How does your mind start its morning? Before you get out of bed or immediately after, does it pass a searchlight over what others have said or done or what they have failed to say or do? Does it automatically scan the upcoming day looking for what "must" be done, what might be potential problems, or mentally engage in possible upcoming conversations? Do you rush about or do you invest your time wisely?

Some spiritual and emotional maturity helps us understand that our morning greatly influences the quality of the rest of our day.

Upon wakening and before our feet hit the floor, we start with an attitude of gratitude: we acknowledge the presence of our indwelling spirit and express thanks for at least five blessings; many of us have learned if we offer prayers of gratitude as we fall asleep, we tend to wake up with grateful thoughts. Then we participate in the most important time of our day: We connect with our spirit; we pray, meditate, and ask for guidance for our thoughts, words, and actions for the upcoming day.

Opening the conduit to receive spiritual power rests on action, not intention or wishes. Some may say, "But I don't have the time to do this!" Really? We make the time if we want peace and happiness.

We have a choice: Do we follow self-directed will or do we try something better?

Prayer: My inner spirit, guide me to establish morning patterns that allow you to help my life. Please let me slow down, open my heart and mind, and welcome you into all areas of my life this day.

Take three relaxing breaths; ask your inner spirit to guide your meditation; pause for a few minutes in silence.

October 30

Even angels need diversion, relaxation, and pleasure.

We may understand that developing our spiritual life is one of the most important tasks we have; we may also know the peace, fulfillment, and rewards that result when we keep an active spiritual connection; however, we live in a world that can be tedious, boring, hectic, and challenging. We may hit those times when chaos overwhelms us. We pause, pray, and try to find peace of mind but still feel discontent.

When feeling like this, we may need to seek activities to occupy our mind and yield pleasant emotional repercussions; we limit our investment in those that are merely mind-numbing escapes from reality; a little of this is alright but too much is not helpful. We don't short-cut the time or effort invested in diversion; this is an indispensable part of healthy life that augments, but does not replace, our spiritual development.

We may take a few days at spiritual retreat, go camping, whitewater rafting, or visit family; we can try ballroom dancing, devote time to an old or new hobby, or enjoy a place or event in which we've long been interested. These are individual choices but should be relaxing, enjoyable, and engage our mind and attention.

Have you truly done something enjoyable lately?

Prayer: Dear God, grant me the insight to see when I should forsake the problems and concerns of this world and seek wholesome diversion. Help me to experience relaxation and pleasure in line with your will.

Take three relaxing breaths; ask your inner spirit to guide your meditation; pause for a few minutes in silence.

October 31

Every day, every moment, we choose either self-will or divine guidance to direct our mind.

Consciously or unconsciously we make this primary decision every day and it establishes the power we have available to face the day.

Going on self-will gives us access to physical, mental, and character resources and this is the way of the world. It is reinforced by culture, society, and most of what we hear and see; it has specific results that produce an inner void, a feeling that something is missing; it yields mediocre relationships, feelings of misery, recurring struggle, and limited happiness and serenity.

Choosing to respond to divine leading is not a decision we make one time and then live happily ever after; we must repeatedly select this alternative for each appropriate decision we face. However, choosing this option opens extra resources to overcome daily challenges; we access an additional reservoir that offers power, wisdom, guidance, peace, and hope that are totally unavailable in the self-directed option. This choice opens a new dimension; it fills the inner void that nothing else can fill. This enhanced depth of soul offers opportunities for extraordinary relationships, the peace that passes all human understanding, and a living integrity to stand against all troubles.

Today, let us choose to forsake self-driven will and participate in the most awesome adventure available to the mortal being, the adventure of the spirit.

Prayer: I pray that I may be conscious of all my choices today and be guided by divine principles.

Take three relaxing breaths; ask your inner spirit to guide your meditation; pause for a few minutes in silence.

November 1

Denial condemns us to mediocrity and misery; we can solve no problem until we admit we have a problem.

We may have some unrecognized challenges that we have gotten used to and accept as part of life: We may spend too much money and say that we need to change; We may have a resentment, guilt, or fear that sits barely below our consciousness waiting to intrude; We may know that daily prayer and meditation improves our life but say we don't have the time. For these continuing disturbances, consider: If we do not have inner peace, we have a problem; we will remain forever non-peaceful until we admit, face, and solve that problem.

Right now, pause and consider: *Do I feel any inner disturbance now or did I feel one yesterday; am I allowing something to keep me from feeling peace and happiness?* We seek to identify those smaller upsets that steal a piece of our happiness and serenity.

If yes, we say a prayer for honesty; we seek the true cause and determine what part we are playing in this: Do I have a hidden fear, anxiety, or contention? Am I procrastinating? Am I allowing another person to control my feelings? Are any selfish, self-centered (including self-pity), or self-righteous thoughts penetrating my mind?

We recognize and accept the problem; then we seek our inner divine guidance and power to find and implement the best solution. We are children of divinity with a birthright of complete and fulfilling peace; only self-driven will can prevent it.

Prayer: I pray that I may honestly look at anything that separates me from peace and happiness, anything that causes me contention or conflict; let me turn to my spiritual source, center, and power for relief.

Take three relaxing breaths; ask your inner spirit to guide your meditation; pause for a few minutes in silence.

November 2

Our conscience tells us to "do right";
our divine inner spark tells us what *is* right.

Our culture and history influence our conscience; one group at a certain time in history may radically disagree with another on morality or "goodness," or what is acceptable.

However, each of us really has an inner guide, the true spirit within, the 'kingdom of heaven' within, the Buddha within. This is the still, small voice or the feeling of inspiration that responds to the spirit of truth; the certainty of absolute knowing that "this is the way."

At times we must make the effort to still our mind, to quiet our clamoring thoughts and listen; we must seek to eliminate the desires and intentions of our self-driven motives and ignore the false truths imbedded by society, culture, and our worldly training. We must listen with the ear of the spirit and hear with love, patience, tolerance, compassion, hope, trust and mercy; we try to respond to the higher calling, the way of the divine and not the way of the world. This day, let us make a conscious effort to listen to our spirit.

Prayer: Dear God, let me listen for your divine leading; quiet my clamoring mind, still my turbulent emotions, and grant me inner silence so that I may hear. Let your peace pervade my body, mind, and soul.

Take three relaxing breaths; ask your inner spirit to guide your meditation; pause for a few minutes in silence.

November 3

Our regrets include words we didn't say, places we didn't see, and acts of love we didn't do. Today, let us make no future regrets.

Do you have that one special place you've always wanted to see? Or that tremendous adventure you long to enjoy? Or a few people that are really important in your life? Complacency, procrastination, and laziness can create hidden regrets.

Simply consider one specific area: the people, especially the loving relationships that contribute so much to our life. We may not always give these wonderful associations the time, effort, and respect that reflect their true value; they are always there, part of our lives; their familiarity and constant presence can lead to our taking them for granted.

Today, actually do something—take an action—that eliminates a future regret.

The relationship may have suffered from one or both ignoring its value; it may not be the vibrant loving association it once was; it may have simply become unexciting and routine; we may need to let down the walls of false isolation, to perhaps become vulnerable and open. We can make that phone call that we know we should make instead of procrastinating; we can visit a friend or relative that we haven't seen for some time; we can sit and write a loving note that expresses our heartfelt appreciation for someone special; we can give our time, energy, and concentration to what is important to someone else; we can take time to spend time, not merely think that we should. We can cook a special meal, gift a surprise, or make something unique that reflects our thoughtfulness and consideration.

Prayer: I pray that I can demonstrate the value and love I feel for another; help me to see that I can add to someone's life today, to lift their heart and spirit.

Take three relaxing breaths; ask your inner spirit to guide your meditation; pause for a few minutes in silence.

November 4

Don't become accustomed to misery and fail to move forward.

We can get to that point where we accept misery and get used to the hurting instead of moving forward: We want to make a career change but are afraid that we may fail; We want out of an abusive relationship but are afraid of being alone; We're drinking or smoking too much and want to quit but don't think we can handle the emotional turmoil without our crutch. We become convinced that the devil we don't know is much worse than the devil we know so we stay mired in misery.

Even a small misery prevents happiness and peace of mind. We may want to feel better but can't make it happen; perhaps we need to remember that each of us has a source of inner power that we can call on to help us.

This power can overcome fear, help us move off the dead center of indecision, and give us the strength to move ahead in spite of our misgivings. It can open our eyes so that we see a different view—we see that we do have value, that we need not be afraid of the unknown, that we can find support, strength, and assistance to move out of this pain. This indwelling spirit can replace our discouragement with hope, our trepidation with confidence, and our worry with peace.

But we must initiate the action—we must pray, ask for help, guidance, and strength and do this over and over until we feel the presence of power within us.

Prayer: Dear God, I ask that I feel the power of your presence within me; give me the courage and strength to make changes in my life that will benefit me and help me live the life you desire for me.

Take three relaxing breaths; ask your inner spirit to guide your meditation; pause for a few minutes in silence.

November 5

Our reaction to another's misfortune reflects our true character.

We may encounter people who break a trust, betray us, take financial advantage or do a hundred other unloving things. And we might be around when something bad happens in their life; they have an accident, someone in their family gets sick, they lose their job, or have their own financial problems. If we take even a little pleasure in their pain we might not be as loving, kind, and compassionate as we pretend.

It may be human to have the "they got what they deserved" feelings but spiritual maturity requires an elevated level of actions, words, and thoughts. If we have that temporary glitch of satisfaction, we recognize it as an opportunity for growth; we don't dwell on guilt or self-incrimination but simply move beyond it.

We limit our growth if we ignore or justify these less-than-righteous attitudes. If this is a repetitive problem, we disclose our secret to a trusted friend or advisor which often provides the incentive to take action and remove this blemish on our character. We access our spiritual foundation, admit our shortcoming, and ask for help knowing that this spiritual reservoir is the source of power and direction for transformation; we seek to be more understanding, compassionate, kind, empathetic, and forgiving; we evaluate if there is any action we can take that would strengthen our resolve to improve—like offering help, condolences, or empathy to the suffering person.

Prayer: My loving inner spirit, please help me be the best I can be. Let your power strengthen me, your love envelop me, and your purpose uplift me. Guide my thoughts, words and actions this day

Take three relaxing breaths; ask your inner spirit to guide your meditation; pause for a few minutes in silence.

November 6

Decisions create character; making a choice for good inherently means that the potential for bad must exist.

Is *courage* desirable? Then must we be reared in an environment which necessitates grappling with hardships and reacting to disappointments.
Is *altruism* desirable? Then we must encounter situations of social inequality.
Is *hope* desirable? Then we must be confronted with insecurities and recurrent uncertainties.
Is *faith* desirable? Then must our mind find itself in that troublesome predicament where it ever knows less than it can believe.
Is the *love of truth* and the willingness to go wherever it leads desirable? Then must we grow up in a world where error is present and falsehood always possible.
Is *idealism* desirable? Then must we struggle in surroundings that stimulate the irrepressible reach for better things.
Is *loyalty* desirable? Then must we carry on amid the possibilities of betrayal and desertion.
Is *unselfishness* desirable? Then must mortal man live face to face with the incessant clamoring of an inescapable self for recognition and honor. We could not choose the divine life if there were no self-life to forsake.
Is *pleasure* desirable? Then must we live in a world where the alternative of pain and the likelihood of suffering are ever-present experiential possibilities.

--Urantia Book p. 51.

Prayer: Help me to see the challenges I face as opportunities necessary for growth; let me not become overwhelmed or discouraged.

Take three relaxing breaths; ask your inner spirit to guide your meditation; pause for a few minutes in silence.

November 7

**Everything happens for a reason;
sometimes the reason is stupidity or selfishness—but it's a reason.**

For every action, there is a reaction; for every cause, an effect. But we must not attribute the wrong cause for what we experience. We are offered a life of peace, love, and hope but will invariably encounter adversity, unfair situations, betrayal, grief, disappointment, and other pain. Let us not rush to blame the universe or God for this turmoil but understand other reasons often actually cause these events:

- Free-will choice—someone (or our self) chooses to act and it affected us; the action may have been based on righteous choices or it may have resulted from false perceptions, ignorance, stupidity, or selfishness.
- Random accidents—someone was simply in the wrong place at the wrong time.
- Misfortunes of nature—we (they) may suffer from a disease or other act of nature that causes pain.

Let's be absolutely clear: A loving God does not afflict his children; he never selects a person to have an accident, suffer disease, or die. We should not blame him; he is not the source of the problem but is the solution. He offers each of us an inner spirit with the strength to triumph over suffering, his healing love to warm our heart when in pain, spiritual insight to understand when confused, the sense of absolute security that we are children of the divine with a purpose and destiny.

Prayer: I pray that I understand the truth about cause and effect. Help me accept in my deepest heart, mind, and soul that my God is a loving God; that he gives only love to each of us; he never harms or afflicts us but is always there to help when the world causes pain.

Take three relaxing breaths; ask your inner spirit to guide your meditation; pause for a few minutes in silence.

November 8

We do not have to accept beliefs that are spiritually repugnant or intellectually dishonest.

Our world hosts a wide variety of religions. We may find it hard to see love in some; others may appear intellectually dishonest or inconsistent. We may search for concepts that seem righteous to us and use a variety of ideas to build our beliefs: We may subscribe to an organized belief system; We may take parts from a certain belief but reject other ideas; We may seek guidance from our inner leadings; We may see what works for others and adopt these. Perhaps a few basic concepts can help in this construction.

Each of us is a child of the divine, the offspring of a loving spiritual parent who has given us specific gifts: 1) Free-will choice that allows us to decide if we do believe, what we believe, and how deeply we engage in the relationship with our source; 2) An indwelling divine presence that provides strength, guidance, and security if we choose to experience it; and 3) A unique personality that makes our approach to God an individual, personal journey.

As we become aware, we experience additional spiritual reassurances: The Spirit of Truth—the certainty of truth resonates throughout our being when we discover truth; Solutions to some challenges appear out of nowhere; A person says the exact words we need to hear; We find a peace that passes all human understanding when our world is in chaos. These and other spirit reassurances guide us in building our relationship with our divine creator.

Prayer: I pray that I am open and receptive to the leadings of the spirit; guide me to find and receive what I need so that I can be the person God wants me to be.

Take three relaxing breaths; ask your inner spirit to guide your meditation; pause for a few minutes in silence.

November 9

"Thank God I got what I got instead of what I deserved" speaks recognition and gratitude for grace.

We may have made a lot of mistakes, hurt others and our self, and not believe that we could correct our errors or change our life; then, something inexplicable happened and we have an opportunity to change. We know that we have received a gift that was bestowed in spite of our actions and intentions—not because of them. This is grace, the reward that we only have to receive. It grants us light where there was only darkness. What we do with this opportunity determines our true gratitude and affects our life course.

Do we bask in the momentary reprieve, give God a "Thank you," and repeat the patterns that caused our troubles? Do we make some short-term changes but then fall prey to self-will and re-create our old problems? Or do we take full advantage of this gift? Are we willing to work for real change? Will we embark on a day-by-day life-long journey to be the best person we can be? Will we make the effort to honestly and fearlessly examine our motives, expectations, and perceptions that led us into misery? Will we seek the true source of strength, direction, and security—that wonderful divine power that dwells in the quiet places of our heart and mind?

Grace brings opportunities and choices; it's up to us what we do with them. Today, let us be aware of opportunities for growth and respond to them.

Prayer: My loving source and divine center, thank you for all that you have given me. Move me to take full advantage of this opportunity today; help me to change so that I keep in constant contact with you and seek your guidance and power in all I do.

Take three relaxing breaths; ask your inner spirit to guide your meditation; pause for a few minutes in silence.

November 10

When I am spiritually weak, other people can control my feelings; I can feel guilty and have done nothing wrong.

We may have loving, supportive friends and family who want the best for us or we may have the opposite—a number of acquaintances who do not care about our well-being but try to control, manipulate, or even destroy us. Likely, we have a mix of these.

If we're human but not approaching sainthood, we'll experience those times when we allow the opinion, words, or actions of these people to affect our emotional life; our source of true strength and impregnable values has eroded. Such a temporary lapse in our spiritual condition does not affect our core but weakens the protective armor that shields us from the world.

We reclaim our power and strength; we make a concentrated effort to open the lines of communication and communion with our inner spirit. The outside world may seem hectic, busy, demanding, or even overwhelming but we know that our priority must be inner peace, that this is what determines the quality of our day. We take time, find that quiet place, pause, practice our relaxation breathing, and pray. We connect; we feel the peace; we feel the flow of energy that brings strength, satisfaction, and security. We know that we are a child of the divine; we do not have to allow anyone else, or our self, to make us less than we are.

Prayer: My divine source I pray that I can come to you as soon as I feel weak, whenever I allow other people to control my feelings, or when I am anxious or afraid. At any inner disturbance, let me quickly turn to you, my source of all power and goodness.

Take three relaxing breaths; ask your inner spirit to guide your meditation; pause for a few minutes in silence.

November 11

If we "do the do," it'll keep getting better one day at a time.

"Do the do." If we want to bake a cake, we find the right recipe, get the ingredients, and mix and bake as instructed. If the instructions say to bake at 350 degrees for 45 minutes, we can't bake it at 400 degrees for 30 minutes. If we want the cake, we need to follow directions. Also, we won't get much of a cake if we meticulously gather all the ingredients, sit back and look at them, drooling and anticipating as we think about our great cake. "Do the do" means that we *follow instructions* and actually *do every step of the work.*

"It'll get better" actually means that "I'll get better." As we find and explore this beautiful and powerful spiritual relationship, as we quiet the incessant clamoring of our mind and find our inner core of strength, power, and purpose, we experience peace. Slowly—day by day, experience by experience and mistake by mistake—we learn to act and react with love, calmness, patience, tolerance, strength, and poise; our attitude and outlook transform; we create fewer problems for others and our self. Our inner peace grants us the ability to accept gifts of love but reject offers of misery from other people.

This changes our place in the world; we live and function *in* the world but have found a haven that is separate from the chaos and misery. "It" gets better one day at a time.

Prayer: Help me to be humble and accept that I need to change; grant that I am willing to follow directions, not do things my way, and persevere in this spiritual journey. Give me strength and peace.

Take three relaxing breaths; ask your inner spirit to guide your meditation; pause for a few minutes in silence.

November 12

We are responsible for our thoughts, feelings, words, and actions today—both for what we do and what we don't do.

Today, will we allow our self-directed ways to determine our thoughts, feelings, words, and actions? Will we live as a merely mediocre human or choose to follow an elevated path? Will we allow our ingrained reactions to control our day or will we try to be aware of all our decisions and pause to find a better way?

We have the power of choice to decide the life we live this day and are responsible for how we use this awesome power

If we change our thoughts, we change our feelings which changes our words and actions; we change our moment and change our day. Our inner spiritual power is often the only energy that can transform our thoughts, shifting them from our selfish, self-centered, self-pitying tendencies to love, patience, tolerance, and service. We have the choice to do it or not do it.

Will we take the time to pray and meditate or will we offer excuses why we are too busy or don't really need to? Will we do something loving for our self and another person—or merely offer lip service to the idea? If we believe God is real and important in our life, will we make the effort to build our relationship or only hope that it happens? If we believe that we must share our blessings in order to keep them, will we actively seek someone with whom to share or hope that we stumble across someone and recognize the opportunity? How do we fulfill our responsibility as child of the divine?

Prayer: My inner guide, help me be responsible today. Stir me to take actions that fulfill my responsibility as a child of God. Let me willingly accept this task with love, courage, and hope.

Take three relaxing breaths; ask your inner spirit to guide your meditation; pause for a few minutes in silence.

November 13

**The Dark Side is always there,
patiently waiting for the opportunity to direct our life.**

The dark side is not some evil force that wants to lead us down the misery path. It is simply our ego plus the materialistic, secular world that elevates and idolizes our self-driven attitudes. If we have allowed selfishness, self-centeredness, self-righteousness, and self-pity to influence many of our decisions, we've established that pattern of action/reaction. The world, situations, and people are always there; they'll invite us to revert to our old way of acting that ultimately cause us pain and misery. This may not happen as a conscious betrayal of our developing divine instincts but just a gradual slipping into old habits.

The outer world offers many opportunities for our regression. Our past choices may have established a pattern that would choose the lower path but we have all the power necessary to overcome any temptation. We have the inner reservoir of strength, source, and conviction that is our birthright as a child of God. We only have to 1) make the conscious choice to access this innate source, 2) take the time to make contact, and 3) open the conduit to allow the power and love to flow from this inner source to direct our mind and dominate our actions. If we do this, the dark side can never prevail against us.

Today, for each choice, do we follow self-direction or do we align with God's will? Do we rely on our own power or do we open the conduit of love and power from our source?

Prayer: I have tasted the great life. Please help me not fall back into my old patterns of feeling and behavior; help me constantly stay aware of your presence, love, and power; let me do my part in our relationship.

Take three relaxing breaths; ask your inner spirit to guide your meditation; pause for a few minutes in silence.

November 14

It's difficult to change habits.

Habits—ingrained patterns—influence much of our daily life. Hopefully, we reach that point where we want to discard old, harmful habits and gain new ones that benefit us. Deeply desiring this doesn't produce any results by itself; we must have a proven plan that yields the desired result and then implement that plan—repeat the desired action over and over until the new habit replaces the old one.

For example, we may sincerely want to replace our self-centered thinking with a conscious contact with God. Part of our plan includes performing dedicated morning exercises. We start to do this but have difficulty; we simply have a problem making it happen. Here, we take specific action: We share our commitment with a trusted friend or spiritual advisor.

When we retire at night, we lay the morning material where it's visible and available. Then, in our nightly prayers, we ask for help—the strength and willingness to carry through on our morning commitment; we set our alarm earlier and dedicate twenty minutes in the morning for spiritual growth. We take a moment to review our day and check our progress. Upon awakening, we say a quick prayer of gratitude before we arise and ask again for help to keep our pledge.

We use any failure to reinforce, not diminish, our commitment; we will not be denied! Thirty days of doing this starts to establish the new habit and we experience the results in our life. Then, we expand and adopt more new habits.

Prayer: I pray that my desire for a better life leads me to change the habits that harm me. Help me to be willing to change; give me the strength and initiative to take action until the new ways replace my old habits.

Take three relaxing breaths; ask your inner spirit to guide your meditation; pause for a few minutes in silence.

November 15

What we see (or think we see) determines our understanding.

> Mentally picture a cave man in your mind's eye: A short, misshapen, ugly, snarling hulk of a man standing, legs spread, club upraised, breathing hate and animosity as he looks fiercely straight ahead. Such a picture hardly depicts the divine dignity of the species. Now, enlarge the picture. In front of this animated human crouches a saber-tooth tiger ready to pounce. Behind him are a woman and two children. Immediately you recognize that such a picture stands for much that is fine and noble in the human race. *But the man is exactly the same in both pictures. Only in the second sketch you are favored with a widened horizon that changed your perception of his attitude.* You can discern the motivation of this early human. Instead of seeing him as belligerent and fearsome, his attitude becomes praiseworthy because you understand him. When you can fathom the motives of your associates, the better you can understand them. (The Urantia Book.)

Understanding produces tolerance; tolerance leads to acceptance and acceptance opens the opportunity for love. When someone behaves objectionably or has blatantly done us wrong, we may not always be able to discern the saber-tooth tiger that is threatening him or her, but be assured there is one. The tiger may be from long ago or today, but such a threat changes anyone. Always remember that people who feel loved, act lovingly; those who feel fear, act un-lovingly.

Prayer: Dear God, grant me tolerance and acceptance of everyone I meet today; help me bestow love where it is most needed; let me respond to belligerence and contention with peace, love, and spiritual awareness.

Take three relaxing breaths; ask your inner spirit to guide your meditation; pause for a few minutes in silence.

November 16

Pride—not a law or ethical code—makes us false martyrs; wisdom may dictate surrender but admitting defeat requires courage and humility.

Surrender: *to cease fighting or resisting and admit defeat*

Do we get bloodied fighting a battle we know we can't win, while thinking "If I change this one thing, it'll turn out different?"—and it never does. Do we keep repeating our actions and getting the same results? Is fear or pride keeping us in a hurtful, abusive relationship while we daydream about salvation? Surrendering requires courage and humility but opens doors that stay closed as long as we fight.

Our need to surrender may involve a crisis area of our life or it may only be a repetitive daily struggle. It's a relief when we finally let go; we feel as if a weight is removed. At first, we may feel hopeless, like we have a big void inside of us and no idea of what we need to do. Then, we notice something.

Our awareness is awakening; we start seeing answers where before we had only problems; unexpected opportunities appear and offer a chance for change. Our mind recognizes new ideas and adopts a more hopeful outlook. Our attitude shifts; we're a little more positive. Our spirit finds entrance into our life and offers peace, strength, direction, and hope that can only flow to the non-resisting, surrendered soul. Today, let us ask our self: *Is there any area in my life which I need to surrender and let go?*

Prayer: Dear God, help me not be afraid of surrender; grant me the humility to accept when I need to let go of my ideas, actions, and habits that harm me or keep me mired in misery or mediocrity; give me the courage to surrender.

Take three relaxing breaths; ask your inner spirit to guide your meditation; pause for a few minutes in silence.

November 17

"It is my will that your will be done" is a consecration of will, not a relinquishing of will.

Our "will" is our power to make decisions and to initiate and consummate action. This is a sovereign power gifted to us by our divine source. Nothing in the universe can override it and make us do what we choose not to do. When some hear that following a spiritual path requires surrendering our will to God, they wonder "What happens to me if I completely relinquish my will? It's as if I'll be nothing."

Using "It is *my will* that *your will* be done" offers a different perception and understanding; this reflects that we are using our power of choice (our will) to align our choices with a new and different purpose and direction. We are not giving up our will but actually using it to choose God's will.

Saying this, even deeply desiring that God's will be done in our life is a great start but must be repeated many times throughout the day. We still retain our will—that power to make decisions and initiate action—and must use it for each decision we face this day; we must choose whether we follow God's will or return to our old path of self-destructive will.

Today, will we do it our way or try something better? How about right now? Will you take time to connect with your spirit or blindly rush into the day?

Prayer: Today, I choose to do your will; guide my decision and let me see what you would have me do. Help my thoughts, words, and acts align with your divine principles of love, compassion, patience, tolerance, and service.

Take three relaxing breaths; ask your inner spirit to guide your meditation; pause for a few minutes in silence.

November 18

The polishing of friction uncovers the gemstone's beauty; character is forged between the hammer of adversity and the anvil of pain.

Loving someone who loves and adores us is easy; loving one who irritates, despises, betrays, or hurts us isn't. Getting the new job, the promotion, or the dream house brings a sense of well-being; getting fired, not have rent money, or suffering illness offer opportunities for anger, anxiety, and sleepless nights. Even if we are trying to live a spirit-centered life, the world, other people, and circumstances can present difficulties and pain. Bad things can happen to us but we have a choice about how deeply we allow them to affect us.

Will we allow fear to overwhelm us and ruin our day(s)—or will we use our new life tools to pause and find peace, power, and direction? Will we regress to anger—or will we patiently strive for love and tolerance? Will we blame another person—or honestly seek to see if we played any part in the situation and take full responsibility if we did? Will we stay stuck in the problem—or daringly search for a solution? Will we allow our dark side of self-driven will to take us into the abyss—or is our faith strong enough to repel all assaults or to help us change direction if we do succumb to temporary temptation?

God does not assure a life free of difficulty but he does promise strength, guidance, and love to surmount all challenges and that we never have to endure anything alone.

Prayer: Help me face this day with confidence that you, my divine source will supply all I need; help me turn to you at any disturbance for I know that you have all the solutions and power.

Take three relaxing breaths; ask your inner spirit to guide your meditation; pause for a few minutes in silence.

November 19

It doesn't take a very big person to carry a grudge but it takes a giant to forgive.

Walking through life with resentments and grudges against others takes a pretty heavy toll on us but we find ourselves doing this without ever being aware of it and then just stay there. We blame, justify, and rationalize why we're right for what we do and how we feel; we don't have to take any responsibility for anything; we don't have to look at our self; we don't have to change; we keep plowing ahead. But forgiving everyone (including our self and God) can take a lot of effort and persistence.

Becoming dissatisfied with our self and the way we feel starts the forgiveness process. We get tired of regurgitating the anger, the blame, and the self-destructive emotions; or we experience an insight, a personal revelation that we cannot grow or improve unless we release this weight of un-forgiveness. We stop thinking we should do this and actually take action.

We pick up pen and paper; we pray for willingness and honesty; we fearlessly write about what happened, what part we had in it, and our honest feelings about it; we discuss this with a trusted friend or spiritual advisor. Then, we release it; we ask God to let us see things differently, to make forgiveness possible; we ask that he remove all the negative, hurtful feelings and to replace them with tolerance, understanding, and love; we pray that the other person enjoy a bounty of love, peace, strength, and hope.

Prayer: Dear God, please open my heart, mind, and soul; help me forgive all real or imagined wrongs done to me. Let me feel the weight lifted; fill me with peace, let me bestow love to everyone.

Take three relaxing breaths; ask your inner spirit to guide your meditation; pause for a few minutes in silence.

November 20

We must judge actions but not value or destiny.

We live in a world of interactions with other people and may sometimes encounter contention and conflict. Some believe that any type of judging is wrong but this can let us repeat mistakes, allow others to take unfair advantage, or blithely ignore acts of evil. Others tend to be overly judgmental and denounce a person's worth based on a few visible acts.

As we mature, we understand that we can disagree with a person's actions while recognizing that he or she is a child of God; we can condemn the act while feeling compassion for the actor.

We invariably face those times when another person's actions interfere with our life. Here, we avoid any emotional reaction or judgment; we take a few minutes to relax and find our center of peace. We ask that any negative feelings—anger, self-pity, anxiety and so on—be removed from our heart, mind, and soul; we ask that we are able to see this situation objectively, that we don't allow any previous bias, shortcoming, or fear to affect our conclusion.

Then we ask: How can I avoid or minimize the effect of this act on my life? If the act is wrong, do I have a responsibility to respond? What is my best response as a maturing child of the divine? How do I weigh staying silent against speaking out or acting? How important is it really? Does this act reflect the actions of a person who feels love and peace—or one who feels animosity and fear? What can I do to impart spiritual values in this situation?

Prayer: My inner guide and source of strength, grant me the insight to see this situation as you would have me see it; grant me the judgment, courage, and power to act according to your plan.

Take three relaxing breaths; ask your inner spirit to guide your meditation; pause for a few minutes in silence.

November 21

Do we have hidden pet vices that hamper happiness and block spiritual growth?

Many of us have that one thing that we really don't want to release or to acknowledge to God. We tell our self that we want to be rid it of but make little or no progress. It causes problems in our relationship with God, our self, and others but we rationalize and justify why we don't have to let it go. Or we may just repeatedly feel contention and wonder why; we don't want to put the searchlight on a character flaw that we hold dear. Procrastination, dishonesty, anger, fear, guilt, self-pity, and self-righteousness represent a few of these pets.

Whenever we feel discouraged, beaten, irritated, afraid, or unloved, we pause and ask our self: "What character trait in me makes me feel this way? Am I willing to release it and feel better?"

We say a prayer asking for courage, humility, and honesty; we root out the underlying cause of our discomfort forsaking blame, excuses, and justification; we seek the help of a trusted friend or spiritual advisor if necessary; we truthfully examine our past to see how often we use this trait and look at the consequences; we become willing to let it go; and then we ask our spirit source to remove it. Our spiritual power is a mighty expulsive energy that can eliminate or minimize the effects of any pet shortcoming.

Prayer: I pray that I may be aware of any trait that keeps me from my best life. Guide me to accept that this does not have to be part of me, that you can and will remove it. Help me be willing to trust you and release it; if needed, help me be willing to be willing.

Take three relaxing breaths; ask your inner spirit to guide your meditation; pause for a few minutes in silence.

November 22

Our mind can be a seething cauldron constantly spewing thoughts to get our attention; we grab the most disturbing one for consideration.

Our self-focused life has trained our mind to respond to life with thought after thought after thought. It continuously offers thoughts that concern our prestige, relationships, finances, or sex life; these can be true, partially true, completely false, or only a fantasy. However, one of them grabs our attention and we build a case why it is the most important thing we face at this moment.

But liberated souls learn to direct the mind; they have discovered that free will, coupled with the indwelling spiritual power can fracture the ego-generated shackles. Prayer and meditation re-train our mind, slowly and progressively replacing the old mental-emotional response habits with healthy and more beneficial patterns.

Today, we commit to freedom; we take action to not automatically react to the disturbing thoughts. We take three or four deep relaxation breaths, connect with our inner spirit and ask that our mind be spiritually directed. We gain stillness and invite the gifts of serenity, love, and security; we savor the embrace of the spirit and feel peace pervade our body. Anytime we notice that our mind has again taken prisoner of our day, we pause, relax, and ask our spirit to melt all thoughts that do not help us and to guide our mind.

Prayer: My loving spirit, I recognize that my self-focused thoughts cause contention and keep me from the light; I cannot control my mind without your aid. I ask that you renew my mind by the transforming power of your indwelling spirit.

Take three relaxing breaths; ask your inner spirit to guide your meditation; pause for a few minutes in silence.

November 23

The world, people, and circumstances have influenced where we stand today; however, it is our choice how much power we give the past.

We start life with beautiful impulses and desires that reflect our divine birthright; then, the world contaminates our beauty. The power of "self" abounds; secular rewards and false adulation flow to the self-focused person although many lack peace, harmony, and love. Atheistic science shouts that we do not need God and organized religion offers little rebuttal that withstands the scrutiny of a modern person. This confusion and chaos has affected our life and brought us to where we are right now but we no longer have to accept what doesn't work. We have discovered the "kingdom of heaven within."

Our spiritual reservoir offers us the power to break the shackles of the past; we remember the experiences to avoid repeating mistakes but release all emotional ties to them. We surrender our disappointments, heartaches, fears, and all misery and watch spiritual love dissolve them. Our inner spirit and the fellowship of our spiritual family help us find solutions for daily problems; we experience peace in the face of tribulation and disappointment; we know that we have an additional power to overcome all tribulations; we have a new direction and purpose for living; we experience an undying hope.

We have come home; the past cannot dominate us.

Prayer: I pray that my spirit may grant me the power to withstand the onslaught of the world. Let me access peace and strength from my divine source; help me to pause and pray at the slightest conflict.

Take three relaxing breaths; ask your inner spirit to guide your meditation; pause for a few minutes in silence.

November 24

Let us acknowledge gratitude for the gifts from our inner spirit.

Each of us has received a precious blessing from our divine source—the indwelling divine spark, the Buddha within, the kingdom of heaven within that is a reservoir of potential power, guidance, courage, peace, and love. Desperation or surrender may open a conduit to receive these transforming gifts but keeping the channel clear requires daily prayer and meditation. Our life improves as we practice these devotions and it is helpful to acknowledge the gifts we receive from our indwelling spirit:

- In the midst of turmoil and contention, you offer peace.
- When fear invades, you offer courage.
- When overcome with anxiety and stress, you offer calmness.
- If our mind is confused, plagued by a whirlwind of thoughts, seemingly without direction and cannot be quieted, you bestow the power to bring order and purpose out of chaos.
- When we are at our darkest time, tortured by pain, facing our limitations and failures, you grant hope—the certainty that anything can be forgiven and repaired, that we can rise again to our place of dignity, value, and wholeness and experience the ever-present love of our divine creator.

My inner spirit, you are always there, patiently awaiting me to call upon you and I am grateful.

Prayer: My dear and loving inner guide, I give thanks for all the help you have given me. Help me never hesitate but to come to you with all the challenges and uncertainty I may face this day and wait quietly until you grant me direction.

Take three relaxing breaths; ask your inner spirit to guide your meditation; pause for a few minutes in silence.

November 25

Initially, my mind got a big belly laugh when I wanted to practice meditation.

I can see it chuckling to itself and saying "Right, go ahead and try it and see what I do. You don't have a chance." For many of us, our mind has ruled our life for years; it goes where it wants and does what it desires. It seems to have a mind of its own and rebels against any form of control. It does not want to relinquish its' power; as we attempt meditation, a myriad of thoughts flit across our consciousness trying to distract us. Controlling this mighty machine requires perseverance and continuous practice.

We are physical, mental, and spiritual beings. In meditation, we can use deep relaxation breathing to calm our body; then we relax our mind, releasing all thoughts, simply letting them go. When thoughts return to interrupt our meditation, we use a sacred, quieting word; we use something that is meaningful to us such as *peace..., love...,* or *serenity...* or '*Be still and listen*' or just '*Shhhh..., be still*' to quiet our wandering mind. We don't resist them but simply do not engage the intruding thoughts; we mentally say, repeat, and keep repeating our sacred word to return to stillness. These repeated distractions are not failures but offer opportunities for us to choose and demonstrate that we desire to be closer to our spiritual source.

A few seconds of inner peace and stillness can open portals to a new dimension and those seconds only get longer and better with practice. You'll never know unless you try.

Prayer: Dear God, I sincerely want to be closer to you. Please quiet my mind, help me enjoy the stillness of the spirit. Renew my mind by the transforming power of your indwelling spirit.

Take three relaxing breaths; ask your inner spirit to guide your meditation; pause for a few minutes in silence.

November 26

You don't have to ride the bull.

Have you ever seen those cowboys ride a 1000 pound bull? They train to stay on the back of this ferocious animal for only eight seconds; if they are thrown off, the animal tries to maim or kill them.

This is similar to anger management techniques that teach skills to manage this ferocious emotion. They may help manage it, but would it not be wiser to eliminate the anger instead of learning to manage it after it's got a hold on us? If we don't get on the bull, we don't have to worry about getting bucked off and facing annihilation.

Accepting anger as "normal" provides automatic excuses to keep doing it; recognizing it as a childish behavior reflecting spiritual and emotional immaturity moves us to take steps to minimize this feeling.

In our morning prayers, we ask to be made aware of any slight inner disturbances that may lead to anger and that we handle these while small; we reflect that we do not want to allow other people to control our feelings; we ask for help to pause when we feel the onset of anger and to remember that an outburst can damage any relationship. When we get angry, we acknowledge it without excuses or blame; we immediately ask our inner spirit to melt this feeling and help us be more tolerant, patient, compassionate, accepting, and loving. We are always wrong when we react in anger and can slowly wean ourselves from this childish behavior.

Prayer: I pray that all feelings of anger melt away. Fill my heart, mind, and soul with love, tolerance, patience and compassion. Grant me that ten second hesitation and guide me to ask for your help before I respond every time I feel irritable, angry, or contentious.

Take three relaxing breaths; ask your inner spirit to guide your meditation; pause for a few minutes in silence.

November 27

Severe suffering and desperation can forge us into the most fortunate people on the planet.

If we have experienced "hell on earth" and have found a spiritual power to overcome this desperate state, we are the fortunate warrior-priest. We have joined the battle, met defeat, discovered our inner reservoir of spiritual energy, and arose victorious. To us, a spiritual transformation is not a theory but a verifiable fact and the foundation of our life. We know the dark side of self-driven will but also know that it can be defeated by the grace and power of God. Such proven results are difficult for any open-minded person to ignore or discount.

Two-fold responsibility comes with this salvation. First, we must continuously strive to fulfill our resurrected potential; we do not let the 'good' become the enemy of the 'best' but stay conscious that we are embarking on a life-long journey of spiritual growth and emotional maturity; we never allow self-satisfaction or complacency stop or delay our growth. We commit to, and perform, daily spiritual maintenance, always recognizing our shortcomings and reaching to become better than we are.

Then we know that we must share this wonderful free gift with all who are seeking; for without sharing, it withers and dies. We make a conscious effort to maintain gratitude, always remembering where we came from and the wonder we now enjoy. Let us be grateful for the bad times we overcame.

Prayer: My loving spirit, guide and sustain me in all areas of my life this day. Help me to grow according to your plan; let me share this wonderful gift of love that flows from our divine source with any willing person.

Take three relaxing breaths; ask your inner spirit to guide your meditation; pause for a few minutes in silence.

November 28

Let us open our heart, mind, and soul to any truth that may enhance our spiritual progress.

Consider the Sermon on the Mount; it is sometimes ignored because of misunderstanding or the belief that it doesn't apply to our modern age. The different translations that yield different presentations increase the challenge: "Happy are the poor in spirit" is different from "Blessed are the poor in spirit." These statements focus on the highest form of happiness that results from experiencing God as a spiritual parent and the ensuing truth that all humanity is one family:

- Happy are the poor in spirit, the humble.
- Happy are those who hunger and thirst for righteousness, for they shall be filled.
- Happy are the meek for they shall inherit the earth.
- Happy are the pure in heart for they shall see God.
- Happy are they who mourn, for they shall be comforted.
- Happy are the merciful, for they shall obtain mercy.
- Happy are the peacemakers, for they shall be called the sons of God.
- Happy are those who are persecuted for righteousness sake, for theirs is the kingdom of heaven. Happy are you when men shall revile you and persecute you and say all manner of evil against you falsely. Rejoice and be exceeding glad, for great is your reward in heaven.

For the next few days, let's reflect on how these traits may affect our happiness today.

Prayer: Dear God, open my eyes that I may see all your truth that I am capable of receiving. Increase my capacity to accept your blessings and let me share all that I receive with others.

Take three relaxing breaths; ask your inner spirit to guide your meditation; pause for a few minutes in silence.

November 29

"Happy are the poor in spirit, the humble."

How can humility lead to happiness? Well, consider how its opposites of pride and self-righteousness lead to misery. How many times in our life have we caused our self problems when we fail to seek help or admit when we're wrong, or when we discount or disregard other opinions and ideas, or when we blindly pursue a path of destruction without opening our eyes to the truth?

Humility is not a groveling, self-loathing, "I'm lower than anything" attitude but is simply realizing that we don't know everything, that we are teachable, that we don't see our self as above or below other people and always knowing that we are less than God. We know and stay constantly aware that the power and direction for the best life comes from our divine source and not from our limited human capabilities.

Consider the wisdom of Lao Tsu when he wrote that "The value of a vessel is its emptiness." If we want to serve our guests a glass of sparkling water but the pitcher is full of dirty water, what value does it have? It must be emptied; then, it can be filled with clean water.

We also must be empty in order to be filled. We experience happiness when we choose the righteous fillers, when we choose to partake of the spiritual bounty that gives us direction, purpose, values, strength and peace that surpass our mortal abilities.

Prayer: Dear God, help me to be humble, to be teachable. Make me aware any time I succumb to self-righteousness or pride and let me seek your grace and power immediately to remove these burdens.

Take three relaxing breaths; ask your inner spirit to guide your meditation; pause for a few minutes in silence.

November 30

"Happy are those who hunger and thirst for righteousness, for they shall be filled."

Righteous: *doing that which is right, just, upright; especially free from wrong, guilt or sin; virtuous, worthy.*

How does hungering to be righteous have anything to do with happiness?

If we are not hungry, we do not long for food. The pangs of true hunger are a tremendous driving force that moves us to seek nourishment, to find that which sustains and fulfills. In the case of righteousness, we find happiness in the seeking; we do not have to attain the goal to get the rewards.

Realizing the immediate and eternal value of "doing that which is right" gives us a goal and purpose in life; accepting that this is a journey lets us appreciate each accomplishment as we move forward.

We enjoy a sense of pleasure each time we overcome one of our shortcomings and act with love, compassion, tolerance, patience, or exhibit other divine qualities. We experience a burst of joy and satisfaction when we hold words that we would have formally uttered in anger; when we help someone anonymously; when we find peace in prayer; when we avoid getting upset over material upheaval; when we see disappointments as opportunities; when we avoid a temptation that previously would have brought us down.

Prayer: I pray that I may find happiness in doing right; let me know the joy of releasing control and aligning my will with God's will for me; make me aware and appreciative of our victories that move me in the path of righteousness.

Take three relaxing breaths; ask your inner spirit to guide your meditation; pause for a few minutes in silence.

December 1

"Happy are the meek for they shall inherit the earth."

Meekness is often a misunderstood quality; it is not weakness and does not reflect a timid, fearful attitude that subjugates our will, values, goals, and desires to what someone else wants. Meekness is simply aligning our will with God's; we choose to follow a divine path rather than a path of self-driven will or the ways of the world.

Patience and forbearance are the hallmarks of meekness. We are certain of our purpose, values, and destiny; we don't have to prove that we are right; we don't have to defend; we don't have to win; we don't have to receive the applause and adulation of others; we can walk away and let others have the last word. Our spiritual foundation grants us a quiet strength and assurance that elevates us to demonstrate integrity and humility. We take a long-distance view of our life and destiny; we know that our seeming success or failure is fleeting—it will change; the current thorn in our shoe may cause temporary pain but does no lasting damage; we recognize that understanding and doing God's will today is our highest life priority.

Happiness springs from the certainty that if we align our motives and action with the divine way, the overriding goodness of the universe inevitably prevails against all temporary upheavals—we can "inherit the earth"; our inner life can dominate over the outer life; we can stay in peace no matter what is happening around us.

Prayer: I pray that I can become meek; grant me patience and understanding. Let me not respond to trifles and trivia but keep my eye, mind, and heart on the spiritual path you have for me.

Take three relaxing breaths; ask your inner spirit to guide your meditation; pause for a few minutes in silence.

December 2

"Happy are the pure in heart for they shall see God."

The phrase "pure in heart" does not imply that we are ready for sainthood but that we have shifted our life from being self-centered or world-centered to being God-centered; we have chosen to live the way we think God wants us to live. This choice and our daily attempt to improve make us "pure in heart"; our motives, purpose, and goals are spiritual and not self-driven. This is a lifelong effort and we strive for daily improvement.

"...they shall see God" implies that we acquire the attitude of spiritual insight; we see things from the viewpoint of the spirit rather than from the viewpoint of the material world. We recognize that disappointments and apparent defeat offer opportunities for growth, that difficulties give us a chance to demonstrate spiritual power and strength, and that rejection and condemnation can enlarge us but not lessen us. We start to see the wonder and love of God in many things—nature, events, relationships, and our personal growth; we acknowledge grace and express our gratitude.

If we have those who attack us or try to use us, we stay aware that they have an indwelling spark of God, they are children of the divine and part of our human family; we respond with dignity, self-respect, and poise; we try to eliminate or minimize their negative impact on our lives without judging their spiritual value or destiny.

Prayer: My loving divine source, grant that I may be pure in heart today; I choose to align my will with yours in all things. Let me see with spiritual vision; let your power shield me from the ways of the world.

Take three relaxing breaths; ask your inner spirit to guide your meditation; pause for a few minutes in silence.

December 3

"Happy are they who mourn, for they shall be comforted."

Yes, mourning includes our traditional understanding of grief and expressing a sense of loss but it also expands beyond these. An enlightened understanding includes tenderheartedness, compassion, and sympathy—being sensitive and responsive to human need.

We see this enhanced consideration of mourning and the desire to love and serve others reflected in the beautiful prayer of St. Francis:

"Lord, make me a channel of thy peace.
Where there is hatred, let me sow love;
Where there is injury, pardon;
Where there is doubt, faith;
Where there is despair, hope;
Where there is darkness, light;
Where there is sadness, joy.
O divine Master, grant that I may not so much seek
To be consoled as to console,
To be understood as to understand,
To be loved as to love.
For it is in giving that we receive;
It is in pardoning that we are pardoned;
It is in dying to self that we are born to eternal life."

Such loving service prepares the way to experience the highest level of happiness available to mortals on this planet—transcendent happiness, the happiness that results from understanding that all we think or do today aligns with a divine purpose, that the good we can do here and now contributes to each person and also to God's plan. This pleasure has more depth, quality, and meaning than happiness from any other source.

Take three relaxing breaths; ask your inner spirit to guide your meditation; pause for a few minutes in silence.

December 4

“Happy are the merciful, for they shall obtain mercy.”

Mercy: *compassion or forgiveness shown toward someone whom it is within one’s power to punish or harm.*

Like all the beatitudes, this applies to our current life and situation and not some promise of the future.

If someone has done us a real wrong, an act of extending mercy denotes loving-kindness, the embodiment of truest friendship. Spiritual growth lets us grant mercy with enlightened forgiveness; we completely relinquish all emotional conflict associated with the event but retain the fact of the experience which helps us avoid getting into similar situations.

Bestowing mercy is like any act of love; it benefits the receiver and the bestower. It demonstrates that we have a maturing spiritual insight; we are developing a point-of view that sees each person the way God sees them. We know that all people are children of God; we recognize that a child is immature and this always results in some degree of problems and mistakes. Our love for each child of God leads us to desire to do good for that person and our forgiveness and compassion are our way of doing good.

Happiness results from this act of actively returning good for evil, of giving love instead of simply remaining neutral and aloof or seeking retaliation.

Prayer: I pray that I may always be led to extend mercy; let my heart be warmed by the glow of forgiveness and compassion. Give me the strength to forgive all real or imagined wrongs against me.

Take three relaxing breaths; ask your inner spirit to guide your meditation; pause for a few minutes in silence.

December 5

"Happy are the peacemakers, for they shall be called the children of God."

No matter our religious beliefs, most accept that Jesus was a man who exemplified peace and he said "My peace I leave with you" and not merely "peace I leave with you." The ultimate peace, his type of peace, is available to us; it's a free gift but we have to follow spiritual guidelines. We must surrender and align our will with God's; then, our moments must reflect a spiritual attitude toward life instead of the worldly attitude.

To be a peace-maker, we must be at peace with our self; this requires that we first be at peace with God. When our peace is shaken, we have allowed our priorities to be misaligned and our dependence on the spirit weakened. Then, we must use all the resources available to us to regain our peace. We immediately pause, seek a moment of quiet, and open the conduit for spiritual power to flow into us.

Remember that we are children of a loving parent; what is happening now is temporary and offers an opportunity to grow; we possess a reservoir of unlimited power to overcome any upset, anxiety, defeat, or disappointment; we ask for guidance, perception, and strength to find peace. The world may assail us; people may injure us; but we have an inner bastion that lets us face any assault with poise, calmness, and equanimity.

When filled with this sublime peace, love dictates that we must share it with others; we desire to let them partake and enjoy the blessings we have received; sharing and helping others inevitably brings happiness.

Prayer: I pray that I may stay aware of your presence in my life, let me know peace and share this blessing.

Take three relaxing breaths; ask your inner spirit to guide your meditation; pause for a few minutes in silence.

December 6

"Happy are those who are persecuted for righteousness sake, for theirs is the kingdom of heaven. Happy are you when men shall revile you and persecute you and say all manner of evil against you falsely. Rejoice and be exceeding glad, for great is your reward in heaven."

Persecution ranges from mild challenges to threats to our physical, mental, emotional, and spiritual well-being. How can this possibly bring happiness? It may be rewarded in heaven but can it actually bring us pleasure today? Believe it or not, it can. But this requires a major shift in our understanding and perception—and a solid foundation in the spiritual life.

The path of the spirit may often deviate from the path of the world. We ask our self: "Are we doing our best to follow what we see as God's will for us?" If so, that is the best we can do. The persecution may rail against our beliefs or may cause us problems in the material, secular world but we have the power to triumph. We return good for evil; we demonstrate a vibrant spiritual faith that rises above the expected worldly reactions. Such a demonstration provides the occasion for the persecutor to experience the power of loving faith and offers us the opportunity for tremendous spiritual growth. In our hearts, we pray for the offender, that he or she may find an insight of God and discover peace and love; we pray for our self, that we may keep our focus on our true priorities and find the wisdom and strength we need.

Persecution always presents an opportunity; we experience happiness when we engage decisions and actions to bring us peace, when we become a living showcase for the spirit, and grow more like our divine parent.

Prayer: My loving God, grant that I may respond to any persecution with thoughts, words, and actions that reflect your attributes, that I can use such opportunities to grow more in your likeness.

Take three relaxing breaths; ask your inner spirit to guide your meditation; pause for a few minutes in silence.

December 7

What price do we put on our life?

To the active alcoholic and addict, the value of their life is the price of the next drink or next drug for if they have a shred of honesty, they know that the next one can kill them. "Normal" people don't have such a precise evaluation of the worth they put on living. Some may consider "Would I forfeit my life for my child, a loved one, or a stranger?" and find some idea of life-value. But each of us should recognize that there is more to life than merely a beating heart and taking a breath.

Medical science is uncovering connections between emotional health and physical health. Resentments, anger, stress, and anxiety have been linked to various diseases and conditions; inner peace has been found to promote physical healing; meditation has been scientifically proven to improve many physical and psychological conditions. Each time we get angry, indulge in self-pity, succumb to stress, blame others or find excuses for our misconduct, we forsake any possibility of peace and happiness and also increase our risk of physical ailments; in effect, we are establishing the value of our life for this day; we are tacitly agreeing that we are not worthy of peace and joy and the best health we can find.

We might ask "How will I value my life—my breath and heartbeat and my peace and happiness—today? Will I place a value that reflects that I am a child of God, a person who wants to be the best version or myself? Or will I sell myself cheaply to self-driven will?"

Prayer: I pray that I may realize my true value and that my feelings, thoughts, words, and actions reflect my worth. Grant that this day I live as my spirit would have me live and demonstrate that I am a child of divinity.

Take three relaxing breaths; ask your inner spirit to guide your meditation; pause for a few minutes in silence.

December 8

We don't need to re-invent the wheel.

It's really very simple to enjoy serenity, happiness, courage, and freedom in our life: we simply find what has actually produced these results in other people's lives, follow the directions, and do the work—do what they did. But our human nature has a few challenges doing something this uncomplicated: 1) we have deeply entrenched habits that rebel against this; 2) we sometimes do not like following directions, and 3) we're lazy; we want to get maximum benefits with minimum efforts.

Many of these clear-cut directions include morning, throughout the day, and nightly recommended practices. Our relationship with our inner spirit, with our Higher Power, is like every relationship we have in life: the quality of our relationship directly depends on our investment of time and effort. If we are losing our peace and allowing people, places, and things to upset us, perhaps we've slipped back into self-will; maybe we are unconsciously refusing to follow directions, taking shortcuts, or still wanting to get something for nothing.

Consider: "Do I really want the best life possible? Am I willing to go to any length? Does my laziness and complacency lead me to settle for the good instead of pushing for the best? Am I following the directions or am I taking shortcuts?"

Prayer: I pray that I may not be complacent, stubborn, or rebellious; grant me the wisdom, willingness, and strength to walk the path of spiritual growth and maturity.

Take three relaxing breaths; ask your inner spirit to guide your meditation; pause for a few minutes in silence.

December 9

The disaster and misfortune hardest to bear are those that never come.

Imaginary misfortune and disaster can only be anticipated but never faced and solved. The fears of tomorrow can destroy today's peace; anxiety, tension, and fear can dominate our day. It's impossible to solve problems that aren't real in this moment but we do face one very real problem: our mind is allowing fear to disrupt our day. We use our physical, mental, and spiritual resources to overcome our self-driven mind:

- Physical: We take a walk and actually focus on the beauty and wonder we see; we listen to an uplifting spiritual or affirmation recording; we make a gratitude list; we pause and practice relaxation breathing.
- Mental: We mentally review the life-transforming moments in our life; we re-capture the way we felt on our wedding day, when our child was born, when we felt humbled by an experience or when we discovered the wonderful relationship with our inner spirit.
- Spiritual: We pause and pray; we acknowledge our dilemma and place it in God's hands; we totally release it. We ask for help, that our mind submits to the guidance of our spirit, that we are able to align our will with his. We ask that peace, security, and hope infuse our total being.

Then we look for someone we can help in any way; service inevitably moves us from being the center of the universe.

Action, not desires or intentions, eliminate the fear.

Prayer: Dear God help me live in the moment throughout this day; grant me the strength and will to let my mind be guided by your spirit; keep me from the evil by-paths of my imagination.

Take three relaxing breaths; ask your inner spirit to guide your meditation; pause for a few minutes in silence.

December 10

Spiritual growth is not a competition; comparing ourselves to others is always self-defeating.

We might wonder how someone else is growing so fast while we still make obvious mistakes.

Each of us is a unique child of God; we grow through our own insights, efforts, desires, experiences, and mistakes—and we will make mistakes. Growth is more important than where we are at any moment or how we compare with other people.

Look back one year and five years if you can. Are you growing? Do you have less contention, anxiety, anger, or worry now than then? Do your moments and days contain more hope, love, and inner peace? This is the face of progress. We want to take action to ensure that our growth continues or even expands; we do not want to waste futile energy in meaningless comparisons or self-flagellation. Improvement only comes from action, not wishes or intentions.

We must devote time to growth; we don't procrastinate or offer excuses as to why we can't do this; we make sure to complete our nightly review to honestly evaluate our positive advances and possible errors; we make an effort to recognize the slightest contention and seek a spiritually-directed solution; we never blame others or give them power over our emotions.

Prayer: I pray that I may walk my own path and not compare myself with other people. Give me the perseverance and strength to do the work I need to do to experience and enjoy my own growth.

Take three relaxing breaths; ask your inner spirit to guide your meditation; pause for a few minutes in silence.

December 11

Be careful in whining about something being unfair or praying for fairness.

If we want things to always be fair, consider the speeding tickets or DUI's we deserved but did not receive, our uttered lies that were never known, and our breaches of trust that were not discovered. We cry "unfair" but often do not want true fairness. We want the immediate challenge to be "fair" as we see what "fair" should be.

The perceived unfairness may be real or imagined but we have to deal with it lest it continue to destroy our peace. We avoid thinking that the whole universe is against us; we remember the times that we faced no consequence or a much less-than-deserved consequence for our actions—those times when we would not really ask for fairness. We put the current situation in a larger context of what is truly important.

We write a gratitude list, specifically naming the people and situations that contribute to our life; we truly consider our blessings. We pray and ask our inner spirit to shift our perception, to re-direct our thoughts, to help us recognize and avoid self-centeredness and self-pity, and to grant us clarity of mind, good judgment in choices, and strength of character. We talk to a trusted friend or confidant to share our turmoil and stay receptive for beneficial ideas. We remind our self that we are not the center of universe and look for another person to help.

It's true that life is not always fair but if we're honest, we likely participate in both sides of the unfairness.

Prayer: Dear God, help me not to react or indulge in self-pity. Help me always remember how blessed I am and what is truly important in my life. Thank you for all you do for me.

Take three relaxing breaths; ask your inner spirit to guide your meditation; pause for a few minutes in silence.

December 12

Sometimes faith is all we have when we step into the darkness.

When you come to the end of all the light you know, and it's time to step into the darkness of the unknown, faith is knowing that one of two things shall happen: Either you will be given something solid to stand on or you will be taught to fly. Edward Teller.

Belief is an intellectual acceptance of an idea, concept, or ideology; faith is when we change the way we live because of that belief. To be effective, our beliefs must align with truth and reality.

When we must choose to either stay in our current misery or step into the unknown, what can we expect of God with absolute certainty? As we step into the darkness, we can be certain that our "leap of faith" will yield specific benefits if we maintain our spiritual connection. We'll discover

- direction—solutions appear that we could not see before;
- strength—an invigorating flow of spiritual energy infuses our body and mind;
- courage—we have an enhanced ability to face and overcome fear and uncertainty;
- purpose—our spiritual direction and values strengthen;
- understanding—our mental acumen shifts to a superior level; we have clarity of mind and an enhanced understanding of values and priorities; and
- peace—we have that inner certainty that all is well and will continue to be well, no matter what is happening around us.

Prayer: Dear God, give me the courage to act according to your will; help me to trust you and your ways; enfold me in your loving protection and guide my mind.

Take three relaxing breaths; ask your inner spirit to guide your meditation; pause for a few minutes in silence.

December 13

A quick check on words and actions:
Is it necessary?
Is it honest?
Is it kind?

We live the day; we think, act, react, and feel the emotions of the moment we are in right now. Hopefully, we start our day with prayer and meditation to give us the best chance of having a peaceful day; we build the spiritual and emotional strength necessary to handle adversity with peace, poise, and equanimity. Then life happens.

We engage with other people; they say or do things that challenge our peace of mind and we want to respond. We are trying to live a better life so we pause and ask our inner spirit for help. In this brief moment before we react, we can also ask our self: Is necessary, honest, and kind?

- Is it necessary? Do I really have to say or do anything right now? Is it truly any of my business? Am I contributing to a solution or to the problem? What is my motive—why do I want to respond? Is my pride or self-esteem wounded; do I want to appear "right?" Is my reply driven by fear or ego?
- Is it honest? Is my reply fully free of deceit? Am I sincere? Do I know all the facts and can I support them with evidence or only opinion, partial information, or hearsay?
- Is it kind? Does it truly demonstrate love, tolerance, gentleness, and compassion?

We also consider: "If God was standing beside me right now, how would I answer?" Remember, he really is there and with us every moment.

Prayer: I pray that I have the willingness, strength, and intelligence to pause today before I act. Guide my words and actions to be necessary, honest, and kind.

Take three relaxing breaths; ask your inner spirit to guide your meditation; pause for a few minutes in silence.

December 14

Fear attacks our serenity as water breaches a dam.

A flash flood can destroy the wall in an instant but a small, persistent trickle can find the weakest path, gradually widen the channel, and overwhelm all resistance.

Each of us may someday face an attack of fear that carries the debris of anger, worry, self-pity, remorse and other misery to infect our weakened and vulnerable mind. If our life is based on self-driven will, we have little defense; we will inevitably yield to a continuous or an overwhelming attack of fear. However, a strengthened and reinforced citadel of inner spiritual power can repel any assault.

We improve and repair the dam before the flood, not after; likewise we maintain and strengthen our spiritual defenses every day with prayer, meditation, and action.

- In prayer, we consciously seek to align our will with divine will, to live a spiritual day rather than a day of self-reliance; we ask our indwelling spirit to direct our thinking and for the willingness, guidance, and strength to overcome any shortcoming.
- In meditation, we sit in quiet receptivity, waiting for the embrace of the spirit. We are nourished and replenished with spiritual essence, the quiet peace and assurance that the spirit lives within us.
- In action, we try to do the right thing; if contention and turmoil invade our peace, we pause and connect with our spiritual power to re-direct our thoughts, re-gain our strength, and remind us of our priorities.

No fear can breach a prepared spiritual shield.

Prayer: Help me stay connected with my divine inner spirit. Let me turn to you as my shield and protector at the smallest sign of any anxiety or fear. Guide my thoughts, actions, and feelings this day.

Take three relaxing breaths; ask your inner spirit to guide your meditation; pause for a few minutes in silence.

December 15

Do we settle for mediocrity or try to be the best we can be? Pursuing this spiritual life requires a balance of perspective; we are trying to grow in an area in which we'll never reach our goals; we must keep our ideals in sight, evaluate our progress and needed areas of improvement but never be too hard on our self. We need to recognize how far we've come as well as how far we have to go. The "Fruits of the Spirit" evident in the lives of the spiritually guided soul offer some guidelines for our evaluation:

- loving service: serving with sublime and healthy affection;
- unselfish devotion: giving support or enthusiasm with no consideration of reward or self-gain;
- courageous loyalty: maintaining strong allegiance that is not lessened by danger or threats;
- sincere fairness; bestowing fairness that proceeds from genuine desire with no pretense or deceit;
- enlightened honesty: expressing honesty that differentiates between truth and fact;
- undying hope: enjoying hope that persists in the face of overwhelming evidence that it is useless;
- confiding trust: communicating those dark secrets and dreams with a trustworthy friend or advisor;
- merciful ministry: ministering with love and compassion to those who have harmed us;
- unfailing goodness: choosing the right thing (righteousness) in face of repeated and overwhelming temptation;
- forgiving tolerance: demonstrating an elevated tolerance in which love and understanding cancel or erase the initial reason tolerance was required; and
- enduring peace: sustaining the peace that passes all human understanding and persists through all upheaval.

Prayer: Help me experience and live the fruits of the spirit.

Take three relaxing breaths; ask your inner spirit to guide your meditation; pause for a few minutes in silence.

December 16

Accepting love makes us more than we were.

Something about us changes when someone bestows love upon us. Feeling that another person cares for us, believes in us, and values us affects our life. They think that we are worthy; they see something in us that others may miss; they are willing to give of themselves, sometimes even sacrificing their own wants and desires, so that our life may improve. Even if we are not aware of it, we start to see our self differently; we hold our head higher; we feel as if we have more value; we believe more in our own abilities and dreams; we have a new confidence in our self; we feel more secure as we know that someone is always there for us; we have found a confiding and trusted companion.

A similar personal expansion happens when we accept the gift of love from our spiritual parent. Like any offered gift, we have the choice to ignore it, reject it, or accept it. The perfection of this divine love exceeds the love from any human source but we must accept the gift to feel its presence and allow it to transform us. This love is infinite, without limits as to how much it can help us grow; it contains the cleansing energy to wash away all past regrets and mistakes, to infuse us with strength, wisdom, and direction that were previously unknown, to grant us a security that encompasses all time and a peace that passes all human understanding.

Love from human or divine sources is always free; it has a true power that can change a life. Today, let us acknowledge this and open our self to receive love and look for opportunities to share this divine gift.

Prayer: I pray that I may not be complacent, stubborn, or rebellious; help me walk the path of spiritual growth and maturity, to receive and bestow love.

Take three relaxing breaths; ask your inner spirit to guide your meditation; pause for a few minutes in silence.

December 17

Our lower power (our self-driven will) offers turmoil, dissatisfaction, and discontent; our Higher Power grants peace, love, and hope.

Power: *the ability to take or cause action*

Our lower power is simply our self-directed will with its myriad of "self" focused traits such as selfishness, self-centeredness, self-righteousness, and self-pity; this clamoring voice constantly tells us that living this way is the only thing that makes sense in this world. This is the root of the "*ism*" of alcohol*ism* and other self-destructive "*isms*"—the overwhelming focus on I, self, and me.

Responding to this lower power generates misery. But the good news is two-fold: 1) We have free-will choice and can choose whether we respond to our Higher Power or our lower power; and 2) Our Higher Power is infinitely more powerful than our lower power; it can absorb, deflect, or over-come our lower power as soon as we surrender and ask for help.

Making a choice about which power will direct our life is not a one-time event; we face many decisions each day and must make a conscious choice in each one whether we'll follow the leadings of our Higher Power or our lower power

We must become aware of each choice and align our will with the path our Higher Power opens for us. If we pause, we can progressively learn to distinguish the push of our lower power from the pull of rightness. The lower side brings tenseness, anxiety, fear, self-importance, hurry, guilt, anger, resentment, and other misery; our higher side yields contentment, love, caring, smiles, security, and peace. Any feeling of disturbance or contention originates from our lower power—the push of self-driven will; our Higher Power brings only light, love, and hope.

Prayer: I pray that I may be aware of each decision today and that I choose the love and peace of my Higher Power.

Take three relaxing breaths; ask your inner spirit to guide your meditation; pause for a few minutes in silence.

December 18

Disagreement does not necessarily mean that someone is wrong; it may only be a difference of experience, attitude, or opinion.

As we try to grow and be the best version of our self, we still encounter those disagreements with other people. When this happens, do we allow our old attitude to determine our response or have we grown sufficiently to welcome differences of opinion? Do we see disagreement as a challenge to our worth, status, or authority? Or as an opportunity to see and consider another viewpoint? Is our instantaneous feeling defensive, looking for ways to prove we are right? Or is it open, willing to hear and evaluate what is said?

Our reaction to disagreement can be a quick check on our spiritual and emotional health.

In any relationship, disagreement can be healthy if we appreciate and respect conflicting opinions. However, this requires that we are comfortable with our self, that we feel the love and power of our inner spirit, that we know our value as a unique individual and a child of God, and that we accept our true assets and limitations.

Only then can we truly respond with the attitude and understanding that all good ideas don't come from us; we do not have a corner on knowledge or experience; we cannot see all the possible views, solutions, and outcomes of a situation; other people may have a better idea or contribute to changes in our own idea so that we share the solution.

Today, let's try to be tolerant, patient, and open-minded.

Prayer: I pray that I can keep conscious, continuous contact with my divine source. Please strengthen my awareness that I am your child and one of your family; let me not need to prove that I am right or above any person.

Take three relaxing breaths; ask your inner spirit to guide your meditation; pause for a few minutes in silence.

December 19

Anytime we react in anger, we are wrong.

No exceptions, no excuses. Anger may be the "dubious luxury" of normal people if we understand that normal is the "norm" or average of anything. Yes, many people get angry; some say it is a natural human emotion that we simply must learn to control. However, normal does not mean that it truly benefits us. If we desire to eliminate anger in our life, we concentrate on increasing our ability to love and to be tolerant, kind, and patient.

We never offer excuses or blame another person for our anger; we learn to recognize and accept even the small internal flare-ups that we are able to hold in check without speaking or acting in anger. We review our life and see the times anger has caused us problems; we look at our state of mind and our feelings when engaged in anger. Perhaps we may enjoy part of this emotion—the feeling of self-righteousness, or power, or of speaking our mind but we must become willing to release this false satisfaction. We have to come to that place of spiritual maturity in which we hunger for freedom from this demeaning emotion.

Then, we turn to our real power—God, our divine inner spirit, or whatever we see as our spiritual source; we acknowledge that we want to be free of anger; we humbly ask for help to lead us to be more loving, tolerant, and patient; we ask for strength and direction to stay committed to our new path. We give thanks for the grace that brought us this far. Improvement may appear slow but it is inevitable as long as we stay committed and persistent.

Prayer: Dear God, kindle in me the desire to be free of anger; make me aware of the harm this emotion causes me and grant me the strength to overcome. Your will, not mine be done.

Take three relaxing breaths; ask your inner spirit to guide your meditation; pause for a few minutes in silence.

December 20

God provides opportunities but doesn't guarantee results.

Serendipity, synchronicity, providence, fate, destiny, and coincidence are some of the terms we use when we think we have been blessed by good fortune including unexpectedly meeting someone who becomes important in our life. Whether we believe that God, universe forces, the angels, or random luck was involved in this fortuitous event, one thing is certain: we have been blessed with a wonderful opportunity but the result is not guaranteed or pre-ordained; the choices and actions of each individual will determine the eventual outcome.

We may have been an addict or alcoholic and offered the opportunity for recovery and we grab the lifeline. The quantity and quality of our recovery is solely dependent on our effort and willingness; do we follow directions and do we do the work? What we want—what we think should happen—what anyone around us wants—mean little if we revert to self-driven will. Complacency, procrastination, lethargy, and excuses of selfishness, self-centeredness, self-righteousness always insure failure over time.

We may have met our soul mate; we are madly in love and the future is brilliant. But the enjoyment of the day-to-day life, the direction of the union (is it growing, stagnant, or regressing?), and the final chorus are not cemented in bliss; a happy ending is not guaranteed but dependent on the daily actions of each person. Even a blessed opportunity only opens the portals of the future; we must earn the long-term rewards.

Prayer: I pray that I recognize the opportunities that God opens before me. Help me take none for granted, today and for the rest of life, and do all that I can to get the best from each one.

Take three relaxing breaths; ask your inner spirit to guide your meditation; pause for a few minutes in silence.

December 21

Love yourself

The admonition to "Love your neighbor *as* yourself" infers that we are only capable of giving or receiving love exactly AS we love our self. Developing a healthy self-love happens in three steps. We must:

1. Know our self. We conduct an honest examination of our patterns—the what, why, and how of everything that has made us who we are. We recount specific acts of what we have done. We seek our true motives for those acts—were we driven by self-focused will or divine will? How did we implement our decisions—did our process reflect divine principles and values or those of the secular world? The end does not justify the means.
2. Accept our self. We are a child of the divine and hopefully slowly maturing toward the image we hold of our God; children can often learn wisdom only through the consequences of mistakes. Denying or ignoring our shortcomings leads to repetition; we acknowledge these and all our assets. Everything can contribute to our growth.
3. Love our self: We know that through grace, God has showered us with mercy, tolerance, and love and we grant our self these same gifts. If God loves us, we are compelled to love our self. We are experiential beings, not made perfect; we earn our advancement through ever-striving to be a better person each day.

Prayer: Dear God, I pray that I may learn to love myself; that I can develop the active and healthy concern for my well-being that I believe you have for me. Help me to grant myself the patience, tolerance, mercy and love that I desire from you and wish to bestow on others.

Take three relaxing breaths; ask your inner spirit to guide your meditation; pause for a few minutes in silence.

December 22

God does not demand of us a uniformity of belief; only a unity of direction.

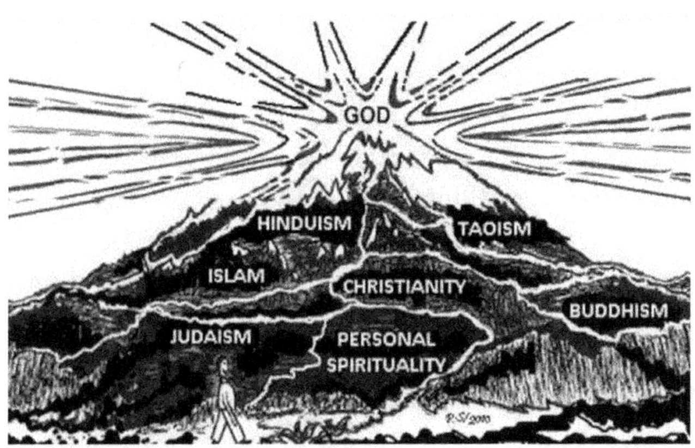

Many paths lead to an ever-increasing understanding of God. He wants us to head toward him and not away from him; he (she) freely offers love, security, peace, compassion, mercy, and grace which must become a personal living experience. Our path is our choice and we can change paths at any time.

If our path does not yield joy, love, and peace, and offer solutions for solving life's daily challenges perhaps we should work harder or consider changing paths.

Prayer: I pray that I make knowing and experiencing the love of my creator a vital part of my day. Help me reflect on the wonderful gifts freely offered every moment of every day; guide my heart, soul, and mind to open and receive this bounty.

Take three relaxing breaths; ask your inner spirit to guide your meditation; pause for a few minutes in silence.

December 23

"Let go and let God."

Great advice but sometimes hard to do. When we face a real or imagined problem that appears disastrous or a series of problems that hit one after another, our mind and emotions engage and we're off into misery. We might know that we need to "Let go and let God" but can't do it; or we manage to do it for a while and then the problem(s) again take control. If we face a real problem, we are responsible to do everything in our power to solve it but we also must release what we can't control.

The main challenge lies with our mind; instead of simply reacting, we invest time and energy to engage our inner spirit to help our thinking.

We make certain to do our morning prayers and meditation; we acknowledge the problem(s) and our certainty that God can and will give us the peace, strength, and insight we seek; we ask for help in seeing the best solutions and in not allowing our mind to pursue thoughts that do not contribute to our well-being.

Throughout the day, we utilize all available resources. We share our problems and concerns with a trusted friend. We pause and connect with our inner spirit during the day; in these, we give thanks for the blessings we recognize and ask for help, strength, and support. We actually use our uplifting music or inspirational messages as soon as our mind starts returning to the problem—before the thought-emotional reaction becomes deeply entrenched.

At night, we again talk to our loving spirit. We listen to our music or read something spiritual before we retire to help us sleep and rest.

Prayer: My loving creator, I pray that I allow your spirit to guide my mind, that your wonderful loving power bring me comfort and peace as we overcome the challenges I face.

Take three relaxing breaths; ask your inner spirit to guide your meditation; pause for a few minutes in silence.

December 24

From whence will we take power to live this day?

Will we depend on our determination, self-reliance, or other people to supply the energy we need to live this day? Will we receive strength and satisfaction from money, things, accomplishments, recognition, or approval of others? Or will we depend on our unseen infinite power that flows within? Which source can truly yield inner peace and happiness?

We may sometimes forget that we have an extra resource, a source of un-tapped power that flows within us. This is the power that can break the shackles of addiction, sever the bonds of self-pity, guilt, anger, and other miseries, and open the gateway to new freedom.

When we access this life-changing energy, our strength, determination, perseverance, and ability to function in the outer world increases. Our mental turmoil lessens and we see solutions that previously eluded us; our lagging spirits are uplifted; we find a peace that passes all human understanding in the face of heartache and disappointment.

Every moment of every day we have a choice: Will we pause and allow this power to work in our life or will we continue to limit our self and live in mediocrity and misery?

Prayer: My loving inner spirit, guide me into the willingness to let go of anything that stands in the way of being of maximum service to you and your children. Help me release my self-driven will and let your loving, supportive energy flow through me.

Take three relaxing breaths; ask your inner spirit to guide your meditation; pause for a few minutes in silence.

December 25

Do you have relatively peaceful days with sporadic turmoil? Or days that move from one misery to the next?

Pain is inevitable; misery is optional. When we love others, we may experience pain from losses, separation, and disappointment. Misery such as anger, resentment, jealousy, self-pity, fear, worry, anxiety, discouragement, some forms of guilt, and other avoidable emotions originate with self-driven will. We experience much less frequent and tumultuous bouts of misery as we allow our spirit to guide our thoughts.

Look across the landscape of your life. How often and how deeply have you allowed the thoughts of the past to affect your day? Or a current invasion to dominate your mind and control your actions, justifying why this is an exception, that "they" shouldn't have done what "they" did, that something is not "fair", that another thing "should" happen according to your desires or expectations?

Do you focus on the darkness or the light in your life, on the problem or on the solution? If you see too much gloom, does it truly reflect your life or your day? If so, do you want to change? Are you willing to take responsibility for your thoughts and actions and do something about it?

At the onset of discontent or irritation, when you first start to feel upset, do something different. Immediately pause and pray; ask for help, strength, and guidance; seek the power and direction of your inner spirit.

Prayer: I pray that my perception encourages me to see the truth and that my attitude replaces self-pity and despair with righteousness and hope. Let the light of the spirit dispel all darkness in me today.

Take three relaxing breaths; ask your inner spirit to guide your meditation; pause for a few minutes in silence.

December 26

Don't miss the treasure hunt today!

God has hidden the prizes and we have to look for them. We already have stumbled on the first one: we woke up; we can breathe and see; we have the opportunity to start our day with gratitude, love, and hope—or we can jump out of bed and rush to chaos.

Our treasure may come when we're stuck in traffic and hear a song that resonates with our spirit, provides an insight, or simply makes us feel better; relief, peace, and happiness suddenly wash over us. We may do some small, special thing for someone; their obvious pleasure lights our day. We may hear a word that illuminates a solution to a problem that has troubled us; the problem dissolves or we realize that it was not as serious as feared. We hold the words of sarcasm or anger that are so eager to spill from our tongue and find a quiet pleasure in our growth. We may look across a room at our parent, our child, our spouse or other loved one and feel an overwhelming sense of affection, gratitude, and fulfillment.

Are we willing to discover wonderful treasures today? Or will we miss the adventure and plod our path of sadness, anxiety, and mediocrity, hurrying to go nowhere?

Prayer: My inner spirit, open my eyes to see the treasure around me; make me aware of and grateful for, the wonderful gifts that you bring to my life.

Take three relaxing breaths; ask your inner spirit to guide your meditation; pause for a few minutes in silence.

December 27

Living in ignorance—yet wise in their own conceit— the deluded go round and round, like the blind led by the blind. (Mundaka Upanishad p.61)

Perhaps we have lived in ignorance, thinking our way was the only way or that we had no alternative. We may even be among those who shouted "There is no God; we do not need a spiritual life; such beliefs and practices are for the weak and afraid." Somehow, we became a little open-minded and willing; our eyes started to open; we experienced the power of a personal relationship with our spirit and did not have to remain "wise in our own conceit."

We know now that God does exist, that we can access an inner spiritual power that transforms our life, and that our individual, personal experience validates this truth. All beliefs, all theories, all fallacious proofs shatter against the impregnable wall of experience.

To the blind who deny the spirit, we can now lovingly reply "I know. I know because I experience the spirit in my life and no person or thing can change or deny my own inner experience."

Prayer: I pray that I may open the eyes of my heart and that I am receptive to the guidance of the spirit of truth and listen to the still, small voice within.

Take three relaxing breaths; ask your inner spirit to guide your meditation; pause for a few minutes in silence.

December 28

Death of a loved one is an interruption and not the end of a loving relationship. It's a comma, not a period in life's sentence.

God is love and learning to bestow and receive healthy love is one our primary tasks as a mortal child of the divine. But it is impossible to fulfill all the potential of love in one short lifetime; we may experience a deep, profound, compassionate affection and feel that we have the ultimate love; but we must realize that this is but a sliver of the potential we have for understanding and experiencing this divine attribute.

Loving someone is of eternal spiritual value which really means the relationship truly lasts forever. When we initiate an act of love here, we are not only participating in a relationship that exists in this time and place but have started something that is a part of our eternal journey. Experiencing the infinite depths and possibilities of love requires much longer than one short mortal life. God, (the universe, the Infinite) knows this and provides time and opportunities for us to fulfill and complete each act of love started here; these building blocks of human love allow us to experience a growing, expanding, and divine love.

Eternity is very real; we have millions (billions, trillions,...) of years to participate and enjoy these wonderful, loving, serving relationships. Death of a loved one is an interruption and not the end of a loving relationship. It's a comma, not a period in the sentence that is life.

Prayer: My divine parent and inner guide, help me to mourn but accept the encompassing power of love; let my tears slowly cleanse the pain; enhance my understanding that love is truly a divine and eternal blessing.

Take three relaxing breaths; ask your inner spirit to guide your meditation; pause for a few minutes in silence.

December 29

It's not all about me;
I am not the center or upholder of the universe.

The world supports the "It's all about me" attitude. It pushes us to take pictures of ourselves, put them on display, and then wait for praise; our opinions, ideas, and feelings are of paramount importance although we have accomplished nothing and know even less; we judge with little or no evidence; then, when someone presents an opposing view, we self-righteously reject it and quickly curse and belittle anyone who has the audacity to disagree. Even some religions may fall into the same pit: "Believe the way I believe or face eternal damnation."

But ...

But a few have discovered a secret; we've learned that our life is happier, more peaceful, and full of love when we do not live as if we are the center of all things; we enjoy better moments and days when our thoughts, words, and actions concern the well-being of others instead of gaining something for our self.

We must remain vigilant; we must maintain our spiritual condition; we must stay consistent with communion, prayer, and meditation to enjoy the flow of power, guidance, and love that springs from our inner divine source. Staying in contact with God helps us avoid thinking we are the center of the universe today.

Prayer: Dear God, grant that today, I release my self-focused perspective. Make me aware when self-directed thoughts penetrate my mind; guide me to take action that prevents their taking hold and growing.

Take three relaxing breaths; ask your inner spirit to guide your meditation; pause for a few minutes in silence.

December 30

Make a difference today.

When we experience the transformation, that inner shift that opens a new life to us, we recognize a responsibility to share this wonderful free gift with others; we discover the paradox that the only way we can keep this is to give it away and the more we share, the more we keep. Growth helps us see that these acts may never impact or change the world; they may not even change the recipients of our bequests; but the smallest, and seemingly least significant act of kindness and love always changes us.

We can listen to someone and offer our experience, strength, and hope. We can open the door, carry a package, or offer a sincere smile to a stranger; we can return a genuine compliment to someone that irritates us; or call an old friend, a parent, a child, or an acquaintance and let them know we are thinking about them. We can volunteer in a soup kitchen, at the local hospital, in a program that distributes food to the less fortunate, or in a hundred other beneficial causes; we can offer transportation to someone, sit with loving patience as they talk and talk, or simply offer a hand to help them rise.

Have we achieved the near-perfection so we only perform great and important deeds? Or do we live at the other extreme where we suffer from an arrogant, self-righteous attitude that rationalizes why we can do the bare minimum to get by?

We will have the opportunity today to do acts that can improve our day. How many will we even recognize? How many will we actually do?

Prayer: Today, let me search for opportunities to share this wonderful gift and become aware of any form of help I can offer to anyone. Grant that I actually do something instead of settling for good intentions.

Take three relaxing breaths; ask your inner spirit to guide your meditation; pause for a few minutes in silence.

December 31

We should not expect others to be perfect until we are.

Tolerance: *to possess endurance, fortitude, stamina in the face of pain and hardship; indulgence for beliefs or practices differing from one's own.*

How much and how often do we allow other people to upset us? Or to simply to diminish our peace, hope, and serenity? We know that we're not perfect and will never achieve perfection in this life; we must also grant that freedom to everyone else.

Intellectual realization of this truth is big step toward spiritual and emotional maturity; however, living this truth—getting to that point where other people's opinions, comments, or approval have little emotional effect of us—requires time, facing situations to learn tolerance (sometimes conquering, sometimes failing, but always learning), and spiritual help.

We may not consciously expect perfection from others but still react when they are less-than-perfect or even when their words, beliefs, and actions oppose ours. Let us be careful with any expectation, especially one such as this in which we are setting unrealistic standards.

Anytime we allow someone to upset us, we can pause, reflect on our own struggle for progress, determine why we are allowing this to bother us; we ask our inner spirit for the insight to see this differently, and the power to change.

Prayer: I pray that I may guard against all expectations; help me have tolerance, compassion, and love for everyone I meet today. I pray that grace grant me the peace that passes all understanding.

Take three relaxing breaths; ask your inner spirit to guide your meditation; pause for a few minutes in silence.

NOTES

Index (A partial reference for topics)

Totally Within

Totally Within

Character	Reaction to another's misfortune reveals our c...	5-Nov
	C.. Is forged between hammer of adversity and anvil	18-Nov
	Decisions create c... Is courage desirable?	6-Nov
Children	C... of God? Why do we expect spiritual maturity?	30-Sep
	Claim your inheritance as child of divine	1-Oct
Choice	It's my c... --bad 5 minutes or bad day	27-Apr
	Turmoil and despair not necessary, my c...	9-Mar
	how will we live this day?	31-May
	Bad things will happen; our c... on our reaction	11-Jun
	Do we invite spirit into our life?	26-Jul
	Every moment we choose to follow self or the spirit	31-Oct
	To choose good, choice for bad must be possible	6-Nov
Coasting	If c.., probably headed downhill	6-May
Comparing	C... our self to others is self-defeating	10-Dec
Compassion	C.. should be guided by wisdom	24-May
Complacency	We slide, don't fall, into c...	16-Jun
	"Resting on our laurels" breeds misery	7-Aug
	Don't become accustomed to misery and stay there	4-Nov
Compromising	C... core values causes misery	29-Aug
Conflict	We have less c... and contention if we listen to God	25-Sep
Congruency	C...teaches us to help but not enable	7-Sep
Conscience	C... tells us to "do right"; divine spark, what is right.	2-Nov
Consequences	Faith and prayer will not eliminate c...	15-May
	Every act has a c...	4-Oct
	Everything happens for a r...; sometimes r... is stupidity	7-Nov
Contempt	Familiarity breeds c...	1-May

ABOUT THE AUTHOR

Thomas Strawser is an international engineer with a master's degree in psychology. Divorce, alcoholism, and numerous losses in his life led him to seek practical solutions to his despair. Combining his spirituality and knowledge of psychology with his engineering know-how, Thomas discovered profound happiness and peace of mind through the process he calls Spiritual Engineering. Thomas has published articles in *Grief* magazine, *New Leaf* magazine, *The Spiritual Fellowship Journal*, and *Guidepost* and authored *Spiritual Engineering: The Harmony of Science and Spirituality.* He and his wife, Patricia, share the transforming power of Spiritual Engineering in bi-lingual seminars around the world guiding thousands through this simple process that produces significant quality-of-life improvements.

PRAYER

Dear God, the infinite, you are the I AM that separated time from eternity, space from infinity to give domain to the universe of universes. You are the only uncaused cause and the first source, center, activator, and upholder of all reality; you contain the potential of all that will ever be. You are the origin of the stars, the suns, the planets and all space; you are the never-beginning, never-ending source that started and sustains creation.

Yet, with your omnipotence and omniscience, you spread your love across your creation; you shared yourself as you created all living beings and bestowed the very breath of life. Then to us, the mortal beings, the ones existing in the deepest reaches of time and space, the ones farthest from your source, you presented the plan for eternal progress that can return us to you and grant us the experience of eternal service, love, and joy. You gave us a fragment of your very self to indwell our mind and then gifted us the command of free-will choice which allows us to decide if we will share our life with you, the degree that we will allow you into our life, or if we ignore and reject you completely.

The life-transforming power you offer grants us peace, strength, courage, and hope to traverse this life and beyond. You are our origin and our destiny; help us to choose wisely this day and unleash the awesome infinite power of your gift.

Totally Within

If you enjoy these daily thoughts/meditations, sign up for free "Daily thought" short version delivered directly to you by just contacting me at:

tjstrawser@comcast.net

Please leave review on Amazon @
https://amzn.to/2us0owX https://amzn.to/3lcntyq

www.ingramcontent.com/pod-product-compliance
Lightning Source LLC
Chambersburg PA
CBHW071403090426
42737CB00011B/1329

* 9 7 8 0 9 7 5 5 6 9 5 4 2 *